MW00450639

HOW TO WOW

PHOTOSHOP CS2 For The Web

Jan Kabili & Colin Smith

Peachpit Press

How to Wow: Photoshop CS2 for the Web
Jan Kabili and Colin Smith

Peachpit Press
1249 Eighth Street
Berkeley, CA 94710
(510) 524-2178
(510) 524-2221 (fax)

Find us on the Web at www.peachpit.com.
To report errors, please send a note to errata@peachpit.com.

Peachpit Press is a division of Pearson Education.

Copyright © 2006 by Jan Kabili and Colin Smith

Project Editor: Rebecca Gulick
Production Coordinator: David Van Ness
Technical Editor: Colin Smith
Compositor: Colin Smith
Proofreader: Liz Welch
Indexer: Karin Arrigoni
Copy Editor: David Van de Water
Cover Design: Jack Davis
Interior Design: Jill Davis

Notice of Rights
All rights reserved. No part of this book may be reproduced or transmitted in any form
by any means, electronic, mechanical, photocopying, recording, or otherwise, without
the prior written permission of the publisher. For information on getting permission for
reprints and excerpts, contact permissions@peachpit.com.

Notice of Liability
The information in this book and the files on the CD-ROM are distributed on an "As Is"
basis, without warranty. While every precaution has been taken in the preparation of the
book and CD-ROM, neither the authors nor Peachpit Press shall have any liability to any
person or entity with respect to any loss or damage caused or alleged to be caused directly
or indirectly by the instructions contained in this book or by the computer software and
hardware products described in it and on the CD-ROM.

Trademarks
Adobe, Photoshop, and ImageReady are either registered trademarks or trademarks of
Adobe Systems Incorporated in the United States and/or other countries.

Many of the designations used by manufacturers and sellers to distinguish their products
are claimed as trademarks. Where those designations appear in this book, and Peachpit
Press was aware of a trademark claim, the designations appear as requested by the owner
of the trademark. All other product names and services identified throughout this book are
used in editorial fashion only and for the benefit of such companies with no intention of
infringement of the trademark. No such use, or the use of any trade name, is intended to
convey endorsement or other affiliation with this book.

ISBN 0-321-39394-5
9 8 7 6 5 4 3 2

Printed and bound in the United States of America

Acknowledgments

As I sit down to write these acknowledgments, the first person who comes to mind is you, the reader. We've never met, but I feel like I know you. You've been on my mind every day for the last few months. I've pictured you choosing this book at the bookstore, sitting down at your computer to give it a try, or grabbing it off the shelf to reread something you found useful. Thank you for buying the book and for being my inspiration.

Thanks to my friend and coauthor, Colin Smith. Colin made all the graphics for these projects, and he let me do all the writing without second–guessing me. He was always there at the other end of my email. And I know that he slept as little as I did. Colin—it's been a pleasure. Thank you for joining me on this journey.

Jack Davis—Thanks for conceiving and nurturing the How to Wow series. Your ideas and the terrific model we had in *How to Wow: Photoshop for Photography* were our touchstones.

Dean Collins—Here's to your memory. I miss your good humor and invaluable advice. Dean was the founder of Software Cinema, Inc., which is publishing the How to Wow training CDs that have grown out of this book.

Thanks to my colleague and partner David Van de Water. He read every word, lending his good eye and good taste to the process.

To all the team at Peachpit Press—our patient editor Rebecca Gulick, production manager David Van Ness, and publisher Nancy Ruenzel—thanks for making this the most pleasant writing experience I've had. Jill Davis—thanks

for creating the InDesign template into which I wrote directly. You can't imagine how much time that saved.

Last, but certainly not least, thanks to my family, Coby Kabili, Kate Kabili, and Ben Kabili, for putting up with me being at the office all the time. I promise dinner will be on time from now on.

—*Jan Kabili*

© Colin Smith

Before I say anything else, I just want to thank all the wonderful and loyal people who read my books and magazine articles, watch my videos, attend my seminars, and visit the Web site photoshopCAFE.com. Thanks for all the encouraging emails. I would not be doing this for a living if it wasn't for you. I am grateful beyond words!

This book that you are holding is the result of the synergy of a great team. It wouldn't be complete without mentioning a few special people.

First of all, thanks to Jan Kabili for putting up with my endless hair-splitting during tech edits and for putting in the all-nighters to make this book happen.

Thanks to Jack Davis for having the confidence in me to work on this project. It's been an honor, and I enjoy bumping into you just about everywhere I go.

The Peachpit team, especially Nancy Ruenzel, Rebecca Gulick, and David Van Ness, you're an awesome team.

Thanks to Gwyn Weisberg and Addy Roff from Adobe Systems; your support is worth more than words.

Thanks to everyone who visits the site at PhotoshopCAFE—especially all the awesome Mods and Admins who keep things going smoothly and in the right spirit during my absence while I have been occupied on this book and others. You are the best!

My buddies in the business, Al Ward from actionFX.com, Scott and Jeff Kelby, Chris Main, Dave Cross, Matt Kloskowski, Bruce Bicknell, Melinda Gotelli, Barbara Thompson, Felix Nelson, and everyone else from KW, your support and inspiration fuels me.

To all my online buddies, Phunk (effectlab), Nina (eyesondesign), Mark Monciardini (designsbymark), Malachi (liquidwerx), Jay (urbangrafixdesigns), Avi (worth1000), Trevor Morris (GFX), Ryan (eyeballdesign), Jens Karlsson (chapter3), and many others I have neglected to mention, thanks for the synergy and making things more fun!

Thanks to my wonderful family and friends; you make it all worthwhile.

Thanks to God for giving me the gifts I have and allowing me to use them in the way I enjoy.

—*Colin Smith*

Contents

3 AUTOMATION 100

4 SITES THAT WOW! 150

Introduction

FRESH IDEAS, cool techniques, and sound advice—if that's what you're after, you've picked up the right book. *How to Wow: Photoshop CS2 for the Web* is not just a collection of recipes. It is designed to teach you the principles you need to create your own Web graphics—including rollovers, sliced and optimized images, animations, interactive page layouts, and more. At the same time, this book will inspire you by providing gorgeous, practical examples on which to practice these techniques, with commands for Mac and Windows users. You'll get ideas for how to incorporate graphics in your own sites, and you'll learn efficient production techniques that will save you time and effort in your own work.

What's New?

Adobe has added some new Web-related features to Photoshop CS2, but has not changed ImageReady since the last version. These conditions are reflected in this edition of this book. We've updated all the projects for CS2, rewritten some of the projects to take place in Photoshop (which now has its own Animation palette), and added some brand–new projects to show off new Photoshop features like variables and datasets, the Image Processor script, and Flash Web Photo Galleries.

Why Do You Need This Book?

The answer is simple. There are very few resources that address how to make content for the Web in Photoshop and ImageReady and that offer step-by-step, inspirational recipes for real-world Web graphics projects. Whether you design sites for a living or work on personal

Web projects, these are things you need to know. That's where we come in. Both of us, Jan and Colin, have been teaching, writing about, and making Web graphics for most of our careers. We're expert Photoshop trainers, and between us we've written more than a dozen Photoshop books. All this is not to blow our own horns, but to let you know that we really can help you.

What's on the CD-ROM?

The CD-ROM at the back of the book contains all the files you need to follow along with the projects. There are also end files for each project to give you a sense of where you're going.

The CD-ROM also has some Photoshop presets—styles, actions, and patterns—that you'll need to complete some of the projects in the book. Please take the time to install the HTW Presets now, following the instructions on the next page. Thanks to How to Wow series editor Jack Davis, you'll also find a collection of Wow Button Style presets in the One-Click Wow Styles folder. These are some of the more than 1,000 presets from the second edition of Jack Davis' book *Adobe Photoshop One-Click Wow!* In addition, there are some third-party offers on the CD-ROM. Check them out.

If you have any questions about the book or problems with the CD-ROM, contact Peachpit Press at ask@peachpit.com.

Getting the most out of this book is a collaborative process. Work through the projects with us, paying particular attention to those things you need to know for your Web work or play. Let's begin.

Working with the Presets and Project Files

The CD-ROM at the back of the book contains two important folders—the *HTW Project Files folder* and the *HTW Presets folder*. Both are essential for working through the projects in this book. Before going any further, please follow these instructions for installing them on your computer.

The Wow Button Style presets in the *One-Click Wow Styles folder* are a gift to you from How to Wow series editor Jack Davis. These button styles are not used in this book. They are for you to enjoy at your leisure. If you want to use them, install and load them the same way you install and load the HTW Presets folder, as explained to the right.

Step 1: Copy

Copy the **HTW Project Files folder** to your hard drive before you begin working through the projects in the book. This folder contains beginning files you'll need to follow along with each project, and end files that show you the finished project. Don't try to work with these project files from the CD.

Copy the **HTW Presets folder**, which contains styles, actions, and patterns for use with the projects in the book **A**, to this specific location on your hard drive: Place the whole HTW Presets folder into the Presets folder, which is inside the Adobe Photoshop CS2 program folder on your hard drive **B**. Then launch or restart Photoshop and ImageReady.

You're not done yet. The next step is to load the preset styles, patterns, and actions into Photoshop's and ImageReady's palettes as described in the column to the right. This is done slightly differently in Photoshop and ImageReady.

Step 2: Load

In Photoshop:
Open the Photoshop Styles palette (Window>Styles), click its side arrow, and choose HTWWeb-Styles **C**. At the prompt: "Replace current styles with the styles from HTWWeb-Styles.asl?" click the OK button. The HTWWeb-Styles are now the only styles visible in the Styles palette.

Open the Photoshop Actions palette (Window>Actions), click its side arrow, and choose HTWWeb-Actions **D**.

In ImageReady:
Open the ImageReady Styles palette, click its side arrow, and choose Replace Styles. The Replace Styles dialog box opens to the Styles presets in the program folder. Scroll to HTW Presets **E**. Then select HTWWeb-Styles.asl and click Open.

If you want HTWWeb-Styles to appear in ImageReady's Styles palette side menu in the future, choose Save Styles from that menu, navigate to the Photoshop CS2 program folder>Presets>Styles, enter Save As: HTWWeb-Styles, and click Save. ▥

1

NAVIGATION

Creating Stylish,
User-Friendly Navigation

NAVIGATION IS THE MOST important graphic element in a Web site. This chapter walks you through a variety of recipes for creating visually exciting graphics that support and enhance navigation.

The navigation system is the engine that drives a viewer through a site and the road map the viewer uses to explore the site. A good navigation scheme is one that is both easy to find on every page and easy to use. It communicates clearly and simply where the viewer is in the site, where she can go from that point, and how to get there.

Graphics play a pivotal role in making navigation successful. Meaningful navigation icons, like symbols on a map, guide the viewer in the search for content. Rollovers offer visual clues to the presence and location of navigation. Button size and color can communicate the importance of particular information in the site hierarchy. The look of a navigation scheme can pack a visual punch that contributes to your site's Wow quotient.

Critical Skills

You'll learn critical skills for building, slicing, and optimizing navigation

graphics from the first two projects in this chapter. You'll use these skills to complete many of the projects in this book and over and over in your personal Web work. We urge you to work through these lessons first, even if you're dying to skip to another juicy lesson later in the book.

In the first project, Building a Navigation Bar, you learn how to put together a set of matching buttons for a navigation bar, taking advantage of time-saving construction techniques and special Web-oriented features in Photoshop CS2. The emphasis here is on efficiency—using one button as a template for an entire bar of matching buttons. The second project, Slicing and Optimizing a Navigation Bar, simplifies the seemingly complex tasks of slicing and optimizing individual components of a navigation bar. We explain how and why to slice, and we show you how to optimize slices in GIF and JPEG formats for fast download and display on the Web. The third project shows you how to use a new feature in Photoshop CS2, Smart Objects, to create and quickly modify a series of navigation buttons. The fourth project, Transparent Buttons, demonstrates how to surround

navigation buttons with transparency to allow your Web page background to show through.

Rollovers

With the basics under your belt, you're ready to tackle rollovers in ImageReady. Rollovers and other interactive graphics are what make the Web special. Rollovers actively involve your audience with your site and offer dynamic information about site content and structure. In this chapter's fifth project, Rollover Navigation, you make JavaScript-powered rollover buttons without the hassle of hands-on programming. The next project, Pointers and Remote Rollovers, cranks things up a notch. Here you learn to make rollovers that trigger a remote event elsewhere on the page, applying that technique to create a stylish navigation bar with mobile pointers.

Image Maps

The last project in this chapter, Image Map Navigation, offers an alternative for those times when you don't want your navigation icons all lined up in neat rows. If it's asymmetry you're after, consider making an image map with hot spots as your navigation points in ImageReady. We invite you to work through all the recipes in this chapter with us to savor these tasty treats.

Starting a New File for the Web

When you create a navigation bar, a page layout, or any Web graphic from scratch, there are some important technical issues to consider up front—including image dimensions, resolution, color mode, and color profile.

You confront most of these issues right off the bat in Photoshop when you set up a new document. We help you unravel these technical mysteries here.

T I P

New Files in ImageReady: When you start a new file for the Web in ImageReady, rather than Photoshop, you're faced with fewer technical decisions (although you have fewer image-building tools available). In ImageReady, files are automatically measured in pixels, are in RGB color mode, and have no color profiles. So your only hard choice is how big to make the file.

Image Dimensions

Files are measured in pixels when you design for the Web, but Photoshop's default for dialog boxes and rulers is set to inches. You can change inches to pixels throughout the program by choosing Photoshop/File>Preferences>Units & Rulers and setting the Rulers field to pixels.

Choose File>New, and enter the Width and Height of a new Web file *in pixels*. A navigation bar or a page layout is best viewed without scrolling, so choose dimensions for those files that will fit within a typical browser window. Unfortunately, browser window sizes vary with each viewer's monitor display settings, choice of browser, and viewing behavior, so we can't give you one foolproof file size recommendation. Many designers make their navigation bars about 760 pixels wide and their page layouts about 760 x 410 pixels, assuming that today's typical monitor is set to at least 800 x 600 pixels and accounting for scroll bars and other browser elements.

It's best to take the time to research the platform, display resolution, and browser that your particular audience is likely to use. Take a screen shot of an open Web browser in that setup, and crop away the browser interface elements to get a measurement in pixels of the area your viewers can see without scrolling. Use those numbers to size Web graphics for your particular audience.

Resolution

Pixels are small rectangles of color information that are the building blocks of bitmapped images. Resolution, as that term is used in Photoshop's dialog boxes, describes the number of pixels per inch (ppi) in an image. If you take our advice in the previous panel and set the dimensions of a file destined for the Web in pixels rather than inches, it doesn't matter what number is in the Resolution field of the New dialog box. Photoshop will create a file with the number of pixels you dictate—without regard for pixels per inch—just as ImageReady does automatically.

However, if you leave the Width and Height fields in Photoshop's New dialog box set to inches, it's important to set the Resolution field to the resolution at which images are displayed in a Web browser on a standard screen–between 72 and 96 ppi depending on a viewer's screen display settings. The same is true if you're resizing an existing image for use on the Web in Photoshop's Image Size dialog box.

Note that your Photoshop settings do not control the absolute size of an image on a viewer's screen. That depends on the display size of each viewer's monitor. For example, if a viewer changes her display from 800 x 600 to 1024 x 768, each pixel becomes smaller, making the same image look smaller on her screen.

Color Mode and Bit Depth

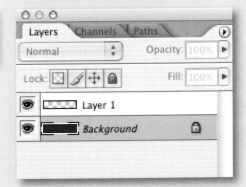

Set Color Mode to **RGB Color** in Photoshop's New dialog box when you are creating a file for the Web. Web browsers cannot see files in any of the other color modes offered—Bitmap, Grayscale, CMYK Color, or Lab Color.

Color mode describes the set of available colors from which an image is built. Each pixel in an RGB file is composed of a combination of red, green, and blue color values.

Bit depth is the amount of color data in each channel of color (red, green, and blue). Leave Bit Depth set to **8 bit**. This creates an image with 24 bits of color information (8 bits in each of the 3 channels of an RGB image), accommodating 16.7 million possible colors.

Background Contents

Every new file begins with a single layer. The nature of that layer depends on how you set the Background Contents field in the New dialog box. If you choose Transparent, the first layer will be composed of transparent pixels represented by a gray and white checkerboard pattern and will be a regular layer. This is the best choice if you plan on optimizing the image as a transparent GIF through which you can see a Web page background.

If you choose either White or Background Color in the New dialog box, the first layer will be a special kind of layer called a *Background* layer. **A Background layer acts differently than a regular layer.** A Background layer cannot have transparent pixels, and you can't change its opacity or move its contents. You also cannot place another layer below a Background layer in the Layers palette. All of these properties can make a Background layer difficult to work with.

To change a Background layer into a regular layer that doesn't have these restrictions, choose Layer>New>Layer from Background, or double-click the Background layer to open the New Layer dialog box, rename the layer, and click OK.

Color Profile

Photoshop's color management system is designed to achieve consistency in the way colors in an image appear on screen and in print. Unfortunately, most Web browsers are not color-managed. So there is no sure-fire way to achieve consistency between the way colors appear on your screen in Photoshop and the way they will appear in each viewer's Web browser.

The best solution we've found is to design an image for the Web in the sRGB color space, so that it appears in Photoshop much the way it would in a Web browser on a typical Windows monitor.

If you're starting a new file from scratch, click the Advanced arrow in Photoshop's New dialog box to reveal the Color Profile menu. Choose the sRGB profile from that menu. If you're using an existing file that has been tagged with a profile other than sRGB, choose Edit>Convert to Profile and choose Profile: sRGB in the Destination Space.

You could also set Photoshop's Color Settings (Edit>Color Settings) to North America Web/Internet. This sets Photoshop's Working Space to sRGB, making sRGB the default profile for new files and untagged files. ▣

Building a Navigation Bar

Add a set of matching buttons to a navigation bar.

INSIGHT

Using Adobe Bridge to open files.
Adobe Bridge is a file viewer and manager that comes with Photoshop CS2. Bridge is a separate program that replaces the old Photoshop File Browser. You can use Bridge to view and open project files as you work through these lessons. Alternatively, you can open project files directly from Photoshop or ImageReady (File>Open).

If a file opens in a program other than Photoshop CS2 or ImageReady CS2 when you double-click its thumbnail in Bridge, you can change the file type association for files with that extension in Bridge preferences (Bridge/ Edit>Preferences).

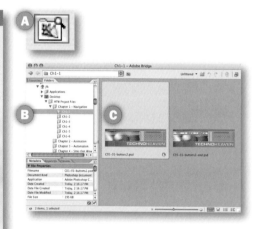

1. Open the Project File in Photoshop
Copy the HTW Project Files folder to your computer if you haven't already. Launch Photoshop CS2 and click the Go to Bridge icon on the right side of Photoshop's Options bar **A** to open Adobe Bridge. In Bridge, browse to the HTW Project Files>Chapter 1-Navigation>Ch1-1 folder **B**. In the Bridge content area, hold the Option/Alt key as you double-click the C01-01-buttons2.psd thumbnail **C** to open that file in Photoshop CS2 and to minimize Bridge.

The project file contains some background artwork for a navigation bar. Your task is to add a series of buttons to this navigation bar. You'll learn an efficient workflow for creating a set of matching buttons. Along the way, you'll become familiar with some object-oriented features new to Photoshop CS2 that come in handy for building Web graphics—multiple layer selection, layer groups, and smart guides.

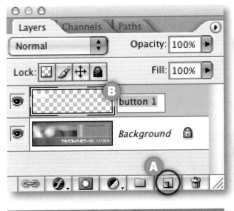

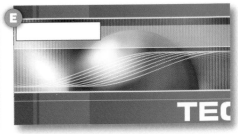

2. Create a Button

Start by creating one rectangular button on its own layer. Click the Create New Layer button at the bottom of the Layers palette **A**. Rename the new layer by double-clicking its Layer 1 name and typing **button 1** **B**. Click on the button 1 layer to make sure it's selected.

Select the Rectangular Marquee tool from Photoshop's toolbox **C**. In the Options bar at the top of the screen, choose Fixed Size from the Style menu and enter Width: 139 px and Height: 29 px **D**. Click in the image to create a rectangular selection.

Press X and then D to set the Foreground color to white. Press Option-Delete/Alt-Backspace to fill the selection with that Foreground color. Press Command-D to deselect. Select the Move tool and drag the button into position on the left side of the translucent white bar, matching the illustration **E**.

TIP

Turning Off Layer Edges. You may see a blue border around your new button, indicating the edges of the artwork on the layer. If you find the border distracting, you can hide it by toggling View>Show>Layer Edges.

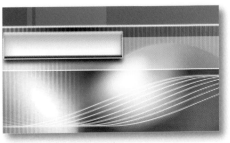

3. Style the Button

Choose Window>Styles to open the Styles palette. With the Button 1 layer selected, click the 01_button style **A** to apply it to button 1. This style is included in the HTW Presets on the CD. If you don't see it, go back to the Introduction and follow the instructions on installing and loading the HTW Presets, or apply a different style from the Styles palette.

TIP

Measuring Type in Pixels. Change Photoshop's type measurements to pixels by choosing Photoshop/ Edit>Preferences>Units and Rulers and choosing Type: pixels.

4. Add Button Text

Select the Type tool. In the Options bar, set Font Family to Arial, Style to Regular, Size to 21 px, anti-aliasing to Sharp, and Color to black **A**. Click on the button in the image and type **home** **B**. This creates a new home type layer above the button 1 layer. Don't worry about where the text is positioned on the button for now. You'll align it to the button later.

TIP

Selecting Multiple Layers. You can select more than one layer at a time in Photoshop CS2, making it easy to group, move, transform, or otherwise affect multiple layers. To select multiple layers, Shift-click if the layers are next to one another in the Layers palette; Command/Ctrl-click if they are not.

5. Group the Button and Its Text

With the home type layer selected, hold the Shift key and click the button 1 layer in the Layers palette, so that both layers are selected **A**. Then choose Layer>Group Layers from the menu bar (or press Command/Ctrl-G). This gathers the two layers into a group labeled Group 1. Click the arrow to the left of Group 1 to see the group contents **B**. Now that the button and text are grouped, it will be easy to duplicate them as a unit.

INSIGHT

Auto Select Group. If an object's layer is part of a group and Auto Select Group is checked in the Options bar, clicking on the object with the Move tool selects the group. If only Auto Select Layer is checked in the Options bar, clicking on the object selects its layer.

6. Make Duplicate Buttons

Select the Move tool **A**. In the Options bar, check Auto Select Groups **B**. If that option is not available, first check Auto Select Layer. You can't enable Auto Select Groups unless Auto Select Layer is checked.

Hold the Option/Alt key as you click on the button in the image (which selects Group 1) and as you drag to the right to duplicate the original button and its text **B**. Thin magenta lines, called smart guides, appear temporarily as you move the duplicate button and text **C**. Use them to align the two buttons horizontally as you drag. If you don't see these lines, choose View>Show>Smart Guides from the menu bar.

Repeat this entire step, creating a third duplicate button and moving it to the right, using the smart guides to align it to the other buttons. You now have three buttons, all displaying the label home **D**. In the Layers palette, you now have three groups.

INSIGHT

Smart Guides. Smart Guides are temporary alignment guides that appear automatically whenever you move or copy items in the document window.

7. Change the Button Text

Select the Type tool and click and drag to highlight the word home on the middle button **A**. Be careful not to click too far from the word or you'll inadvertently create a new type layer. Type *about us* and click the checkmark on the Options bar **B**. Repeat on the third button, renaming that button *contact us.*

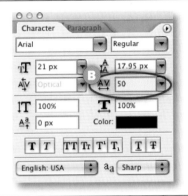

8. Edit Multiple Layers Together

Save time and effort by editing multiple layers at the same time. In the Layers palette, Command/Ctrl-click on each of the type layers—home, about us, and contact us—to select all three **A**. Open the Character palette (Window>Character). With the Type tool selected, choose 50 in the Tracking field **B** to increase the space between the letters on all three type layers at once.

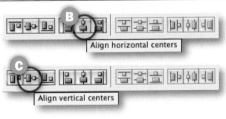

9. Align Text to Buttons

Now align each text label to its button. Start with the home button. Shift-click the home type layer and the button 1 layer to select them both in the Layers palette **A**. Select the Move tool. In the Options bar, click the Align Layer Horizontal Centers button to move the text to the horizontal center of the button **B**. Then click the Align Layer Vertical Centers button to move the text to the vertical center of the button **C**. Repeat this step on the other two buttons.

Congratulations! You've created a navigation bar of matching buttons with a minimum of fuss. The file is still in PSD (Photoshop Document format), which is a good format in which to save a master file because it retains layers. However, this image is not ready to upload to a Web site. Web browsers cannot display a PSD file; it must be converted to a Web-ready format, like JPEG or GIF, as you learn to do in the next project. ▣

JPEG Optimization Settings

Optimizing reduces the size of an image so it will load faster in a Web browser. JPEG, is the best format for optimizing photographs. JPEG is also useful for optimizing Web graphics that contain graduated colors, like gradients, glows, or shadows. Optimize an image as a JPEG using the following settings in Photoshop's Save for Web window or ImageReady's Optimize palette.

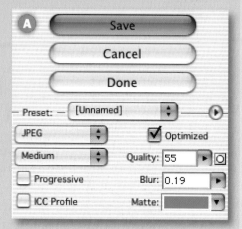

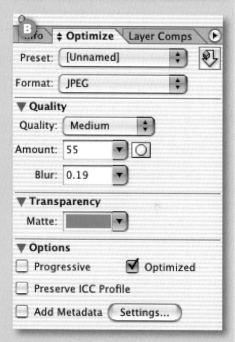

File Format

In Photoshop, choose File>Save for Web to open the Save for Web window **A**. In Image-Ready, choose Window>Optimize to open the Optimize palette **B** and expand the Optimize palette to see all its settings, as explained in the tip on the opposite page. Choose JPEG from the Format menu, or start with a pre-made collection of JPEG settings from the Preset menu.

Quality

Quality is the variable that has the most significant impact on the file size and appearance of a JPEG. The lower the quality setting, the more compression is applied. This reduces the file size, but can degrade the appearance of the image. Choose a preset from the Quality menu. Fine-tune that setting with the slider in Photoshop's Quality field or ImageReady's Amount field. The circle icon to the right of Photoshop's Quality field and ImageReady's Amount field opens a dialog box in which you can set different quality levels for text layers, vector layers, and individual channels in an image.

Blur

Blurring an image decreases its file size. Add blur by dragging the slider in the Blur field to the right. Don't overdo it or your image will look too soft.

Optimized

Leave this setting checked to lower file size slightly.

Progressive

This setting causes an image to appear progressively while it's downloading, so the viewer sees a low-resolution version before she sees the real thing. Leave this setting unchecked unless you like this effect.

T I P

Expand ImageReady's Optimize palette. To see all the ImageReady optimization settings, click the double-pointed arrow on the Optimize palette tab.

ICC Profile

ICC Profiles contain color management information. Many designers choose not to include ICC Profiles with Web files because most Web browsers can't read them and they increase the size of a file. To do this, uncheck ICC Profile.

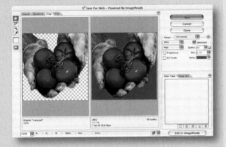

Matte

The Matte field is only relevant if there are transparent pixels in the source image. Because JPEG format does not allow transparency, any transparent pixels in the source image will be filled with the color in the Matte field when you optimize as JPEG. If you plan to use a solid-color Web page background, set the JPEG's Matte field to the same color as the page background. This will cause the areas of the image that were transparent to blend in with the Web page background, creating the illusion of transparency.

Color Table

Ignore the Color Table in Photoshop's Save for Web window when you're optimizing a JPEG. We mention the Color Table here only to confirm that it should be blank when format is set to JPEG. That's because JPEGs, unlike GIFs, do not map the colors in the source file to a limited color palette.

Image Size

Reducing the dimensions of an image will always reduce the file size. In Photoshop, you can reduce the dimensions of the optimized file without affecting the source file. Click the Image Size tab in the Save for Web window **A**. Check Constrain Proportions to avoid distorting the image **B**. Reduce Width and Height to fixed numbers of pixels or by Percent **C**. Changing image size—particularly sizing up—can degrade image quality. To minimize the negative effect on image quality, set Quality to Bicubic Sharper when you're sizing down and to Bicubic Smoother when you're sizing up **D**. In ImageReady, resizing is done on the source file, using similar settings in the Image Size dialog box (Image>Image Size).

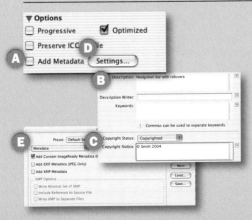

Metadata

Metadata is file information. You can choose to attach various kinds of metadata to a Web file from ImageReady's Optimize palette. Metadata adds to file size, so we usually uncheck Add Metadata **A**. If you leave Add Metadata checked, by default ImageReady adds any information that's in the Description **B** and Copyright Notice **C** fields of the File Info dialog box (File>File Info), increasing file size slightly. In rare cases, you may want to include EXIF data (information stored in a digital photograph, such as camera settings) or XMP data (keywords and other information about a file for use by other applications). To do that, click the Settings button in ImageReady's Optimize palette **D** to open the Output Settings dialog box and choose a metadata option there **E**. ▥

GIF Optimization Settings

GIF, which stands for Graphics Interchange Format, is the ideal format for optimizing areas of solid color and lines, like illustrations, logos, cartoons, line art, and text. Use the following settings in Photoshop's Save for Web window or ImageReady's Optimize palette to optimize a GIF.

File Format

Open Photoshop's Save for Web window (File>Save for Web) **A** or ImageReady's Optimize palette (Window>Optimize) **B**. Choose GIF from the Format menu, or choose a collection of GIF settings from the Preset menu. (Two PNG formats are also available—PNG-8, which is similar to GIF, and PNG-24, which can contain varying degrees of transparency. These formats are less popular than GIF and JPEG because not all Web browsers display PNGs correctly, and because PNG-24 files can be relatively large in file size.)

Reduction Method

When you optimize a file as GIF, all the colors in the original image are converted to a limited palette of colors. The Reduction setting determines how that color palette is generated. Choose Selective, Perceptual, or Adaptive from the Reduction menu to create a palette based on the colors in your original image. Avoid the other choices, because they are fixed palettes unrelated to the original image and can cause a noticeable change in image color. Don't feel compelled to choose Web (which generates a fixed palette of the 216 "Web-safe" colors), because today most monitors are 24-bit and can display a much wider range of colors. Use the Mask icon next to the Reduction menu to generate different palettes for text layers, vector layers, and selections you've saved to alpha channels.

Number of Colors

The Colors setting determines how many colors are included in a GIF's color palette, up to a maximum of 256 colors. This setting has the most significant impact on the file size and the appearance of a GIF. Fewer colors will reduce the file size, but may cause the image to lose important details. Choose the lowest preset from the Colors menu that produces an image that looks good to you. Then fine-tune your choice by typing a slightly lower number into the Colors field. To avoid losing particular colors as you reduce the Colors setting, first select those colors in the image with the Eyedropper tool (Shift+click to select multiple colors) and click the Lock icon at the bottom of the Color Table (see description on facing page); then reduce the Colors setting.

Web-Snap

Leave Web-Snap set to 0%. This setting converts some of the colors in your palette to Web-safe without allowing you to choose which colors are converted. If you want to use Web-safe colors, it's preferable to select those colors in the image with the Eyedropper tool (Shift+click to select multiple colors), and then click the Web Shift icon (the cube) at the bottom of the Color Table. This method gives you more control over the conversion.

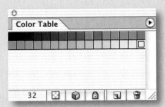

Color Table

The Color Table displays and allows you to edit the colors in a GIF's color palette. You can select colors in the Color Table to convert them to other colors, make them transparent, shift them to Web-safe, or lock them down. Photoshop's Color Table is located in the Save for Web window. ImageReady's Color Table is located in a separate palette. Choose Window>Color Table, or click the Color Table Palette icon in the Optimize palette to open ImageReady's Color Table palette.

Dither

Dither (a pattern of colored dots) is used to simulate a color that's not in the Color Table. No Dither is usually the best choice, because dither increases file size. Dither is useful to avoid banding if you must optimize a photograph, gradient, or glow in GIF format. The Dither and Amount menus offer several dither patterns to choose from. Click the Mask icon to add different amounts of dither to text, vector objects, or alpha channels.

Transparency

GIFs, unlike JPEGs, can include transparency. If the original image has transparent areas, make sure there's a checkmark in the Transparency checkbox to retain transparency in the GIF. You can convert individual colors to transparency by selecting colors in the image with the Eyedropper tool and clicking the Map Transparency icon in the Color Table.

Matte

The Matte setting affects the edges of a transparent GIF. If Matte is set to None, the edges of the graphic will appear jagged when the GIF is placed on a Web page. If Matte is set to a color that matches a Web page background, the edges of the graphic will appear smooth against that background. If Matte is left at its default of white, the graphic may display an unsightly white halo against a Web page background.

Transparency Dither

Transparency Dither creates dots of color at the edge of a transparent GIF, so you can place the same transparent GIF on different backgrounds without seeing a halo of color. Choose No Dither if, like us, you find this look too chunky for your taste.

Other Options

Increase the Lossy slider slightly to reduce file size. Click the Mask icon to add different amounts of Lossy compression to text, vector objects, or alpha channels. Check Interlaced if you want a low-resolution pre-download. Check Unified Color to apply the same Color Table to all states of a rollover graphic. Uncheck Metadata to keep file size down. Use the preview controls to view animation frames in the Save for Web window. ▥

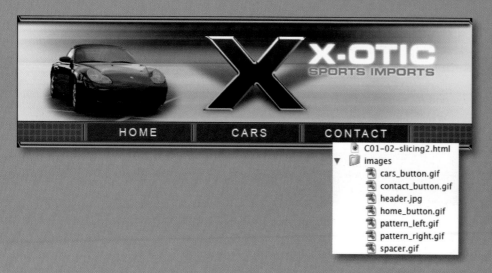

Slicing and Optimizing a Navigation Bar

Slice a navigation bar and optimize each slice as a separate GIF or JPEG, as you learn how and why to slice Web graphics.

1. Slice the Buttons

Open C01-02-slicing2.psd from the Chapter 1-Navigation>Ch1-2 folder into Photoshop CS2. This project is done in Photoshop, although you can slice and optimize in ImageReady too.

Slicing carves an image into pieces, each of which becomes a separate Web file. It's common to slice buttons so that you can attach a separate link to each button file when you build your site.

Select all three button layers in the Layers palette by holding the Shift key as you click on the Home Button layer and then the Contact Button layer **A**. Choose Layer>New Layer-Based Slices from the menu bar. This creates a tight, rectangular *layer-based slice* (identifiable by a blue symbol) around each button **B**, and some surrounding slices called *auto slices* (identified by gray symbols) to fill in the gaps **C**.

Layer-based slicing is quick and easy, and creates slices that move with the underlying art so you can change your design after slicing. But this slicing method works only if each button is alone on a separate layer.

INSIGHT

Develop a Slicing Strategy. Slice with a specific purpose in mind so you don't end up with random slices that produce unnecessary files. Valid reasons to slice are:

- To add discrete links to multiple buttons.
- To optimize each area of an image in the appropriate format.
- To make rollover buttons or remote rollovers.
- To animate part of an image.
- But *not* to try to accelerate download to viewers' browsers. Lots of small images aren't guaranteed to load faster than one large image.

TIP

Adjusting Slices. User slices can be adjusted at any time by clicking and dragging slice borders with the Slice Select tool. Layer-based slices and auto slices cannot be adjusted until they are converted to user slices. To do that, select a slice with the Slice Select tool and click the Promote button in Photoshop's Options bar or choose Slices>Promote to User Slice in ImageReady.

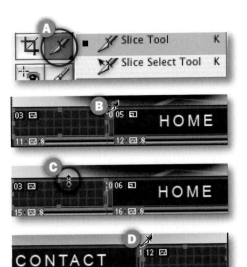

2. Slice the Pattern Graphics

The patterns on each side of the buttons will optimize best as GIFs, because they are illustrations. The rest of the image will optimize best as JPEGs because it contains photos, bevels, and gradients. In this step you'll slice the patterns in order to optimize them separately. You can't use layer-based slicing because the patterns are not on individual layers. This is a job for the Slice tool.

Select the Slice tool in the toolbox **A**. Click and drag around the pattern on the left to create a manually drawn slice called a ***user slice*** **B**. As you drag, use the magenta smart guides to align this slice to the button slices. If the slice needs adjusting, click on any of the slice borders and drag **C**. Repeat to slice the pattern on the right **D**.

TIP

Slice Naming. Avoid using spaces or odd characters in slice names to ensure that the GIFs and JPEGs generated from the slices have names that are server friendly.

3. Name the Slices

Give the major slices meaningful names so the files they produce are recognizable later. Select the Slice Select tool in the toolbox **A**, and click on the slice around the Home button. Click the Slice Options button in the Options bar **B** to open the Slice Options palette. Type ***home_button*** in the Name field and click OK **C**. Repeat for each button slice and for the large graphic slice at the top of the image, giving each a recognizable name. Naming the large graphic slice automatically promotes it to a user slice.

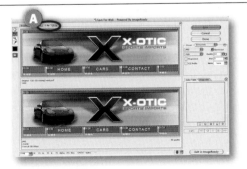

4. Open the Save for Web Window

Choose File>Save for Web to open the Save for Web window—where optimizing is done in Photoshop. Click the 2-Up tab **A** so that you can compare the original image at the top of the window to a preview of the optimized image at the bottom of the window.

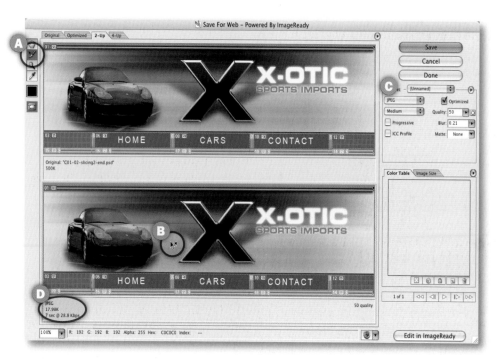

5. Optimize the Top Graphic Slice

Apply different optimization settings to individual slices to minimize file size and maximize appearance. Start with the top graphic slice, which is likely to optimize best as JPEG due to the photo and the gradient background in this slice. Choose the Save for Web Slice Select tool **A**, and click on the large graphic slice in the preview pane **B**. Choose the following optimization settings **C** (described in the preceding **JPEG Optimization Settings**) for this slice:

- Optimized File Format: JPEG.

- Quality pop-up menu: Medium. Then increase the Quality slider to 50 to reduce remaining color artifacts.

- Blur slider: Increase slightly to 0.21.

- Optimized: Checked.

- ICC Profile: Unchecked.

- Progressive: Unchecked.

The size of this slice is reduced to around 17.98K **D**.

6. Optimize the Buttons

In the preview pane, Shift-click the three button slices to select them all. Choose the following settings **A** (described in **GIF Optimization Settings**):

- Optimized File Format: GIF.

- Color Reduction Algorithm: Selective.

- Colors: 16 (seen in the Color Table).

- Dither Algorithm: No Dither.

- Lossy: 10.

- Interlaced: Unchecked.

- Web-Snap: 0%.

- Transparency, Matte: Not relevant.

All the buttons together are just 1.59K **B**.

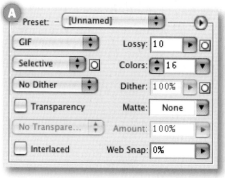

TIP

Balance File Size and Appearance.
Always choose optimization settings that minimize the file size of a slice, without degrading its appearance too much. This is a balancing act that usually requires compromise. Keep your eye on the file size under the selected preview pane and the appearance of the image in the preview pane. To get a better look at the preview, click the Slice Visibility toggle to hide slices.

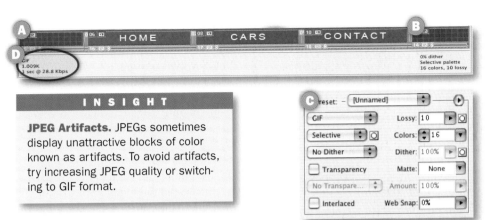

7. Optimize the Patterns

Shift-click on the two square pattern slices with the Slice Select tool to select them both **A**, **B**. These graphics display artifacts when optimized as JPEGs, so you'll optimize them as GIFs. Use the same GIF optimization settings you applied to the buttons **C**.

With those settings, file size for both pattern slices is just 1.006K **D**. This size may vary depending on how you drew these slices.

INSIGHT

JPEG Artifacts. JPEGs sometimes display unattractive blocks of color known as artifacts. To avoid artifacts, try increasing JPEG quality or switching to GIF format.

8. Optimize the Auto Slices

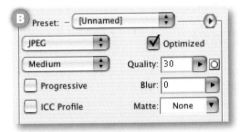

The auto slices (those with gray numbers) are automatically linked for optimization. So optimizing one auto slice will optimize them all, saving time and effort. Use the Slice Select tool to select any one of the auto slices in the preview pane **A**. It's difficult to predict whether these auto slices will optimize best as GIF or JPEG. The best approach is to try both, observing the appearance and file size of all the auto slices as you choose optimization settings. We settled on **B**:

- Optimized File Format: JPEG.
- Quality pop-up menu: Medium.
- Blur slider: 0.
- Optimized: Checked.
- ICC Profile: Unchecked.
- Progressive: Unchecked.

All of the auto slices now share these settings.

Select all the slices by clicking and dragging with the Slice Select tool across all the slices in the preview pane of the Save for Web window. The file size readout now reports the total file size of the whole navigation bar as 25.66K **C**.

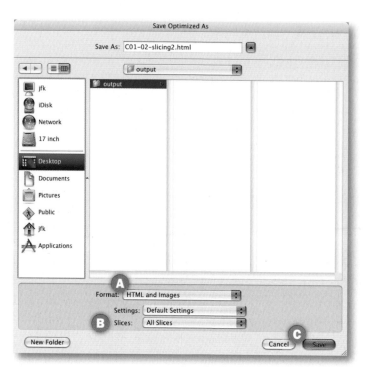

9. Save the Optimized Files

Photoshop will save each of the slices in this image as a separate GIF or JPEG, along with an HTML file containing a table to reassemble all the individual images into a navigation bar. Click Save in the Save for Web window. In the Save Optimized As window, choose HTML and Images from the Format/Save as Type menu to generate the HTML file **A**. (If you choose Images, Photoshop will save only individual GIFs and JPEGs, which you could take into a site-building program for assembly there.) Leave the Slices menu set to All Slices **B**, choose a destination, and click Save **C**.

On your hard drive, there will now be an HTML file and an Images folder containing all the optimized GIFs and JPEGs. Don't separate the HTML file and the Images folder or the links to the images will break. Open the HTML file in a Web browser to see the results of your hard work. Each slice has become a separate image in a cell of an HTML table that holds all the images in place.

I N S I G H T

Slicing and Optimizing a Web Page Layout. Everything you learned here applies to preparing any large image for the Web. Try using these skills to prepare an entire page layout for the Web, slicing, optimizing, and saving its individual components just as you did here with a navigation bar.

10. Save the Source File

Before you close your original PSD file, choose File>Save As to save a copy of the source file that preserves your optimization settings and slices. Choose a destination, check Layers to preserve any layers in the file **A**, and click Save **B**. Use this source file to make changes to the Web files in the future, rather than try to edit and recompress the optimized versions of the files. 🔲

Slice Options

These settings impact how the contents of a selected slice appear in a Web browser. Use them only if you plan to save an HTML file with your slices. To access these settings, choose the Slice Select tool and select a slice. In Photoshop open the **Slice Options dialog box** A (click the Slice Options button in the Options bar). In Image-Ready, open the **Slice palette** B (click the Slice palette icon in the Options bar).

Slice Type

Leave Slice Type set to Image if a slice contains an image you want to display. Change Slice Type to No Image to leave a sliced area blank. No Image is a good choice for auto slices that have no important image content and for areas to which you plan to add HTML text. Rather than entering your HTML text in the text box that appears, add it later in a site-building program like GoLive or Dreamweaver, where you'll have more control.

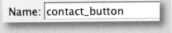

Name

Enter a meaningful name, without spaces or odd characters, for the slice and the image file it will produce. Otherwise, the program automatically generates a complex name.

URL

To add a link from a slice to an external Web site, type the entire URL of that site here. Links to pages in the same site are easier to add later in a site-building program.

Target

Use the Target field to control how the browser window behaves. Enter **_blank** to open a linked-to page in another browser window so viewers aren't drawn away from your site. The other choices are used with frames and are best added in a site-building program.

Message Text

The content of this field appears in the status bar at the bottom of a Web browser when a viewer mouses over the sliced area. Use it to offer extra information to viewers.

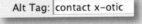

Alt Tag

Use Alt Tag to add identifying information to an image slice for non-sighted visitors.

Dimensions

These settings add file dimensions to the HTML code. They're available only for user slices.

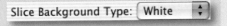

Slice Background Type

Use this field to add a color behind a No Image slice or a transparent GIF. ▥

Creating a Navigation Bar with Smart Objects

Use Smart Objects to edit multiple buttons all at once and to apply transformations without losing image quality.

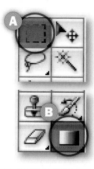

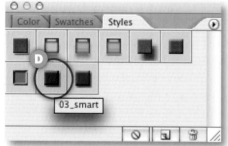

1. Create a Button

Open C01-03-smart2.psd from the Chapter 1-Navigation>Ch1-3 folder into Photoshop CS2. We started this navigation bar for you. You'll add a series of buttons, using Smart Objects to make the design process efficient and flexible.

First, make a simple button. Select the Background layer, choose Layer>New>Layer, type **button1** in the Name field of the New Layer dialog box, and click OK. Select the Rectangular Marquee tool **A**. In the Options bar, choose Style: Fixed Size and enter Width: 114 px and Height: 30 px. Click in the image to create a rectangular selection. Press D to set the Foreground color to black and the Background color to white. Select the Gradient tool **B** and drag from top to bottom of the selection to fill it with a black-to-white gradient **C**. Press Command/Ctrl-D to deselect. In the Styles palette, click the 03_smart style **D** to apply it to the button **E**. If you don't see this style, which is included in the HTW Presets, you may choose to create a different style or create your own.

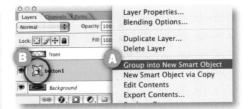

INSIGHT

How a Smart Object Works. When you convert layers into Smart Objects, the contents of the layers are tucked away behind the scenes. What you see is a thumbnail telling you that you're working on a reference to the layers. You can manipulate the Smart Object without harming the original content. Double-click on the thumbnail to open a new document that contains all the original pixels. Change and save this document and the changes will be reflected in your main document.

2. Make a Smart Object

To create a Smart Object from the button1 layer, Control/right-click that layer and choose Group Into New Smart Object from the contextual menu **A**. (This command is also available from the Layer>Smart Objects menu and from the Layers palette menu.) The button1 layer is converted into a layer with a Smart Object thumbnail **B**. The original data from the button layer is now embedded in this PSD file. The Smart Object is a composite created from that data.

CAUTION

Duplicating Smart Objects. If you want changes to one Smart Object to also occur in another Smart Object, use the commands listed in this step to duplicate the Smart Object. If you choose other commands, like Layer>Smart Objects>New Smart Object via Copy, you won't get this reflective effect between Smart Objects.

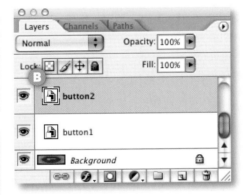

3. Duplicate the Smart Object

In this step you create three duplicates of your Smart Object for the other three buttons in the image.

Control/right-click the Smart Object layer and choose Duplicate Layer **A**. (This command is also available from the Layers palette menu or by pressing Command/Ctrl-J.) Name the duplicate button2. There's now a second Smart Object layer in the Layers palette **B**. Repeat twice more for button3 and button4. You won't see multiple buttons in the image yet because the duplicates are directly on top of one another.

The duplicate Smart Objects are associated with one another so that if you open, edit, and save changes to one, all the Smart Objects will change.

4. Distribute the Buttons

Select the Move tool in the toolbox. Make sure Auto Select Layer is checked in the Options bar. Click on the button in the image and drag to the right **A**. Repeat to separate the four buttons.

INSIGHT

Smart Objects Transform Without Degrading. The image quality of pixel-based (raster) layers suffers every time you rotate, scale, warp, or otherwise transform layer content. The beauty of Smart Objects is that they protect the original image from degradation. For example, you might scale down an item with Free Transform. If you change your mind and scale it back up to the original size, the image is not harmed. But as always, don't scale raster images much larger than their original size.

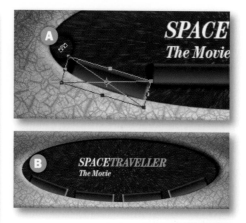

TIP

Editing Smart Objects. You're limited in the kinds of edits you can apply directly to a Smart Object. Features you can use on a Smart Object include transform commands, layer styles, layer masks, opacity adjustment, and blending mode. Other kinds of edits, like filtering, cropping, painting, and more, require opening a Smart Object to edit its contents.

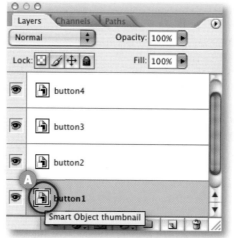

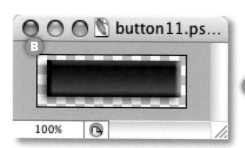

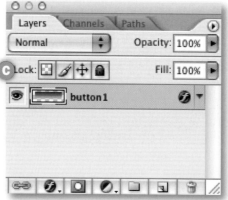

5. Rotate and Position the Buttons

One reason to turn these buttons into Smart Objects is to rotate them without degrading their image quality. Select the button1 Smart Object in the Layers palette, and choose Edit>Transform>Rotate. When the cursor changes to a curved arrow, click and drag to rotate the button **A**. Drag the button under the lip of the interface. Press Return/Enter to commit the transformation. Repeat as many times as necessary, without fear that your actions will degrade the image. Do the same on each of the other three buttons to match the illustration **B**.

6. Open a Smart Object to Edit

The biggest advantage of using Smart Objects in a navigation bar is that when you edit one Smart Object, the change ripples through all duplicate Smart Objects. If you convert all the navigation buttons to duplicate Smart Objects, as you did here, you can edit them all at once. This comes in handy if you want to try out matching styles on your buttons in the design process, or if a client wants a change to all the buttons in a navigation bar.

Double-click directly on the Smart Object thumbnail on the button1 layer **A** to begin editing the content of that Smart Object. Alternatively, choose Edit Contents from the Layer>Smart Objects menu or from the Layers palette menu. Click OK at the prompt that explains how to save your edits.

A new document window opens with the button image **B**. The Layers palette displays the original layer from which the Smart Object was made **C**. If this Smart Object had been made from multiple layers, you would see them all in this Layers palette.

INSIGHT

PSB Format. When you open a Smart Object for editing, the format of the document to be edited is PSB, Photoshop's Large Document format.

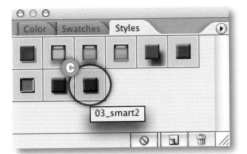

03_smart2

7. Edit the Smart Object

In this step you'll change the shape and style of the Smart Object. Select the Elliptical Marquee tool in the toolbox **A**, and drag an oval selection in the document window. Choose Select>Inverse to select everything but the oval shape **B**. Choose Edit>Delete and Command/Ctrl-D to deselect. The button is now a blue oval.

In the Styles palette, click the 03_smart2 style **C**, which came with the HTW Presets. If you don't see this style, reinstall the HTW Presets following the instructions in the Introduction or click on a style of your own choosing. The button is now a brown, beveled oval **D**.

8. Save the Edits

Choose File>Save to commit your edits. It's important that you save to the same location from which this file opened to maintain the connection to the original file. Avoid using File>Save As.

Click on the open file that contains the navigation bar, C01-03-smart2.psd. As soon as you do, the edits you performed on one Smart Object ripple through all the duplicate Smart Objects, changing all the buttons in the navigation bar to brown, beveled ovals.

9. Add Text to the Buttons

Select the Type tool and add four layers of text that read Home, Trailer, Story, and Links. Use Edit>Free Transform on each of the four Type layers to rotate and position each piece of type on top of its button.

Experiment with Smart Objects on some projects of your own. They are the wave of the future. ▣

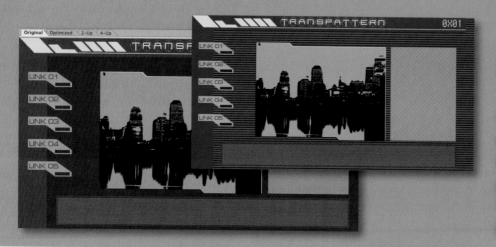

Transparent Buttons

Place transparent buttons on a Web page without the telltale halo you often see around Web graphics. This project is done in ImageReady.

1. Delete the Background Layer

Open into ImageReady C01-04-trans.psd from Chapter 1-Navigation>Ch1-4. This file has been sliced and optimized for you. If the slices aren't visible, click the Slice Visibility toggle in ImageReady's toolbox **A**.

Saving the solid gray background slices as GIF files would inflate the total file size of this page. Instead, make these areas transparent to let the Web page background show through. The page background color is created with HTML code, which has less impact on file size than do image files. Choose the Original tab in ImageReady's document window **B**. In the Layers palette, select the Background layer and drag it to the trash icon **C**. This creates transparency (represented by a checkerboard pattern) in the source file.

INSIGHT

Why Design with Transparency?
Transparency can add visual interest to a Web page by giving shape to the graphics. Without transparency all bitmapped graphics look rectangular, like the patterned boxes in this Web page layout.

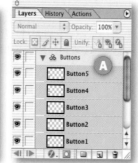

2. Slice the Buttons

Click the Button5 layer and hold the Shift key while clicking the Button1 layer in the Layers palette to select all the button layers **A**. Choose Layer>New Layer Based Slices from the menu bar to create a layer-based slice around each button **B**. Slices are always rectangular, so each slice encompasses some of the transparent area that surrounds the button.

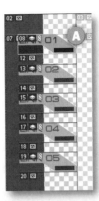

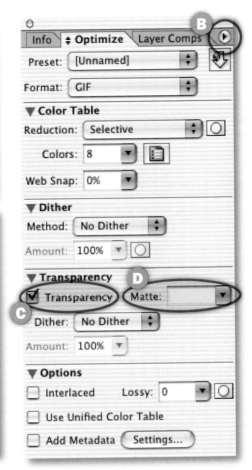

3. Optimize the Button Slices

Click on the Optimized tab in the document window to view the slices optimized for the Web. With all the button slices still selected (displaying yellow borders) choose Slices>Link Slices for Optimization from the menu bar. Select any button slice **A** with the Slice Select tool, and choose the following settings in the Optimize palette. (To expand the Optimize palette choose Show Options from the palette side menu **B**.)

- Format: GIF.
- Reduction: Selective.
- Colors: 8.
- Web-Snap: 0%.
- Dither Method: No Dither.
- Transparency: Make sure **Transparency** is checked or you won't see transparency around your buttons **C**.
- Matte: Leave the Matte field set to white temporarily **D**.
- Lossy: 0.
- Interlaced, Use Unified Color Table, and Add Metadata: Unchecked.

TIP

Optimizing in ImageReady. Optimizing in ImageReady is just like optimizing in Photoshop, except that the features are located in different places. In ImageReady the Slice and Slice Select tools each have a separate spot in the toolbox, the preview pane tabs are in the document window, optimization settings are in the Optimize palette (Window>Optimize), and the Color Table is in its own palette (Window>Color Table or click the Color Table Palette icon in the Optimize palette).

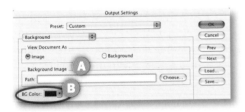

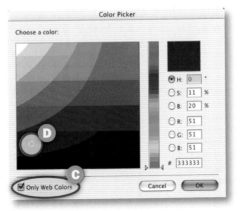

CAUTION

Web-Safe Backgrounds. Earlier we told you not to feel compelled to stick to Web-safe colors when you're making GIFs for the Web. However, when you're specifying a page background color that will be generated by HTML code we suggest you do use a Web-safe color so the color doesn't shift in a browser.

4. Specify a Page Background Color

Now set a color for a Web page background that will show through wherever there is transparency in a slice. Choose File>Output Settings>Background from the menu bar. Make sure that View Document As is set to Image, and the Path field is blank **A**.

Click in the BG Color field **B** to open the Color Picker. Activate the Only Web Colors checkbox **C**, click on the darkest Web-safe gray **D**, and click OK. This sets the Web page background color in the HTML file that will be saved with the sliced images. Click OK in the Output Settings dialog box.

INSIGHT

Soft Edges Become Halos.
A transparent GIF will have a halo if the graphic in the original file has soft edges. Soft edges can be created by a selection tool or painting tool that creates anti-aliased edges (edges with graduated levels of opacity), a feather, a blur, or a drop shadow.

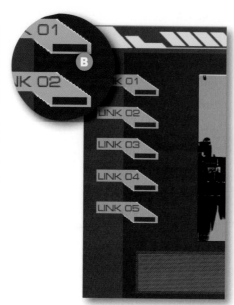

5. Preview the Buttons with Halos

Choose a Web browser from the Preview in Browser button in the toolbox **A** to preview your sliced images against a gray Web page background in a browser.

Notice that there are white pixels along the diagonal edges of each button **B**. This is not part of the design; it is a halo that takes its color from the default white Matte setting in the Optimize palette. The original file is in PSD format, which allows many levels of transparency. You are previewing the optimized file as a GIF, which allows only one level of transparency—completely transparent or completely opaque. The semitransparent pixels along the diagonal edges of the buttons have become opaque white, as specified in the Matte setting, creating the unsightly halo. The vertical and horizontal edges are not soft, so they have no halo. (Don't be confused by the white lines around the skyline graphic; they are part of this design.)

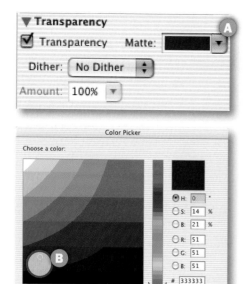

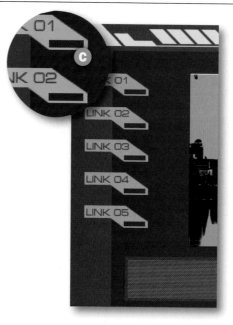

6. Hide the Halo

To camouflage the halo against a solid color background, simply set the Matte field in the Optimize palette to the same color as the Web page background. In the Optimize palette, click the Matte field **A** to open the Color Picker. Make sure Only Web Colors is checked, choose the same gray color you chose for the page background **B**, and click OK.

Click the Preview in Browser button again. This time you won't see the halo around the buttons in your Web browser **C**. It's still there, but it blends perfectly with the background of the same color.

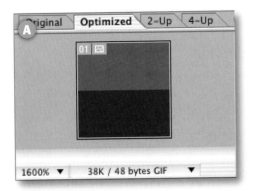

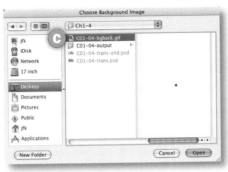

T I P

Patterned Backgrounds That Hide a Halo. Not all patterned backgrounds do a good job of camouflaging a transparent GIF's halo. Patterns with thin lines and similar colors work best. Thicker patterns with contrasting colors often reveal the halo.

7. Add a Repeating Patterned Background

You can use the same technique to camouflage a halo against some patterned backgrounds. To make a patterned background that is small in file size, take advantage of the tiling nature of an HTML background image. Start with a small patterned GIF file. This simple pattern, magnified here to 1600% so you can see it **A**, is six pixels wide by six pixels high and has a file size of less than 1K. The pattern file will be downloaded only once to a viewer's Web browser, but will be displayed over and over to fill any size browser window.

In the sliced document, choose File>Output Settings>Background. Click the Choose button next to the Path field **B** to open the Choose Background Image window. Navigate to the pattern file C01-04-bgback.gif in Chapter 1-Navigation>Ch1-4 and click Open **C**. Click OK. This identifies the pattern as a background image in the HTML file that will be saved with the slices.

8. Hide the Halo Against the Pattern

Open C01-04-bgback.gif and click on the lighter gray in the pattern with the Eyedropper tool to set the foreground color. In the Optimize palette, click the Matte field arrow and choose Foreground Color **A**. Click the Preview in Browser button. The halo blends into the pattern of horizontal stripes created from the repeated pattern file **B**.

9. Set Slice Options and Save

Select each auto slice (those with gray symbols) and set Type to No Image in the Slice palette (Window>Slice) **A**. Select each button slice and name it in the Slice palette **B**. Choose File>Save Optimized As, set Format to HTML and Images, and click Save. ▥

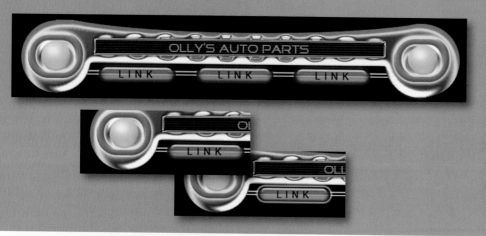

Rollover Navigation

Make a matched set of working rollover buttons in ImageReady the easy way, by creating and applying a rollover style.

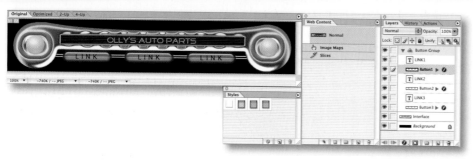

1. Set Up Your Workspace

Open the ImageReady palettes you'll use to create rollover buttons in this navigation bar—the Web Content, Styles, and Layers palettes. Click the Styles tab and drag the Styles palette away from the Web Content palette so you can see them both. Make sure you've loaded the HTWWeb-Styles preset into the Styles palette, as explained in the Introduction.

T I P

Create Rollovers in ImageReady. You can make artwork for rollover buttons in Photoshop, but when it's time to add rollover functionality, switch to ImageReady. Of the two programs, only ImageReady can write JavaScript code behind the scenes to make your rollovers work.

2. Create a Layer-Based Rollover

Open C01-05-roll.psd into ImageReady from Chapter 1-Navigation>C1-P5. The default Normal state of an image is the way the image looks when it first loads in a Web browser. If you add an Over state, the appearance changes when a viewer mouses over a trigger area that's defined by a slice.

Start by simultaneously creating a slice and an Over state for Button1. You have to use layer-based slicing because that slicing method is a prerequisite for creating rollover styles. Select the Button1 layer in the Layers palette **A**. Then click the Create Layer-Based Rollover icon at the bottom of the Web Content palette **B**. This generates a layer-based slice around the content of the Button1 layer **C** and an Over state for that slice, both listed in the Web Content palette.

3. Rename the Slice

Give your new slice a more manageable name by double-clicking its default name in the Web Content palette and typing **btn1** A, or by changing its name in the Slice palette B.

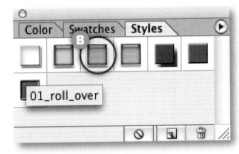

4. Change the Look of the Over State

Next you'll change the appearance of the sliced button in the Over state by applying a style. Other ways to change the appearance of a rollover graphic are to vary its position, opacity, layer blending mode, or layer visibility.

Select the Over state of the btn1 slice in the Web Content palette A. Then click on the 01_roll_over style in the Styles palette to change the button's color and effects in the Over state C. (If the HTW-Web-Styles aren't accessible in your Styles palette, choose a different style.)

CAUTION

Exit Preview Mode. After previewing a rollover in ImageReady, you must click the Preview button again to exit preview mode, or you'll be unable to perform other program functions.

5. Preview the Over State

Click the Preview button in the toolbox, and move your mouse over the first button in the image to see the Over state in action. Click the Preview button again to exit preview mode.

TIP

Changing States. States are applied in a default order (Over, Down, Selected, Out, Up, Click), but you can change a state to another at any time. Double-click a state in the Web Content palette. In the Rollover State Options palette that opens choose another state and click OK.

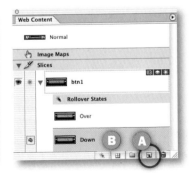

6. Add a Down State

A rollover can have multiple states. Next you'll add a Down state to this rollover button. The Down state occurs in a Web browser when a viewer clicks and holds on an area defined by a slice.

With the Over state of the btn1 slice selected in the Web Content palette, click the Create New Rollover State icon at the bottom of that palette A. The new Down state B starts out looking just like the Over state.

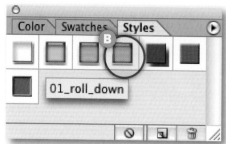

7. Change the Look of the Down State

With the Down state selected in the Web Content palette **A**, change the appearance of the button again by clicking the 01_roll_down style in the Styles palette **B**. Preview the Down state by activating the Preview button in the toolbox, and clicking and holding the first Link button in the image **C**. Exit preview.

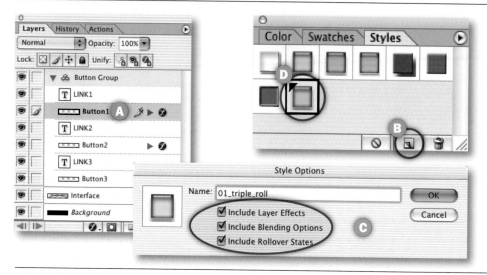

8. Create a Rollover Style

Now you'll save all the states of your rollover as a reusable rollover style. With the Button1 layer selected in the Layers palette **A**, click the Create New Style icon at the bottom of the Styles palette **B**. In the Style Options dialog box that opens, make sure Include Layer Effects, Include Blending Options, and Include Rollover States are checked to retain all the content and functionality of your original rollover **C**. Name the style *01_triple_roll*, and click OK. The style appears in the Styles palette with a black triangle, which indicates that it's a rollover style rather than a static style **D**.

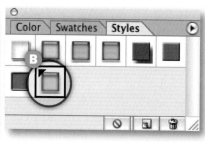

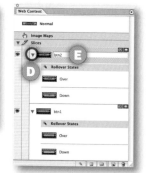

9. Apply the Rollover Style to Button2

Now you'll reap the rewards of your hard work. It's quick and easy to create a set of matching rollover buttons by applying the rollover style to the other two buttons in this navigation bar.

Select the Button2 layer in the Layers palette **A**. In the Styles palette, click the new rollover style 01_triple_roll **B**. This creates a layer-based slice around the content of the Button2 layer **C**, generates an Over state and a Down state for this slice along with the JavaScript to make the states function, and changes the appearance of the button on each state—all with a single click. Click the triangle next to the new slice in the Web Content palette to see the rollover states for the new slice **D**. Double-click the slice name and rename this slice *btn2* **E**.

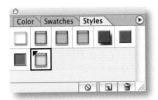

10. Apply the Rollover Style to Button3

Repeat the preceding step with the Button3 layer selected to complete your set of rollover buttons. Rename the resulting slice **btn3**.

11. Preview in a Web Browser

Click the Preview in Browser button in the toolbox to test your rollovers in your default Web browser.

12. Optimize and Save

Optimize each slice for fast download using the settings in the Optimize palette. When you optimize a slice, you affect all states of its rollover, so check the appearance of all three states of the rollover buttons. Choose File>Save Optimized As. In the Save Optimized As dialog box, set Format to HTML and Images **A** so that ImageReady generates an HTML file containing the JavaScript that will make your rollovers function. (If you prefer to create rollovers in a site-building program or write your own JavaScript, choose Format: Images Only.) In addition, the program creates an Image folder in which it saves GIFs and JPEGs from the slices and rollovers in the source file **B**.

Choose File>Save to resave the PSD file with all of the slicing and rollover information you've added.

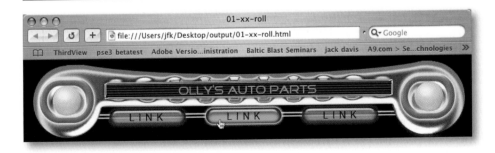

13. Open the HTML File in a Browser

Open the saved HTML file in a Web browser to see the results of your work. Each button should change appearance when you mouse over it and when you hold it down. ▥

Pointers and Remote Rollovers

These rollovers look great, but they're not just eye candy. Combine local rollovers that point to a link with informational remote rollovers.

TIP

Slices and Rollovers. Slices and rollovers go hand in hand. Slices define the area that triggers a rollover and the areas that change with the rollover states. Layer-based slices work best for rollovers because they automatically expand to fit the largest graphic on a rollover's states.

1. Design with Layers

In this project you apply both local and remote rollovers to navigation graphics, pointing your viewers to links and providing descriptions of where the links lead. The key to creating a complex rollover scheme like this one is to make ample use of layers. Open C01-06-pointer.psd from Chapter1-Navigation>Ch1-6. Notice that we've put each element involved in the rollovers—the pointer graphics, the link graphics, the text messages, and the LCD box—on its own layer **A**. We've organized the layers into layer sets, and sliced and optimized the background graphics for you so you can concentrate on creating rollovers.

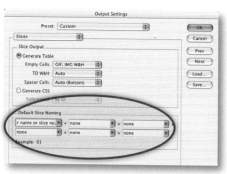

2. Simplify Slice Names

You'll do lots of work with slices in this project. By default, ImageReady creates long, unwieldy slice names. Change the default slice-naming convention to generate simpler names by choosing File>Output Settings>Slices to open the Output Settings dialog box. Click the arrow on the top left slice name field and choose Layer Name or Slice No. from the pop-up menu. Choose None in each of the other slice name menus and click OK.

3. Confirm the Normal State

Select the Normal state at the top of the Web Content palette **A**. This is the way the page will look when it first appears in a Web browser. None of the pointers are visible and there is no text in the LCD on the top right of the page **B**.

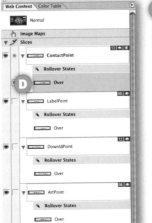

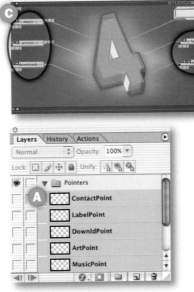

4. Create Layer-Based Rollovers for the Pointers

When a viewer moves his mouse over a link, a pointer will appear on that link. To create this effect, select all the pointer layers by holding the Shift key while clicking on the ContactPoint and MusicPoint layers in the Layers palette **A**. Then click the Create Layer-Based Rollover icon at the bottom of the Web Content palette **B**. This single click creates a layer-based slice around each of the five pointers **C**, along with an Over state for each of those pointer slices **D**. All the slices and rollover states are listed in the Web Content palette. You don't see the pointers in the image because they have not yet been made visible in this state.

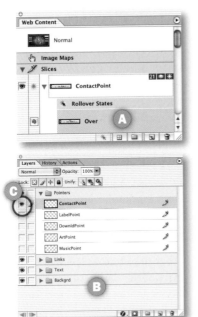

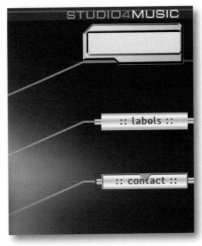

5. Make a Pointer Visible on the Over State

Next you'll change the appearance of the ContactPoint slice in its Over state. Select the Over state of the ContactPoint slice in the Web Content palette **A**. In the Layers palette, click in a blank area **B** to deselect all selected layers. Then click in the Visibility field to the left of the ContactPoint layer to display that layer's Eye icon **C** and to make that layer's contents visible in the image **D**. Now when a viewer mouses over the contact link in a browser, a pointer will appear on that link.

6. Repeat Step 5 on the Other Pointer Slices

Create a similar rollover for each of the other pointer slices—the LabelPoint slice, DownldPoint slice, ArtPoint slice, and MusicPoint slice—by repeating Step 5. Make only the pointer layer of the same name **A** visible on the Over state **B** of each pointer slice.

This is a good time to preview what you've done so far by clicking the Preview button in the toolbox **C** and moving your mouse over each link to display its pointer. Click the Preview button again to exit preview mode.

7. Slice the Remote Area

Next you'll add a second rollover event to the Over state of the ContactPoint slice—a text message that will appear in the LCD box at the top right of the page when a viewer mouses over the contact link in a browser. First you'll create a slice for the remote area involved in the rollover. Open the Backgrd layer set in the Layers palette and select the LCD layer **A**. Choose Layer>New Layer Based Slice from the menu bar to create a slice around the LCD box **B**.

8. Create a Remote Rollover

Select the Over state of the ContactPoint slice in the Web Content palette **A**. In the Layers palette, open the Text layer set and click in the Visibility field of the topmost text layer ("contact studio 4") to turn on that layer's Eye icon **B**.

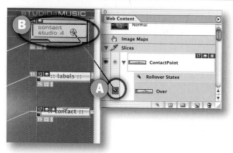

TIP

Turn Off Slice Visibility. It's useful to hide distracting slices temporarily when you preview in ImageReady. Click the Slice Visibility toggle in the toolbox to hide and show slices.

9. Target the Remote Slice

This is the fun part! When you make a remote rollover, you have to target the slice where the remote event occurs. In the Web Content palette, press the spiral icon (the pickwhip) next to the Over state of the ContactPoint slice **A**. Drag a line from the pickwhip to the LCD box in the image to target the LCD slice **B**.

T I P

Links. You can make links active in ImageReady or in a site-building program like GoLive or Dreamweaver. In ImageReady, select one of the link slices in the Web Content palette. In the Slice palette (Window>Slice) type the URL of the linked-to page in the URL field. Type the entire URL, including the http:// prefix, if you're linking to a page in another site.

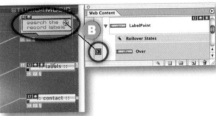

10. Repeat Steps 8 and 9 on the Other Pointer Slices

Create a similar remote rollover for each of the other pointer slices. Repeat Steps 8 and 9 on the Over state of each pointer slice, turning on the Eye icon for the matching text layer **A**:

- LabelPoint Slice: "search the record labels"
- DownldPoint Slice: "download the newest mp3"
- ArtPoint Slice: "search the artists"
- MusicPoint Slice: "search the music"

Target the LCD slice each time, by clicking and dragging from the pickwhip icon next to the Over state of each pointer slice in the Web Content palette to the LCD box in the image **B**.

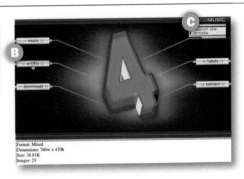

11. Preview in a Web Browser

Click the Preview in Browser button in the toolbox **A** to test the rollovers in your default Web browser. When you mouse over a link, a pointer appears on the link **B**, and a text message describing the link appears in the LCD box **C**. As you can see, these rollovers are not just eye candy. They identify which graphics are links and offer additional information about each link, making your navigation scheme user-friendly.

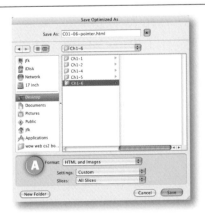

12. Save

Normally you would optimize each slice at this point. That's been done for you, so just choose File>Save Optimized As, and in the dialog box that appears choose Format: HTML and Images **A**. This causes ImageReady to generate an HTML file with rollover JavaScript along with image files for each state of all the rollovers on the page **B**. Choose File>Save to re-save the PSD file with the slice and rollover data you've added. 🖮

Image Map Navigation

Create image map hot spots in ImageReady to link a single image to multiple pages.

INSIGHT

What Is an Image Map? An image map is a single image with multiple links. It's a useful alternative to defining links with slices, particularly if your link regions are distributed around an image (like cities on a country map) or would overlap if defined by rectangular slices.

Under the hood of an image map, coordinates are "mapped" mathematically on the image so that when a mouse travels through a mapped region it is detected and a click will send the viewer to a linked file.

1. Draw a Tool-Based Hot Spot

Open into ImageReady C01-07-imap.psd from Chapter 1-Navigation>Ch1-7. You'll define each of the button links on this page with image map link regions (hot spots) in ImageReady. Photoshop doesn't have image map tools.

Start by drawing a hot spot around the Home button with the Polygon Image Map tool. If that tool isn't showing, press whichever image map tool is displayed in your toolbox and choose the Polygon Image Map tool from the flyout menu **A**. Zoom in and then click in each corner of the Home button to draw a hot spot in the approximate shape of the button. To close the hot spot border, move toward the starting point until you see a small circle and click **B** or just double-click.

TIP

Image Map Tools. The Polygon Image Map tool draws connecting line segments, giving you the most control over the shape of a hot spot. The Rectangle Image Map tool and the Circle Image Map tool draw hot spots in those geometric shapes.

2. Adjust the Hot Spot

Adjust the hot spot to fit the button by clicking on the anchor points with the Image Map Select tool **A** and dragging **B**. For more precision, Shift-click to add an anchor point **C** or Option/Alt-click to delete an anchor point **D**.

3. Duplicate a Hot Spot

Repeat Steps 1 and 2 to make another hot spot on the Games button **A**. With the Image Map Select tool active, click the Image Map palette icon in the Options bar **B** to open the Image Map palette (or choose Window>Image Map). From the palette's side menu **C** choose Duplicate Image Map. Alternatively Option/Alt-drag the hot spot to copy it. Drag the new hot spot on top of the Help button **D**.

4. Make Layer-Based Hot Spots

The Tips, D-Loads, and Support buttons were created on separate layers—so you can use a quick, layer-based command to make their hot spots. Select the TipsBtn layer in the Layers palette **A**. Choose Layer>New Layer Based Image Map Area from the menu bar. By default this makes a rectangular hot spot around the Tips button that doesn't match the shape of this button **B**. To fix that, in the Image Map palette choose Polygon from the Shape pop-up menu **C**. Then click the arrow on the Quality field and drag the Quality slider to the right until the hot spot matches the shape of the button **D**. (We set our Quality field to 100 and got a perfect fit **E**.) Repeat this step for the D-Loads and Support buttons, each of which is on its own layer too.

T I P

Fitting Hot Spots. An image map hot spot is an active link area in a viewer's browser. The viewer's main clue to the presence of a hot spot is the underlying graphic (along with a tiny hand icon that appears when he mouses over a hot spot in a browser). It's important that the hot spot fit the underlying graphic as closely as possible so the viewer knows where to click.

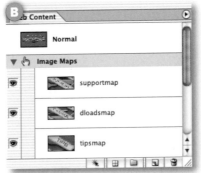

5. Name the Hot Spots

Each of your hot spots is listed in the Web Content palette with default names **A**. Give your hot spots more meaningful names by double-clicking their names in the Web Content palette and typing **helpmap, gamesmap, homemap, tipsmap, dloadsmap,** and **supportmap** respectively **B**. (Or select each hot spot in the Web Content palette and name it in the Image Map palette.)

INSIGHT

Relative Links. We recommend assigning relative links when you're linking to files within the same Web site, so that the site can be moved without the links breaking. Relative links are relative to the location of the current page. So to use them you have to plan in advance how you're going to structure your site files. For example, the relative link from the helpmap hot spot on the current page to the help.html page would be:

help.html if the help page is in the same folder as the current page;

/helpfiles/help.html if the help page is in a folder called helpfiles that's one level down from the current page;

../help.html if the help page is one level up from the current page;

../games/help.html if the help page is in a folder called games that's one level up from the current page.

Absolute Links. Absolute links are best when you're linking to an external site. They are links that include the complete path to a site file. For example, http://www.flightgames.com/help.html includes:

• the Internet protocol (http://).

• the site domain (www.flightgames.com).

• the page name (help.html).

6. Add Links to the Hot Spots

Select the helpmap hot spot in the Web Content palette. In the Image Map palette, type ***help.html*** in the URL field. Repeat this step for each of the other hot spots, typing ***index.html*** (for the home button), ***games.html, tips.html, dloads. html*** and ***support.html***, respectively.

Each of these is a relative link, which means that its path is relative to this image map page. The relative link help.html, for example, assumes that the help page will be in the same folder with this page on a Web server. (See the sidebar for more about relative links.) If you don't yet know what your Web site's file structure will be, you can leave this field blank and use a WYSIWYG site-building program like GoLive or Dreamweaver to make relative links for you later.

7. Make a Rollover in the Image Map

You can include rollovers in image maps. When you add a rollover to an image map hot spot, a slice is created behind the scenes. Select the Rectangle Image Map tool in the toolbox **A**, and drag a rectangular hot spot around the FGI logo in the image **B**. Then click the Create Rollover State icon at the bottom of the Web Content palette **C** to create an Over state in the hot spot **D**. To change the appearance of the FGI logo in the Over state of the rollover, click the ***f*** icon at the bottom of the Layers palette **E** and choose Outer Glow from the Layer Effects pop-up menu. Click OK in the Layer Style dialog box to accept the default options for this layer effect. Click the Image Map Visibility button in the toolbox **F** and then the Preview button **G** and mouse over the logo to preview the rollover. Click the Preview button again to exit Preview mode.

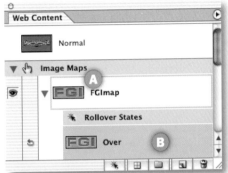

8. Add a Remote Rollover

You can even include a remote rollover in an image map.

In the Web Content palette, double-click the name of the new image map and rename it *FGImap* **A**. Select the Over state of FGImap in the Web Content palette **B**. In the Layers palette, click in the Visibility field of the Flight Games Inc. layer to display an Eye icon **C**. This makes the Flight Games Inc. text visible on the Over state of the FGImap rollover.

9. Preview in a Web Browser

Click the Preview in Browser button in the toolbox **A** to test the rollovers in a Web browser. When you mouse over the FGI logo in the browser, a glow appears around that logo, and the Flight Games Inc. appears in the image **B**.

10. Save

We already optimized this image as a JPEG. These optimization settings apply to the entire image map and its rollovers.

Choose File>Save Optimized As, and in the dialog box that appears choose Format: HTML and Images **A**, make a destination folder, and click Save **B** to save imap.html with the image map data and rollover JavaScript, along with a folder of images. Choose File>Save to resave the PSD file with all of its image map, slice, and rollover information.

Congratulations on completing this chapter on navigation. In the next chapter you'll learn how to make amazing animations in Photoshop and ImageReady. 🖾

ANIMATION

Moving Things Along with Unusual, Exciting Animation Projects for the Web

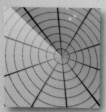

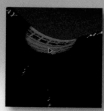

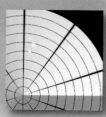

SEX SELLS, AND SO DOES MOTION, as advertisers well know. That's why everywhere you turn on the Web there's an animated banner, logo, or text message dancing as fast as it can to catch your attention. Animated Web graphics are scene stealers. So it's worth your while to learn all you can about Web animation. It's the pulse of today's Web and it's sure to remain a core feature of the Web in the future.

In this chapter we offer you fresh ideas and techniques for making effective, tasteful animations for the Web, each of which has a special Wow factor. We show you how do to some of these projects in Photoshop, and others in ImageReady. Photoshop CS2 is the first version of Photoshop to have animation capability. The animation features in Photoshop are almost identical to those in ImageReady, except that you can't export animations as SWFs or create animated rollovers in Photoshop.

These Aren't Your Father's GIFs

Most of the animations we'll make together are animated GIFs. You may be surprised at how much you can do with animation in this format. These projects help you understand how to design and optimize GIF animations that run smoothly and are small enough to be of real use on the Web.

We take you places you may not have known you could go with animated GIFs. In the Rollover-Triggered Animation project, you'll learn how to use rollovers in conjunction with multiple animations to make an animated Web banner with a three-dimensional illustration. You'll continue in that vein with the Image Map-Triggered Animation project, where you learn when and how to use an image map rather than a slice to trigger a remote animation.

It's All Very Moving

The moving spotlight you'll make in the Layer Mask Animation project is one of the coolest of the animation projects. The spotlight moves around highlighting different parts of the building using a special layer mask technique.

We're partial to the realistic animated scene you'll build in the project called Bringing a Picture to Life. It's an unusual example of the use of subtle, small animations to enhance a design. Don't miss the first project, Radar Screen Animation, which shows you how to build a realistic radar screen from scratch, complete with an animating gradient and radar blips.

Try Animating a Layer Style or Animating Warped Text—projects that are quick and easy with stunning results. And of course all you photographers will want to know how to create an Animated Slide Show of photo thumbnails complete with cross-dissolves.

Flashy Format

Animated GIFs aren't all you learn about here. In this chapter you'll find a whole project devoted to creating a Vector-Based Flash Movie. That's right, you can now export animations from ImageReady in SWF format.

So get ready to dig into an entertaining and useful chapter. Once you've digested our recipes, you'll be ready to go out and whip up a batch of tasty animations on your own.

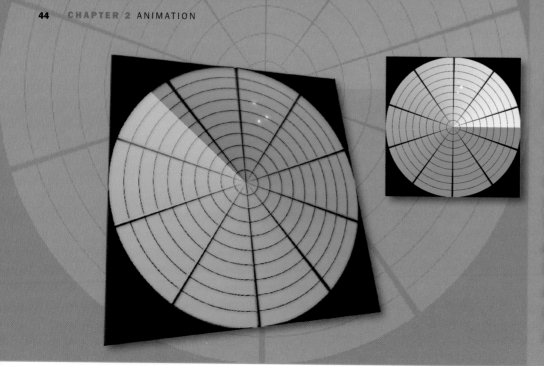

Radar Screen Animation

This animation may look complex, but it's so simple you can build it from scratch. Varying the angle of a gradient layer style on each frame makes the screen appear to rotate. Add some radar blips and you have a realistic radar screen.

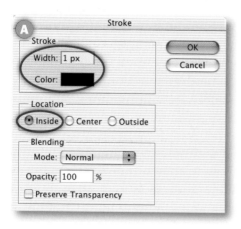

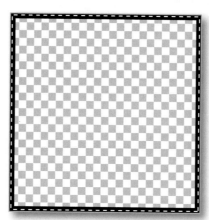

1. Make a Pattern Image

Build the layered artwork for this animation in Photoshop. The graphics are easy to make from scratch, so there is no start file on the CD-ROM for this project.

First, make a custom pattern you'll use to create the segmented circles. In Photoshop, choose File>New and create a 50 x 50 pixel RGB document with Background Contents set to Transparent. Zoom in (Command/Ctrl-+). Choose Select>All. Choose Edit>Stroke, and in the Stroke dialog box **A** set Width to 1 px, Color to Black, and Location to Inside, and click OK.

TIP

Saving a Pattern. Save a newly defined pattern or you'll lose it if you switch pattern sets. Choose Edit>Preset Manager and choose Patterns from the Preset Type menu. A thumbnail of your new pattern appears at the bottom of the current pattern set. Click to select that pattern thumbnail (or Shift-click multiple thumbnails), click the Save Set button, and name the set. Restart Photoshop so your new set appears in the list of pattern sets. Make your set active by clicking the Load Set button in the Preset Manager and choosing your set.

2. Define the Image as a Pattern

With the selection still active, choose Edit>Define Pattern to create a repeating pattern you'll apply to your radar screen image. Name the pattern *50px Grid,* and click OK. Close the pattern image without saving.

3. Make a Radar Screen Image

Click the Background Color box in the toolbox and in the Color Picker uncheck Only Web Colors and choose green (R: 83, G: 149, B:61). Create a new 500 x 500 pixel RGB file with Background Contents set to Background Color. Resolution can be left at its default since this file is measured in pixels. (See *"Starting a New File for the Web"* in Chapter 1.)

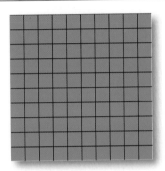
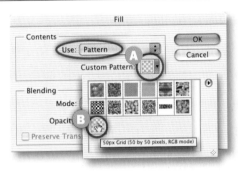

4. Fill with the Pattern

Click the Create New Layer icon at the bottom of the Layers palette and name the new layer **Grid**. With the Grid layer selected, choose Edit>Fill. In the Fill dialog box, choose Pattern from the Use menu. Click in the Custom Pattern field **A** to open the active pattern set. Select the 50px Grid pattern **B**, and click OK to fill the layer with a repeating grid.

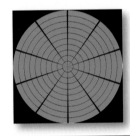
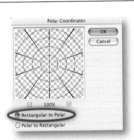

5. Change Squares to Circles

It's easy to change the squares into a circular pattern. With the Grid layer selected, choose Filter>Distort>Polar Coordinates. Choose Rectangular to Polar and click OK. The circular grid of a radar screen is created automatically!

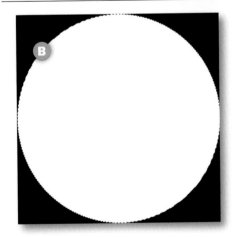
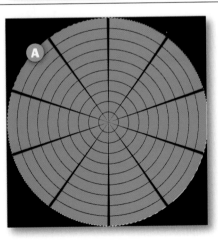

6. Create a White Screen

With the Grid layer selected, click the Create New Layer icon in the Layers palette and name the layer **Screen**. Select the Screen layer. Select the Elliptical Marquee tool from behind the Rectangular Marquee. Hold the Option/Alt key (to draw from the center) and the Shift key (to constrain to a circle), click in the center of the circular grid, and drag out a selection to the edge of the circular grid **A**. Choose Edit>Fill, choose White from the Use menu in the Fill dialog box, and click OK to fill the circle with white **B**. Choose Select>Deselect.

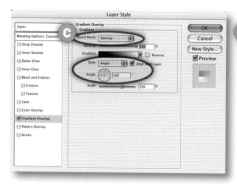
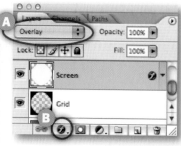

7. Apply a Gradient to the Screen

With the Screen layer selected, choose Overlay from the Blending Mode pop-up menu at the top of the Layers palette **A**. Click the *f* icon at the bottom of the Layers palette **B** and choose the Gradient Overlay layer style. In the Layer Style dialog box **C**, set the following options for the Gradient Overlay layer style—Blend Mode: Overlay, Style: Angle, and Angle: *180°*. Click OK to apply the layer style to the Screen layer.

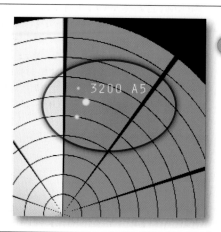
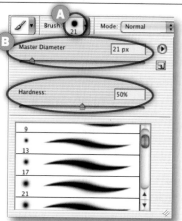

8. Add Radar Blips

Create a new layer above the Screen layer, name it *Blips* and select it. Press D and X on your keyboard to set the Foreground color to white. Select the Brush tool. In the Options bar, click the brush sample **A** to open the Brush pop-up palette (not to be confused with the Brushes palette). Choose a 21-pixel Soft Round Brush, and set the Hardness slider to 50%. Click in the image to paint a blip. Reduce the Master Diameter slider **B** slightly and paint a few smaller blips.

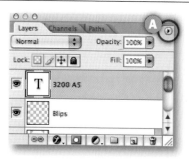

9. Add Radar Coordinates

Select the Type tool, and choose a font and small font size in the Options bar. Type some official-looking coordinates (3200 A5) for your blips. With the type layer selected, click the side menu arrow on the Layers palette **A** and choose Merge Down to merge the type layer into the Blips layer.

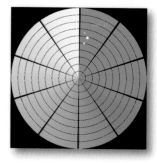
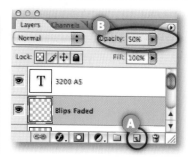

10. Fade the Blips

Click and drag the Blips layer to the Create New Layer icon at the bottom of the Layers palette to duplicate it **A**. Rename the Blips Copy layer to *Blips Faded*. With the Blips Faded layer selected, press 5 on your keyboard to lower the layer's opacity to 50% **B**. You've completed all the artwork for the animation!

INSIGHT

Manual Animation. This is a manual animation, as opposed to a tweened animation. This means that you'll create the animation frames and alter the artwork on each frame yourself, rather than have the program create intermediate frames automatically.

INSIGHT

Content for the Frames. You'll create the content of the animation frames in this project two ways—by varying the visibility of layers of artwork, and by changing the angle of the Gradient Overlay layer style on the Screen layer.

11. Open the Animation Palette

Photoshop CS2 is the first version of Photoshop to have an Animation palette. Consequently you do not have to jump to ImageReady CS2 to animate this file. In Photoshop, choose Window>Animation to open the Animation palette. The first frame of the animation is displayed automatically in the Animation palette **A**.

12. Set Up Frame 1

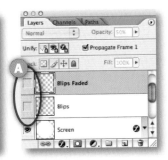

Set up the artwork for this frame by hiding some layers and displaying others. In the Layers palette, click in the Visibility fields of the Blips layer and the Blips Faded layer to turn off those Eye icons **A**. Leave the Eye icons next to all the other layers turned on throughout the animation.

13. Add Frame 2

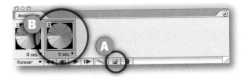

Click the Duplicate Selected Frames button at the bottom of the Animation palette **A** to generate Frame 2 **B**. Each time you create a new frame this way, the content of the new frame (2) is a copy of the content of the preceding frame (1). In the next step you'll change the content of Frame 2.

14. Change the Gradient on Frame 2

On Frame 2 vary the angle of the radar screen's gradient so a light begins to move around the circle. Make sure Frame 2 is selected in the Animation palette. In the Layers palette, click the *f* icon on the Screen layer to display the Effects sublayers. Double-click the Gradient Overlay sublayer to open the Layer Styles dialog box. In the Layer Styles dialog box, change the Gradient Overlay Angle field to *135°* **A** and click OK.

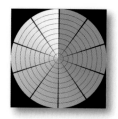
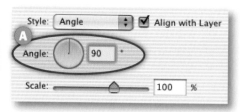

15. Add Frame 3

With Frame 2 selected in the Animation palette, click the Duplicate Selected Frames button to create Frame 3. With Frame 3 selected, double-click the Screen layer's Gradient Overlay effect and set the Gradient Overlay Angle field to **90° A**.

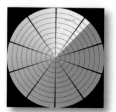
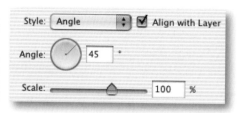

16. Add Frame 4

With Frame 3 selected in the Animation palette, click the Duplicate Selected Frames button to make Frame 4. With Frame 4 selected, double-click the Screen layer's Gradient Overlay effect and set the Angle field to **45°**.

17. Make Blips Visible on Frame 4

Add another artwork change to Frame 4. With Frame 4 selected in the Animation palette, click in the Visibility field of the Blips layer in the Layers palette to turn on that Eye icon **A**. This makes radar blips appear on the screen as the bright part of the gradient moves over them.

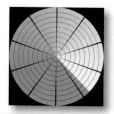
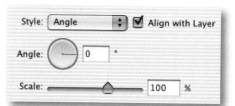

18. Add Frame 5

With Frame 4 selected in the Animation palette, click the Duplicate Selected Frames button to make Frame 5. Double-click the Screen layer's Gradient Overlay effect and set the Angle field to **0°**.

19. Add Frame 6

With Frame 5 selected in the Animation palette, click the Duplicate Selected Frames button to make Frame 6. With Frame 6 selected, double-click the Screen layer's Gradient Overlay effect and set the Angle field to **−45°**. Click in the Visibility field of the Blips layer in the Layers palette to turn that Eye icon off. Click in the Visibility field of the Blips Faded layer to turn that Eye icon on. This makes the blips begin to fade as the bright part of the gradient moves past them.

I N S I G H T

Frame Summary. Use this chart as a reference as you build this animation.

Frame	Gradient Angle	Blips Layer	Blips Faded Layer
1	180	Off	Off
2	135	Off	Off
3	90	Off	Off
4	45	On	Off
5	0	On	Off
6	−45	Off	On
7	−90	Off	On
8	−135	Off	On

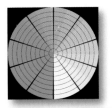
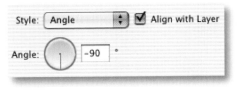

20. Add Frame 7

With Frame 6 selected, duplicate the frame and set Frame 7's Gradient Overlay layer style Angle to **–90°**. Leave the Blips layer off and the Blips Faded layer on, as they were in the preceding frame.

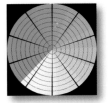

21. Add Frame

With Frame 7 selected, duplicate the frame and set Frame 8's Gradient Overlay Angle field to **–135°** Leave the Blips layer off and the Blips Faded layer on. You've finished building the animation!

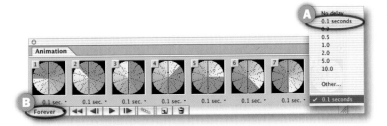

22. Set the Animation Timing

Now slow the animation down from the default setting. Click on the Animation palette side menu and choose Select All Frames. Click on the frame delay setting under any frame and choose 0.1 sec **A**. Leave the Loop setting to Forever so the animation will play continuously **B**.

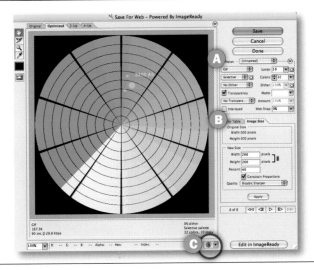

23. Optimize and Preview

Optimization settings apply to all frames in an animation. Choose File>Save for Web. In the Save for Web window choose Format: GIF, Lossy: 10, Reduction: Selective, Colors: 32, Dither Method: No Dither, Transparency: Checked, Interlaced: Unchecked, Web-Snap: 0% **A**. The file size is still quite large. Reduce it by clicking the Image Size tab **B** and reducing Width and Height to 200 pixels. Click the Preview in Browser button **C** to preview in a Web browser. Back in the Save for Web window, click Save.

24. Save

In the Save Optimized As window, leave Format/Save as Type set to Images Only **A** and click Save. There's no need to save an HTML file because animated GIFs function on their own. Choose File>Save to resave the PSD file. And you're done! ▦

how2wow!

Animating Warped Text

Use the Warp Text feature to add twists and turns to text as you create animation frames in Photoshop. Learn the technique here, and then try it on text of your own to animate a text-based logo or Web banner.

T I P

Animating with Effects. In this animation you vary the Warp Text effect on a single layer as you move from frame to frame in the Animation palette. You don't have to make a separate layer of artwork for each animation frame. This is similar to animating a layer style.

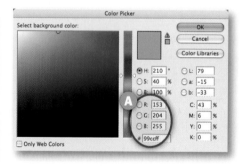

1. Create a New File in Photoshop

This text-based animation is easy to make from scratch so there is no start file on the CD. You'll create some text and give it a twist by applying the Flag style in the Warp Text dialog box. Then you'll create animation frames and tween. Finally, you'll copy, paste, and reverse some of the frames to make the text appear to move back and forth. The Warp Text feature is available in both Photoshop and ImageReady. For this project you'll work in Photoshop.

Start by making a new file in Photoshop CS2. Click the Background color box in the toolbox. In the Color Picker, enter R: 153, G:204, B:255 and click OK **A**. Choose File>New. In the New dialog box **B**, set Width to 760 pixels and Height to 210 pixels. Ignore the Resolution field. Choose Color Mode: RGB Color and Background Contents: Background Color. Click OK to open a new image.

2. Add Text

Choose Photoshop/Edit>Preferences> Units & Rulers, set Type to pixels, and click OK. Select the Type tool in the toolbox. Set the following type options in the Options bar **A**:

- Font Family: Impact
- Font Style: Regular
- Font Size: Enter *116 px*
- Anti-aliasing: Sharp
- Color: Choose White in the Color Picker that opens when you click the Color field.

Click the image and type *how2wow!* **B**.

3. Recolor the Text

Select the *2* by clicking and dragging over it with the Type tool **A**. In the Options bar, set Color to red (R: 255, G: 0, B:0). Click the checkmark in the Options bar to commit this type edit **B**. Click and drag across the letters *wow!*, change them to black (R: 0, G:0, B:0), and commit the edit **C**. Don't be confused if you see a question mark in the Options bar Color field. That indicates there is more than one color in this type layer.

4. Format the Text

With the Type tool selected, click the Character and Paragraph palette icon on the Options bar **A** to open the Character palette. Again select the *2* in the image by clicking and dragging over it. In the Character palette, set Font Size to 145 px **B**. Then move the cursor over the icon on the Baseline Shift field until it becomes a double-pointed arrow. Drag to the left to –20 **C**. Click the checkmark in the Options bar to commit these type edits **D**.

5. Center the Text

Choose Select>All or press Command/Control-A. Select the Move tool. In the Options bar, click the Align Vertical Centers button **A** and then the Align Horizontal Centers button **B**. Press Command/Control-D to deselect. This is a handy way to center an item to the document window.

6. Open the Animation Palette

Now you'll start creating the animation. If the Animation palette is not open, choose Window>Animation to open it. Frame 1 of the animation is automatically displayed in the Animation palette **A**.

7. Open the Warp Text Dialog Box

Next you'll bend the text on Frame 1. Check that the how2wow! type layer is selected in the Layers palette **A**. Select the Type tool, and click the Warp icon in the Options bar **B** to open the Warp Text dialog box.

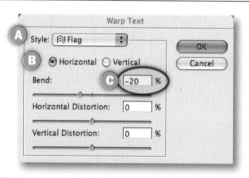

8. Set Warp Text Options for Frame 1

In the Warp Text dialog box, choose the Flag style from the Style menu **A**. Leave the Horizontal button selected to establish the horizontal orientation of the warp **B**. Move the Bend slider to −20% to set the amount and direction of the distortion **C**. Leave the Horizontal Distortion and Vertical Distortion sliders set to 0%. Click OK.

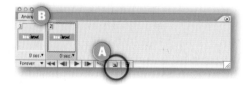

9. Add Frame 2

Click the Duplicate Selected Frames button in the Animation palette **A** to create Frame 2 **B**. Frame 2 is currently an exact copy of Frame 1. You'll change its content in the next step.

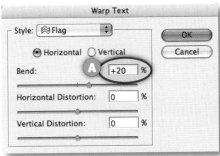

10. Change the Warp on Frame 2

Check that Frame 2 is selected in the Animation palette, the how2wow! type layer is active in the Layers palette, and the Type tool is selected in the toolbox. Click the Warp icon in the Options bar to reopen the Warp Text dialog box. In the Warp Text dialog box, drag the Horizontal Distortion slider to +20% **A**. Leave the other settings as they are, and click OK. Leave this frame selected in preparation for another new frame.

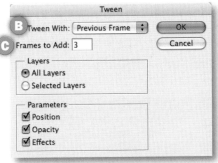

11. Tween

Now you'll tell Photoshop to make some in-between frames for you. With Frame 2 selected, click the Tween button at the bottom of the Animation palette **A**. In the Tween dialog box choose Tween With: Previous Frame **B** and enter Frames to Add: *3* **C**. Click OK. This causes Photoshop to create three intermediate frames—now frames 2, 3, and 4—between the two frames that you made.

T I P

Deleting Frames. You can delete frames at any time by selecting them and clicking the trash icon at the bottom of the Animation palette. To delete an entire animation, click the side arrow on the Animation palette and choose Delete Animation.

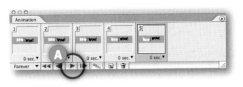

12. Preview in Photoshop

Preview what you've made so far by clicking the Play arrow at the bottom of the Animation palette **A**. The animation plays in Photoshop's document window. Click the Stop button that replaces the Play arrow to pause the animation. We recommend doing this from time to time as you build an animation to check that the animation works as expected.

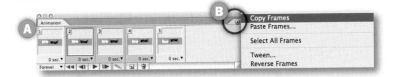

13. Copy Frames 2 through 4

Click on Frame 2 in the Animation palette, hold the Shift key, and then click on Frame 4 to select Frames 2 through 4 **A**. Click the side arrow on the Animation palette and choose Copy Frames **B**.

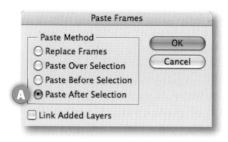

14. Paste the Copied Frames

Select Frame 5 in the Animation palette. Click the side arrow and choose Paste Frames. In the Paste Frames dialog box choose Paste After Selection **A** and click OK. You now have a total of 8 frames in the Animation palette. The frames you just copied and pasted are Frames 6 through 8. Leave those frames selected.

15. Reverse the Copied Frames

With Frames 6 through 8 selected, click the side arrow on the Animation palette and choose Reverse Frames. This reverses the order of the copied frames, so your animation moves in both directions.

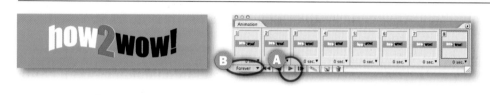

16. Preview Again in Photoshop

Preview the animation again by clicking the Play button on the Animation palette **A**. The text will move up and down in a sinuous curve. It repeats because you left the Looping option set to its default of Forever **B**.

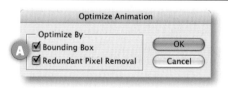

17. Confirm Optimization Options

Click the side arrow on the Animation palette and choose Optimize Animation. Make sure that Bounding Box and Redundant Pixel Removal are checked **A**. Bounding Box crops each frame to include only the area that has changed since the last frame. Redundant Pixel Removal makes pixels that have not changed since the last frame transparent. You must check Transparency in the Save for Web window, as you'll do in the next step, to enable Redundant Pixel Removal.

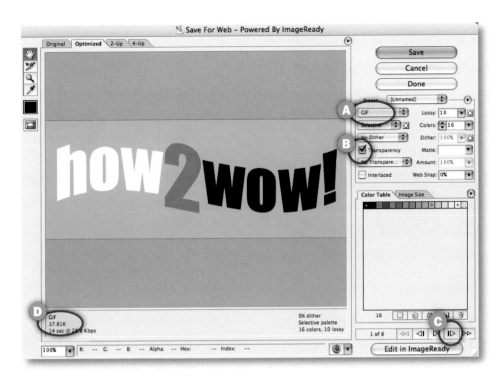

18. Optimize in Save for Web Window

Choose File>Save for Web. In the Save for Web window, click on the Optimized tab to see a preview of your image with the optimization settings you choose. Set Format to GIF **A**. An animated GIF is saved in the same format as a static GIF. You cannot optimize an animation as a JPEG or PNG because those formats do not support animation.

Choose GIF optimization settings with the goal of reducing file size while maintaining appearance. (See *GIF Optimization Settings* in Chapter 1.) Try: Reduction algorithm: Selective, Colors: 16, Lossy: 10, Dither: No Dither, Interlaced: unchecked, WebSnap: 0%. Be sure to check Transparency **B** to enable Redundant Pixel Removal.

The settings you choose here apply to all the frames of the animation. Click the Select Next Frame control **C** to move through the frames of the animation, checking that they all look good with the current optimization settings. Animated GIFs tend to get big, so keep your eye on the file size **D**.

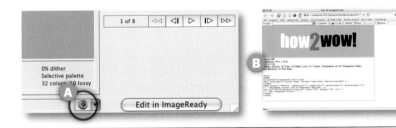

19. Preview in a Web Browser

Click the Preview in Browser button at the bottom of the Save for Web window **A** to preview the animation in your default browser. The preview includes file information and HTML **B** that you won't see in your final file.

TIP

Reopening the Animation. To make changes to the animation in the future, reopen the PSD source file, edit, and output a new GIF. You can't edit the GIF version of an animation because Photoshop will not display its frames in the Animation palette.

20. Save

In the Save Optimized As dialog box, set Format/Save as Type to Images only **A**, and click Save. Photoshop saves a single GIF file containing the whole animation.

Choose File>Save As to resave the PSD source image. 🖚

Bringing a Picture to Life

Add life to a scene by creating multiple animations of traffic signals and lights. This project is done in ImageReady.

INSIGHT

Animating a Photograph. Image-Ready creates animations in GIF format by default. If you're including a photograph in a GIF animation, you'll have to optimize the photo with GIF settings, even though GIF limits the number of colors in a photograph and can compromise its appearance. To make a photograph look better in GIF format, try increasing the number of colors and adding dither; but use these tactics judiciously to keep the file size of the animation from skyrocketing. Although JPEG is usually the format of choice for photographs, JPEG does not support animation.

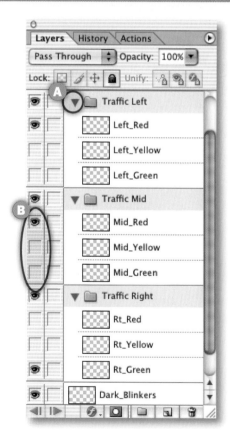

1. Deconstruct the Layers

Let's face it—Web animations can be distracting, if not downright overwhelming. But when applied subtly, as in this project, animation can add a realistic touch that makes an otherwise static scene come alive on the Web. You'll create several animations in sliced areas of this photograph, making traffic lights change and parking lights blink on and off.

In ImageReady, open C02-03-scene.psd from the Chapter 2-Animation>Ch2-3 folder. Take a minute to familiarize yourself with the contents of the layers in this file before you start animating. In the Layers palette, click the arrow to the left of each of the three Traffic layer sets, opening them so you can see the layers they contain **A**. Option/Alt-click in the Visibility field to the left of any layer **B** to see only the artwork on that layer. Option/Alt-click again to see all the layered artwork that was originally visible.

2. Turn on Slice Visibility

We already made and optimized some slices in this image, so that you can concentrate on creating the animations. The user slices we made have blue numbers. The auto slices ImageReady added are ghosted and have gray numbers. If you don't see these slices, click the Slice Visibility toggle near the bottom of the toolbox. If the ghosted auto slices are obscuring your view, choose Image-Ready/Edit>Preferences>Slices and lower the percentage of color adjustment in the Auto Slices field.

3. Slice the Traffic Lights

In this project you'll be creating several independent animations in a large image. You'll slice the areas where the animations will occur to separate them from the rest of the image. ImageReady will generate a separate animated GIF file from each slice that contains animation frames.

Start by adding slices around the traffic lights so that you can animate those areas. Select the Slice tool in the toolbox, zoom in, and draw a slice around all three lights in the traffic signal on the left **A**, another around the lights in the middle traffic signal **B**, and one more slice around the lights in the traffic signal on the right **C**. You can make the red, yellow, and green traffic light layers visible temporarily to make it easier to see where to slice. Turn those layers off when you're done slicing.

4. Slice the Truck Blinkers

Draw another slice with the Slice tool around the darkened blinkers on the left side of the truck to prepare that area for animation. You can make the Dark_Blinkers layer visible temporarily to help position your slice. Turn that layer off when you're done slicing.

TIP

Layer Visibility. Control the visibility of the artwork on a layer by clicking in the Visibility field to the left of the layer to show or hide its Eye icon. A layer is on when the Eye icon is showing and off when it's not showing.

All the layers sets in this file will display an Eye icon throughout the animation, because at least one layer in each of the layer sets is always set to on.

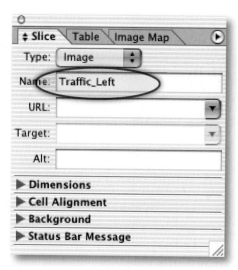

5. Name the Animation Slices

ImageReady assigns a default name to each slice. The GIFs produced from the slices will inherit those names. To ensure that you can recognize your animated GIFs among the many image files that will be generated, give each of your animation slices a meaningful name. Choose Window>Slice to open the Slice palette. Select the Slice Select tool in the toolbox and click on the slice you drew around the traffic signal on the left. Type *Traffic_Left* in the Name field of the Slice palette. Repeat this for the other three slices you just created, naming them *Traffic_Mid, Traffic_Rt,* and *Blinkers* respectively. Don't use spaces or special characters in slice names.

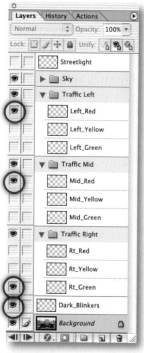

6. Set Up Frame 1

Choose Window>Animation to open the Animation palette. Frame 1 of the animation is displayed in that palette. Go to the Layers palette and click in the Visibility field of the following layers, turning on their Eye icons, to make the artwork on these layers visible on Frame 1 of the animation. All the other traffic light layers should be off.

- Left_Red (This turns the traffic light on the left to red **A**.)

- Mid_Red (This turns the traffic light in the middle to red **B**.)

- Rt_Green (This turns the traffic light on the right to green **C**.)

- Dark_Blinkers (Don't be confused by the on/off terminology here. When this layer is **on**, the blinkers on the left side of the truck look dark **D**.)

7. Add a Time Delay

Click the Time Delay menu under Frame 1 and choose 0.5 seconds to set the approximate timing of Frame 1 and all subsequent frames.

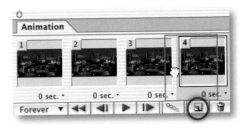

8. Add Frames 2 through 4

The next three frames are copies of Frame 1. Click the Duplicate Animation Frame button at the bottom of the Animation palette three times. Or hold down the Option/Alt key on your keyboard while clicking and dragging Frame 1 to the right and repeat twice more so you have a total of four frames.

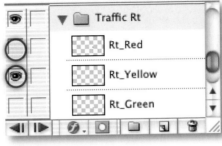

9. Create Frame 5

On Frame 5, the traffic light on the right changes to yellow. Create Frame 5 by selecting Frame 4 and clicking the Duplicate Animation Frame button at the bottom of the Animation palette. Now change the artwork on Frame 5 by going to the Layers palette, turning on the Rt_Yellow layer, and turning off the Rt_Green layer.

10. Add Frames 6 through 8

The next three frames are copies of Frame 5. With Frame 5 selected, click the Duplicate Animation Frame button three times. You should have a total of eight frames.

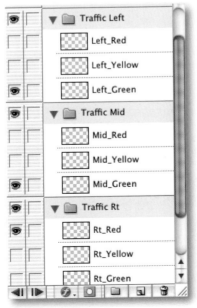

11. Create Frame 9

On Frame 9, the traffic light on the left changes to green, the traffic light in the middle changes to green, and the traffic light on the right changes to red. Create Frame 9 by selecting Frame 8 and clicking the Duplicate Animation Frame button. Change the artwork on Frame 9 by doing the following in the Layers palette:

- Turn off the Left_Red layer
- Turn on the Left_Green layer
- Turn off the Mid_Red layer
- Turn on the Mid_Green layer
- Turn off the Rt_Yellow layer
- Turn on the Rt_Red layer

12. Add Frames 10 through 26

The next 17 frames are copies of Frame 9. With Frame 9 selected, click the Duplicate Animation Frame button 17 times. You have a total of 26 frames.

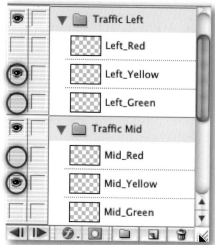

13. Create Frame 27

You're almost done. On Frame 27, the traffic light on the left changes to yellow, and the middle traffic light changes to yellow. The light on the right stays red. Create Frame 27 by selecting Frame 26 and clicking the Duplicate Animation Frame button. Change the artwork on Frame 27 by doing the following in the Layers palette:

- Turn off the Left_Green layer
- Turn on the Left_Yellow layer
- Turn off the Mid_Green layer
- Turn on the Mid_Yellow layer

14. Add Frames 28 through 30

The next three frames are copies of Frame 27. With Frame 27 selected, click the Duplicate Animation Frame button three times. You now have 30 frames.

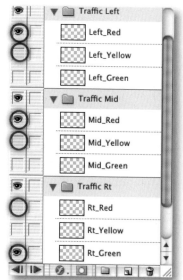

15. Create Frame 31

On Frame 31, the traffic light on the left changes to red, the middle traffic light changes to red, and the traffic light on the right changes to green. Select Frame 30 and click the Duplicate Animation Frame button. Change the artwork on Frame 31 by doing the following in the Layers palette:

- Turn off the Left_Yellow layer
- Turn on the Left_Red layer
- Turn off the Mid_Yellow layer
- Turn on the Mid_Red layer
- Turn off the Rt_Red layer
- Turn on the Rt_Green layer

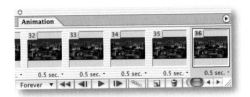

16. Add Frames 32 through 36

The next five frames are copies of Frame 31. With Frame 31 selected, click the Duplicate Animation Frame button five times. You should have a total of 36 frames. You're done creating frames.

17. Preview in ImageReady

Preview what you've made so far by clicking the Play arrow at the bottom of the Animation palette. The animation plays in ImageReady's document window. Click the Stop button that replaces the Play arrow to pause the animation.

18. Add the Blinking Truck Lights

Click the diagonal lines at the bottom right of the Animation palette and stretch the palette out so you can see as many frames as possible **A**. Click on Frame 2. Then hold the Command/Ctrl key as you click on every other frame (Frames 4, 6, 8, 10, 12, 14, 16, 18, 20, 22, 24, 26, 28, 30, 32, 34, 36). In the Layers palette, click in the Visibility field of the Dark_Blinkers layer to turn the visibility of that layer off **B**, so that the colored lights on the back of the truck are visible on the selected frames. Preview again to see these lights blink on and off throughout the animation.

19. Turn on the Streetlight

Select any frame in the animation. In the Layers palette, turn on the visibility of the Streetlight layer **A**. Then click on the Streetlight layer to select it and click the Unify Visibility button in the Layers palette **B**. In the prompt that appears, click Match. This causes the Streetlight layer to become visible on every frame of the animation. The symbol you now see on the Streetlight layer indicates that the change you made to the visibility of this layer has been applied to all frames in the animation.

20. Preview in a Web Browser

Click the Preview in Web Browser icon in the toolbox to play the animation in your default Web browser. The traffic lights will change color synchronistically and the lights on the truck blink on and off, adding a touch of realism to the scene. If your animation isn't working as expected, debug it by clicking on each frame in the Animation palette and matching layer visibility to the Frame Summary on the facing page.

T I P

All Frames Optimize the Same. When you optimize an animation (a single file or a slice to which you've applied animation frames), all frames in the animation use the same optimization settings. With the Optimized tab selected in the document window, turn off slice visibility and click through the frames in the Animation palette to check the appearance of the optimized image on each frame.

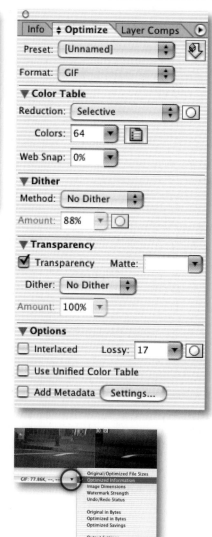

21. Optimize and Save

Click the Optimized tab in your document window. Wait a second while the program works through all the frames to generate an optimized preview. At this point you would normally optimize each part of the scene by selecting each user slice and one of the auto slices separately and choosing optimization settings in the Optimize palette (Window>Optimize). However, we had already optimized the existing slices, and the slices you drew took their optimization settings from our underlying slices. Select the slices you drew in the scene and notice the settings in the Optimize palette. Each of them was optimized as a GIF with 64 colors, No Dither, and a Lossy setting of 17 to keep the file size down while maintaining the appearance of the image. Transparency is checked because it is a prerequisite for Redundant Pixel Removal.

Click the arrow on either of the information fields at the bottom of the document window and choose Optimized Information to see the file size of the optimized animated scene. Depending on how you drew your slices, it's about 77K. Choose File>Save Optimized As, leave Format/Save as Type set to Images Only, and click Save. Choose File>Save to save the original with your changes. ◫

Frame Summary. Here's a summary of layer visibility on each animation frame (in addition to the Streetlight, Sky, and Background layers which are always on).

Frame	Left_ Red Layer	Left_ Yellow Layer	Left_ Green Layer	Mid_ Red Layer	Mid_ Yellow Layer	Mid_ Green Layer	Rt_ Red Layer	Rt_ Yellow Layer	Rt_ Green Layer	Dark Blinkers Layer
1	ON	OFF	OFF	ON	OFF	OFF	OFF	OFF	ON	ON
2	ON	OFF	OFF	ON	OFF	OFF	OFF	OFF	ON	OFF
3	ON	OFF	OFF	ON	OFF	OFF	OFF	OFF	ON	ON
4	ON	OFF	OFF	ON	OFF	OFF	OFF	OFF	ON	OFF
5	ON	OFF	OFF	ON	OFF	OFF	OFF	ON	OFF	ON
6	ON	OFF	OFF	ON	OFF	OFF	OFF	ON	OFF	OFF
7	ON	OFF	OFF	ON	OFF	OFF	OFF	ON	OFF	ON
8	ON	OFF	OFF	ON	OFF	OFF	OFF	ON	OFF	OFF
9	OFF	OFF	ON	OFF	OFF	ON	ON	OFF	OFF	ON
10	OFF	OFF	ON	OFF	OFF	ON	ON	OFF	OFF	OFF
11	OFF	OFF	ON	OFF	OFF	ON	ON	OFF	OFF	ON
12	OFF	OFF	ON	OFF	OFF	ON	ON	OFF	OFF	OFF
13	OFF	OFF	ON	OFF	OFF	ON	ON	OFF	OFF	ON
14	OFF	OFF	ON	OFF	OFF	ON	ON	OFF	OFF	OFF
15	OFF	OFF	ON	OFF	OFF	ON	ON	OFF	OFF	ON
16	OFF	OFF	ON	OFF	OFF	ON	ON	OFF	OFF	OFF
17	OFF	OFF	ON	OFF	OFF	ON	ON	OFF	OFF	ON
18	OFF	OFF	ON	OFF	OFF	ON	ON	OFF	OFF	OFF
19	OFF	OFF	ON	OFF	OFF	ON	ON	OFF	OFF	ON
20	OFF	OFF	ON	OFF	OFF	ON	ON	OFF	OFF	OFF
21	OFF	OFF	ON	OFF	OFF	ON	ON	OFF	OFF	ON
22	OFF	OFF	ON	OFF	OFF	ON	ON	OFF	OFF	OFF
23	OFF	OFF	ON	OFF	OFF	ON	ON	OFF	OFF	ON
24	OFF	OFF	ON	OFF	OFF	ON	ON	OFF	OFF	OFF
25	OFF	OFF	ON	OFF	OFF	ON	ON	OFF	OFF	ON
26	OFF	OFF	ON	OFF	OFF	ON	ON	OFF	OFF	OFF
27	OFF	ON	OFF	OFF	ON	OFF	ON	OFF	OFF	ON
28	OFF	ON	OFF	OFF	ON	OFF	ON	OFF	OFF	OFF
29	OFF	ON	OFF	OFF	ON	OFF	ON	OFF	OFF	ON
30	OFF	ON	OFF	OFF	ON	OFF	ON	OFF	OFF	OFF
31	ON	OFF	OFF	ON	OFF	OFF	OFF	OFF	ON	ON
32	ON	OFF	OFF	ON	OFF	OFF	OFF	OFF	ON	OFF
33	ON	OFF	OFF	ON	OFF	OFF	OFF	OFF	ON	ON
34	ON	OFF	OFF	ON	OFF	OFF	OFF	OFF	ON	OFF
35	ON	OFF	OFF	ON	OFF	OFF	OFF	OFF	ON	ON
36	ON	OFF	OFF	ON	OFF	OFF	OFF	OFF	ON	OFF

Animated Slide Show

Display thumbnails of your photos on the Web in an animated slide show with professional-looking dissolves made in ImageReady.

istockphoto.com

TIP

Protecting Photo Quality. JPEG is a lossy format that compresses a file by throwing away image data. So each time you make a change to a JPEG and resave, you lose a little image quality. This is true even if all you do is rotate and save the image. If you shoot JPEGs with your digital camera, as soon as you bring the photos into your computer, save a copy in PSD format for editing and archive the JPEGs.

1. Create a New File in ImageReady

In this project you'll learn how simple it is to show off a selection of your photos in an animated slide show. Try it with these photos and then substitute your own. If you use your own photos, resize them so that they are all the same size along at least one dimension, create a new folder, and move your prepared photos into that folder.

Start by creating a new file in Image-Ready. (There is no start file on the CD.) We chose to work in ImageReady over Photoshop because here you can import files to separate layers automatically, as in the next step. Choose File>New from the menu bar. In the New dialog box, set Width to 300 pixels and Height to 224 pixels. Set Contents of First Layer to White. Click OK to open a new image.

istockphoto.com

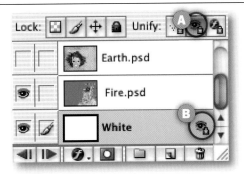

2. Import Photos as Frames

Choose File>Import>Folder as Frames from ImageReady's menu bar. Navigate to a folder of photos (for example, the Chapter 2-Animation>C02-04-photos folder) and click Choose. ImageReady automatically does all of the following for you:

- Places each item in the folder onto a separate layer in the Layers palette **A**.

- Creates a frame in the Animation palette (Window>Animation) for each layer **B**.

- Makes the contents of a single layer visible on each frame (by turning on just one layer's Eye icon per frame) **C**.

This shortcut bypasses the long-winded process of dragging individual photos into the slide show file, creating animation frames one-by-one, and adjusting layer visibility manually on each frame.

T I P

Frame Order. The Import>Folder as Frames command imports files in alphabetical order. After you import frames, you can change their order by clicking and dragging frames left or right in the Animation palette.

3. Create a White Layer

Click the Create New Layer icon at the bottom of the Layers palette **A**. Double-click the name of the new layer in the Layers palette and rename it *White.* Press D on the keyboard to set the Background Color in the toolbox to white. Press Command-Delete/Ctrl-Backspace to fill the new layer with white. Then drag the new layer to the bottom of the layer stack in the Layers palette **B**.

4. Match the Layer Across Frames

Next you'll make the White layer visible on all frames of the animation so that the semitransparent tweened frames you'll be creating shortly will all have the same solid white background. Select the White layer and click the Unify Visibility button at the top of the Layers palette **A**. The symbol on the White layer **B** indicates that it is visible on all frames.

5. Tween Frame 2

The rest of the frames in this animation will be created automatically by Tweening.

Select Frame 2 in the Animation palette and click the Tween button at the bottom of the Animation palette **A** (or click the arrow on the right side of the Animation palette **B** and choose Tween from the side menu).

6. Choose Tween Settings

Choose the following settings in the Tween dialog box:

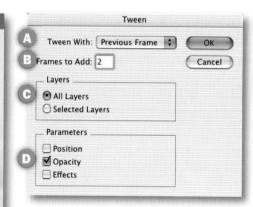

- Make sure Tween With is set to Previous Frame to add tweened frames between the selected frame and the previous frame **A**.

- Type the number *2* in the Frames to Add field. This tells the program to create two additional tweened frames **B**.

- Leave Layers set to All Layers **C**.

- Make sure that Opacity is checked, because this is the layer property that you want to change across the tweened frames **D**. We usually leave all three parameters checked just to be safe.

Click OK to add two semitransparent tweened frames **E** between the earth and fire photos. This will create a dissolve between these photos that resembles the slide dissolve you'd get by using two professional slide projectors in the analog world.

INSIGHT

What Can You Tween? ImageReady will tween only the following properties of artwork. So, for example, you can't use tweening to morph two images.

- Position — Use the Move tool to change the location of layered art.
- Opacity — Vary the opacity of one or more layers in the Opacity field of the Layers palette.
- Effects — Apply one or more Layer Styles and vary their options in the Layer Styles dialog box; change Blending Modes in the Layers palette or vary Blending Options in the Layer Styles dialog box; apply a warp text effect to type and change options in the Warp Text dialog box.

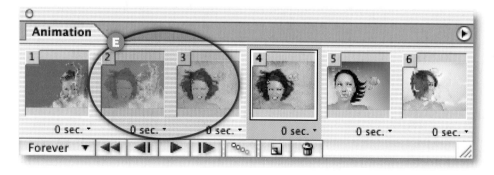

7. Preview the Tween

Select Frame 1 in the Animation palette. Then click the Select Next Frame button at the bottom of the Animation palette **A** to move through the frames one at a time. Notice that both the fire and earth photos are partially transparent on Frames 2 and 3, creating a dissolve.

8. Tween Frame 5

The water photo now appears on Frame 5. Select Frame 5 and click the Tween icon in the Animation palette again **A**. Leave all the Tween settings as are and click OK to add two tweened frames **B** between the earth and water photos.

9. Tween Frame 8

The wind photo is now on Frame 8. Select Frame 8 and click the Tween icon again. Leave all the Tween settings as they are, and click OK to tween the wind photo with the water photo.

10. Preview the Animation

Click the Play button at the bottom of the Animation palette to preview the animation in the document window. Notice that there's a jump between the wind photo and the fire photo. That's caused by the animation looping back to to the beginning of the animation with no partially transparent fames between the wind photo on Frame 10 and the fire photo on Frame 1. You'll fix that in the next step.

Click the Stop button (the square icon) at the bottom of the Animation palette to stop the preview.

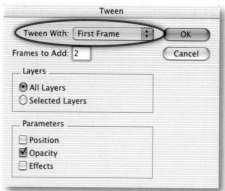

11. Tween the First and Last Frames

Select Frame 10—the last frame in the Animation palette. Click the Tween button. In the Tween dialog box, change the Tween With field to First Frame. Leave the other tween settings as they are, and click OK. There are now two partially transparent frames at the end of the animation. They create a dissolve between the wind photo in Frame 10 and the fire photo in Frame 1, smoothing the look of the animation when it loops back to the beginning to repeat itself.

CAUTION

Must Be a GIF. If you see a warning when you try to preview in a browser, click Cancel and change the Format field in your Optimize palette to GIF. Re-click the Preview in Browser button.

12. Preview in a Web Browser

Click the Preview in Browser button on the toolbox to preview the finished animation in a Web browser. Notice that it plays very fast and that it repeats over and over. You'll address those two issues in the next steps.

TIP

Forever Is Too Long. ImageReady animations are set to loop forever by default. A continuously repeating Web animation can be distracting, if not downright annoying. It's often better to limit the number of repetitions by adjusting the looping option in the Animation palette.

13. Set the Repetitions

The looping option at the bottom of the Animation palette is set to Forever by default. This would create an animation that continuously repeats without end. You'll limit the number of repetitions of your slide show in this step. Click the looping option and choose Other from the pop-up menu. In the Set Loop Count dialog box that appears, type **2** into the Play field and click OK. Your slide show will play through twice in a viewer's Web browser.

TIP

Once Is Not Enough. If you set your animation to play once, it might finish playing before it is completely downloaded to a viewer's Web browser. To ensure that viewers see your complete animation, set animations to loop at least two times when that is appropriate to your design.

14. Reduce the Speed

Slow this animation down so viewers have time to appreciate the photographs. Select all the frames by clicking on Frame 1, holding down the Shift key, and then clicking on Frame 12. Click the time delay setting beneath any frame and choose 0.2 seconds. This sets the same timing for all frames.

15. Pause on Selected Frames.

Now increase the timing on the four frames that display opaque photos so that the animation pauses on those frames. Click on Frame 1, hold the Command/Ctrl key and click on Frames 4, 7, and 10. Choose 2 seconds from the time delay menu beneath any one of those frames. Preview again to see the results.

T I P

Interpolation Method. When you reduce image size, some pixels are discarded from the image. The method by which pixels are discarded (the interpolation method) can affect the appearance of the image. Bicubic Sharper is usually the best interpolation method for reducing image size. Use it when you're making small Web images like photo thumbnails.

16. Optimize the Animation

Although this file contains photos, it can't be optimized in JPEG format because JPEG doesn't support animation. Instead, you'll have to optimize the entire file as one animated GIF, choosing the maximum number of GIF colors (256), and adding dither to smooth the bands of color in the photos. Click the Optimized tab in the document window. In the Optimize palette, choose Format: GIF, Colors: 256, Dither Method: Diffusion, Dither Amount: 100%, Lossy: 17, and Add Metadata: Unchecked. Leave the other optimization settings at their defaults, as shown here.

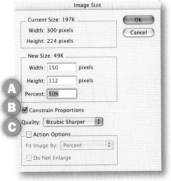

17. Reduce the Image Size

Click the box at the bottom of the Optimized tab of the document window and choose Optimized Information. The file size reported there is quite large for the Web. To reduce file size, you'll have to reduce the physical dimensions of the image. Choose Image>Image Size. Type 50% in the Percent field **A**, make sure Constrain Proportions is checked **B**, and choose Quality: Bicubic Sharper **C**.

C02-04-show-end.gif

18. Save

Choose File>Save Optimized As. Leave Format/Save as Type set to Images Only, and click Save. ImageReady saves a single animated GIF file. To display this slide show on the Web add a link to the GIF in any HTML file. Choose File>Save As to save the PSD source file. 📖

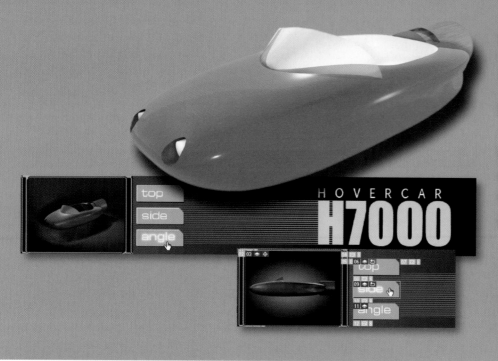

Rollover-Triggered Animation

Use rollover buttons to start animations playing in a Web banner in this interactive project.

1. Set Up Your Workspace

This ImageReady uber-project combines remote rollovers with animations. Open C02-05-hover.psd from the Chapter 2-Animation>Ch2-5 folder. You'll use lots of palettes, so start off by setting up your workspace. Open the Layers palette, the Web Content palette, the Animation palette, and the Optimize palette. Arrange them on your screen so you can see them all **A**.

ImageReady's Web Content palette (not to be confused with the similar-looking Layers palette) is a management center that keeps track of all the slices, rollover states and animation frames you'll be making. Animation frames are hidden in the Web Content palette by default. Configure the Web Content palette to display animation frames by clicking the palette's side arrow **B** and choosing Palette Options. In the Palette Options dialog box choose Include Animation Frames **C** and click OK.

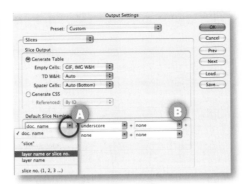

INSIGHT

Where You're Going. You'll be making three separate animations—all located in black frame on the left. Each animation will start playing when a visitor moves his mouse over the corresponding rollover button (top, side, or angle) in a Web browser.

2. Set the Slice Naming Convention

ImageReady automatically names slices for you. The slice name contributes to the name of the GIF that each slice ultimately generates. Default slice names are long and complicated. Make them simpler by changing the slice naming convention. Choose File>Output Settings>Slices. In the Default Slice Naming area of the Output Settings dialog box, click the arrow on the first field and choose Layer name or slice No. **A**. Repeat in the third field and choose None **B**. Leave the other fields at None.

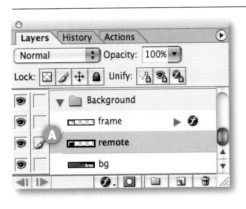

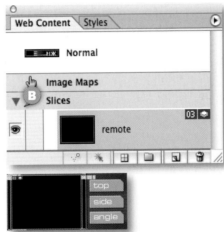

3. Slice the Remote Area

Start by creating a slice around the space in which the animations will occur. We'll call this the remote slice because it's removed from the buttons that will trigger the animations.

In the Layers palette, select the remote layer in the Background layer set **A**, and choose Layer>New Layer Based Slice. A new slice named remote appears in the Web content palette with a thumbnail displaying the slice content **B**. Notice that the slice name is taken from the corresponding layer.

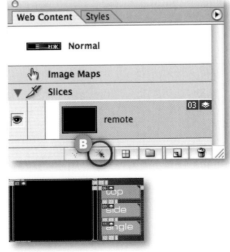

4. Slice the Rollover Buttons

Now you'll slice and add an Over state to each of the three rollover buttons—the top, side, and angle buttons. Fortunately, you can do all this at once. Open the Buttons layer set if it's closed. Select the three layers by clicking on the topbutton layer, pressing the Shift key and clicking on the anglebutton layer **A**. Now click the Create Layer-Based Rollover icon at the bottom of the Web Content palette **B**. This causes ImageReady to create a separate layer-based slice around each of the three buttons.

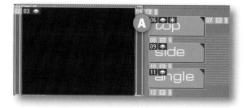

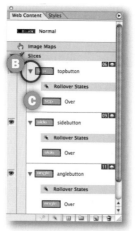

5. View the Slices and Over States

You can see the slices you just made in the image **A**, and they are listed in the Web Content palette. Each slice in the Web Content palette has an arrow on its left side **B** that opens a list of the rollover states for that slice. Each of the three new button slices has an Over state listed beneath it **C**. When you add animation frames to a rollover state, they will be listed under that rollover state. You can think of the Web Content palette as a visual outline of the interactive features in the image.

INSIGHT

Rollover States and Slices. Rollover states are attached to slices, which mark the area that triggers a rollover and the place local rollover effects will occur. A rollover slice will produce an image file for each state of the rollover. To learn more about rollovers, review the rollover projects in **Chapter 1, Navigation**.

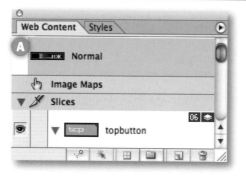

6. Set Up the Normal State

The Normal state is the way the image will look when it first loads into a viewer's Web browser. When you're working with your own files, select the Normal state at the top of the Web Content palette **A**, and use the Visibility icons in the Layers palette to make only those layers visible that you want showing when the page loads. We've already done that for you. So this step is a freebie.

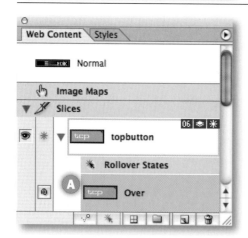

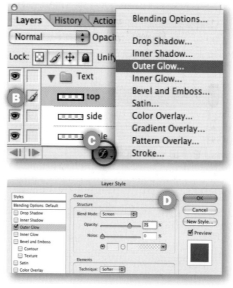

7. Add a Glow on the Over State

The Over states you made for the three rollover buttons are copies of the Normal state of each button. Now you'll change the appearance of those buttons on their Over states.

Select the Over state of the topbutton slice in the Web Content palette **A**. Then go to the Layers palette and select the top layer in the Text layer set **B**. Click the *f* icon at the bottom of the Layers palette **C** and choose Outer Glow from the pop-up menu. Click OK in the Layer Style dialog box to accept the default options for the Outer Glow style **D**. The text on the top button will now glow when a user moves his mouse over that button in a browser.

8. Add Glows to the Other Buttons

Repeat the preceding step on the side-button slice, selecting its Over state in the Web Content palette and then adding an Outer Glow to the side layer in the Text layer set. Repeat on the angle-button slice, selecting its Over state and adding an Outer Glow to the angle layer in the Text layer set.

CAUTION

Preview Often. We strongly suggest that you preview often as you build this complex file. That way, if you discover that a rollover or animation isn't working properly, you can fix the problem by moving back a few states in the History palette and then redoing only a few steps.

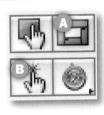

9. Preview the Rollover Buttons

Click the Slice Visibility button in the toolbox A to make the slices temporarily invisible for a clearer view of the image. Click the Preview button in the toolbox B. Move your cursor over the top button in the image. Its text will glow. Move your mouse away and the glow disappears. Mouse over the side and angle buttons, which behave the same way.

10. Exit Preview Mode

Click the Preview button again in the toolbox to exit Preview Mode. It's easy to forget to do this. If you do forget, you'll see a warning when you try to perform other commands.

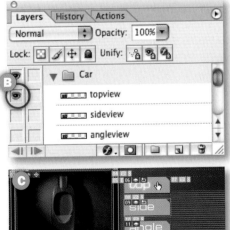

11. Set Up the Over State

You'll add another rollover effect, an animation that plays in the remote slice, to each of the three buttons. Each button will trigger a different animation—a fade-in of a top, side, or angled view of a futuristic hover car.

Select the Over state of the topbutton slice in the Web Content palette A. This is important because it identifies the trigger that will play the first animation—a viewer moving his mouse *over* the top button.

In the Layers palette, click in the Visibility field of the topview layer in the Car layer set B (but don't select the topview layer yet). The top view of the car is now visible in the image C.

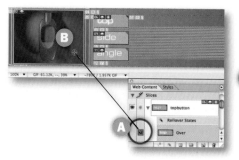

12. Target the Remote Slice

Now you'll tell ImageReady where you want the animation of the top view of the car to occur. To do that you'll target the remote slice from the Over state of the topbutton slice.

Go to the Web Content palette and click on the pickwhip icon (the spiral) to the left of the Over state of the topbutton slice **A**. Drag out a line from there to the remote slice in the image **B**. You'll see a target symbol next to the remote slice in the Web Content palette **C**.

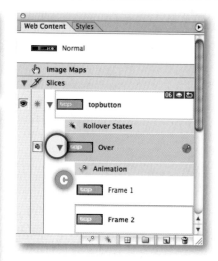

TIP

Two Locations. You can view, add, and manage frames in either the Web Content palette or the Animation palette. Each has its advantages. The Web Content palette shows everything in one place—animation frames with their related slices and rollover states. The Animation palette has a user-friendly graphic interface.

13. Create Frame 2

You're ready to build the animation that will be triggered by the Over state of the top button. In the Animation palette, click the Duplicate Animation Frame button **A** to create Frame 2 **B**.

Frames 1 and 2 are now visible in both the Animation palette and the Web Content palette. You can view them in the Web Content palette by clicking the arrow on the Over state of the topbutton slice **C**. If you don't see any animation frames in the Web Content palette, return to Step 1 and follow the instructions there for configuring the Web Content palette.

CAUTION

Work in This Order. Be careful to perform all steps in the order we've laid out for you. Otherwise your rollover animations won't work.

14. Disable Propagate Frame 1

Select Frame 1 in the Animation palette **A**. Now select the topview layer in the Car layer set in the Layers palette **B**.

Then click the side arrow on the Layers palette and choose Propagate Frame 1 Changes, removing the checkmark from that item **C**. This disables a feature that automatically copies changes made on Frame 1 to the other frames in an animation. Now you can change the opacity of the sideview layer on Frame 1, as you'll do in the next step, without affecting layer opacity on Frame 2.

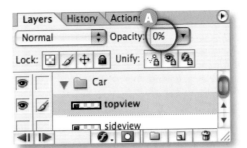

15. Change Layer Opacity on Frame 1

With Frame 1 and the topview layer still selected, enter **0%** in the Opacity field at the top of the Layers palette **A**. The top view of the car is now invisible on Frame 1 and visible on Frame 2 of the animation.

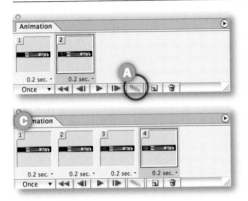

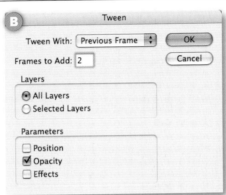

16. Tween Layer Opacity

Smooth the transition between the frames by automatically adding some in-between frames that have partial opacity. Select Frame 2 in the Animation palette. Click the Tween button on the Animation palette **A**. In the Tween dialog box, choose these settings **B**:

- Tween With: Previous Frame
- Frames to Add: Enter **2**
- Opacity: Checked

Click OK. There are now four frames of gradually increasing opacity **C**.

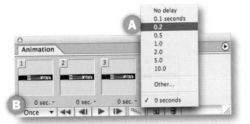

17. Set Time and Duration

Click on Frame 1 in the Animation palette, hold the Shift key, and click Frame 4 to select all frames. Click the time delay pop-up menu under any of the frames and choose 0.2 seconds **A**. Click the looping option and set it to Once **B**.

18. Preview the Tween

Click the Preview button in the toolbox. Mouse over the top button. It glows and the animation plays, causing the top view of the care to fade into view. Click the Preview button to exit preview.

If you see a problem, use the History palette to back up to a point before the problem occurs. Then redo the steps from that point on. When you're satisfied, save your work.

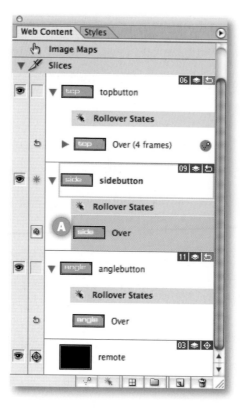

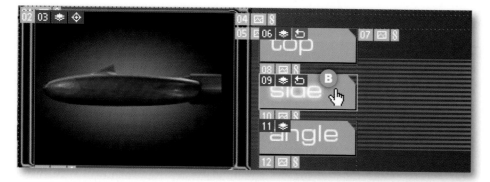

19. Repeat for the Side Button

You've completed one of the three roll-over animations. Now you'll just repeat the same steps on the side button and angle button. Follow this summary of steps 10 through 18 to program the side button:

- Select the Over state of the sidebutton slice in the Web Content palette **A**.

- Make the sideview layer visible (turn on its eye icon) in the Layers palette.

- Target the remote slice by dragging from the spiral icon on the Over state of the sidebutton slice in the Web Content palette to the remote slice in the image.

- Click the Duplicate Animation Frame button in the Animation palette to create Frame 2.

- Select Frame 1 in the Animation palette

- Select the sideview layer in the Layers palette.

- Disable Propagate Frame 1 Changes from the Layers palette side menu.

- Change the Opacity of the sideview layer to 0% in the Layers palette.

- Select Frame 2 and click the Tween button in the Animation palette. Add 2 frames, check Opacity, and choose Tween With: Previous Frame in the Tween dialog box.

- Select all four frames in the Animation palette. Set the time delay to 0.2 seconds and set looping to Once.

- Click the Preview button. Mouse over the side button in the image **B**. The side illustration fades into view. Mouse out and the area turns black. Exit Preview.

- Save.

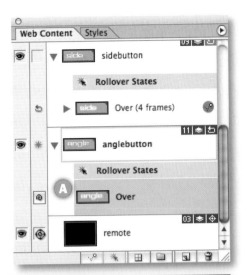

20. Repeat for the Angle Button

Now program the angle button the same way. You've done the same steps twice, so we'll be very brief here:

- Select the Over state of the angle-button **A**.
- Make the angleview layer visible.
- Target the remote slice from the Over state of the anglebutton slice.
- Create Frame 2.
- Select Frame 1.
- Select the angleview layer.
- Disable Propagate Frame 1 Changes.
- Change the Opacity of the angleview layer to 0%.
- Select Frame 2 and tween, adding two frames.
- Set the time delay for all four frames to 0.2 seconds.
- Set looping to Once.
- Preview **B**, and exit preview.
- Debug if necessary and save.

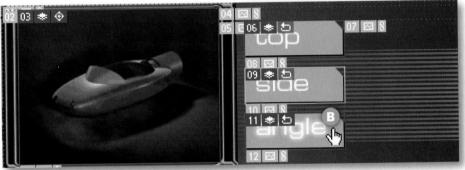

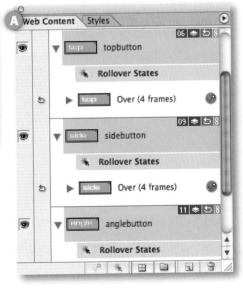

21. Link Slices for Optimization

In the Web Content palette, click the topbutton slice, hold the Shift key, and click the anglebutton slice to select all three slices **A**. Choose Slices>Link Slices for Optimization. A link symbol appears in the three button slices in the image **B**.

Now the optimization settings you choose for any one button will affect all three buttons automatically.

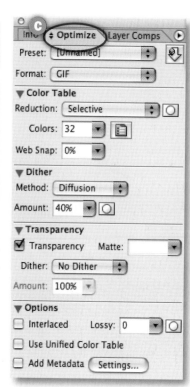

I N S I G H T

Why Select the Over State? Selecting the Over state of one of the buttons you linked for optimization lets you see the effect of the optimization settings on the glow that appears on the Over state of that button. At the same time you can see the effect on the Normal state of the other two buttons.

I N S I G H T

Why These Settings? The illustrations in the remote slice might look better as JPEGs because they are 3D, but Format has to be set to GIF because this slice contains animations. Setting Colors to the maximum of 256 and adding Dither helps retain the appearance of these 3D illustrations optimized in GIF format.

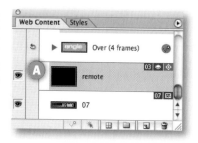

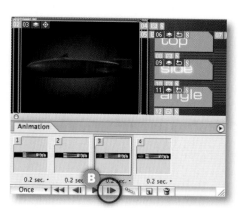

22. Optimize the Button Slices

Click on the Optimize tab in the document window to preview the optimized image **A**. Select the Over state of any button in the Web content palette **B**.

Option/Alt-click the double-pointed arrow on the Optimize palette tab to fully expand the palette **C**. Choose these optimization settings in the Optimize palette:

- Format: GIF
- Colors: 32
- Dither Method: Diffusion
- Dither Amount: 40%
- Add Metadata: Unchecked
- Leave the other optimization settings at their defaults, as shown here.

The three buttons now share these settings. These settings affect both the Normal and Over states of each button.

23. Optimize the Remote Slice

Select the remote slice in the Web Content palette **A**. In the Optimize palette, choose:

- Format: GIF
- Colors: 256
- Dither Method: Diffusion
- Dither Amount: 40%
- Add Metadata: Unchecked
- Leave the other optimization settings at their defaults.

These settings affect all the frames of all three animations. Check the appearance of other frames by selecting the Over state of a button slice in the Web Content palette and clicking the Select Next Frame button at the bottom of the Animation palette to scroll through the frames **B**.

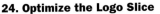

24. Optimize the Logo Slice

Notice that there is an auto slice (with a gray symbol) around the Hovercar logo **A**. This slice will probably need to be optimized with more colors than the other, plainer auto slices. Select the Slice Select tool from the toolbox and click in the Hovercar slice. Choose Slice>Promote to User Slice. Now you can optimize this slice independently of the auto slices. In the Optimize palette choose: GIF, Selected, 128 Colors, No Dither, Metadata unchecked.

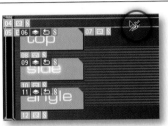

25. Optimize the Auto Slices

Click in any of the auto slices (the ones with the gray symbols). In the Optimize palette choose: GIF, Selected, 16 Colors, No Dither, Metadata unchecked. These settings automatically apply to all of the auto slices.

26. Save

Choose File>Save Optimized As. Leave Format/Save as Type set to HTML and Images, leave Slices set to All Slices, and click Save. Each slice in the image generates at least one image file. The button slices produce two GIFs each—one for the Normal state and one for the Over state **A**. The remote slice produces three GIF files containing animations and a GIF for the Normal state of that slice **B**. Each auto slice produces a numbered GIF **C**. ImageReady also makes an HTML file for you **D** that contains a table that reassembles all the individual images and that includes JavaScript to make the rollovers function. Choose File>Save to resave the PSD source file with the information you've added.

This has been a complex project. You may have to read it through more than once to remember its concepts so that you can create your own rollover-triggered animations.

Layer Mask Animation

An animated layer mask moves a spotlight across a Las Vegas landmark. This animation looks like a masters-level project, but it's really a snap to put together.

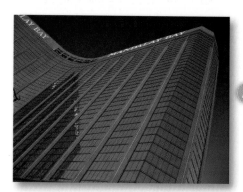

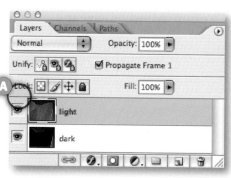

1. Start with Two Layers

A spotlight scans the face of a Las Vegas resort in this animation. The animation looks complicated, but it's really very simple to make using a layer mask in Photoshop.

Open C02-07-mask2.psd from the Chapter 2-Animation>Ch2-7 folder. Click the Eye icon on the top layer off and on **A** to see that you're starting with two versions of the same image—a photo shot in daylight and a copy that's been doctored with Curves to look like a night shot. The lighter photo is on the top layer, the dark copy is on the bottom layer.

You'll add a layer mask to the top layer, and move the layer mask independently of the artwork to create a spotlight that appears to move around the building.

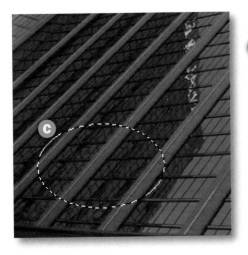

2. Make an Elliptical Selection

Start by making an elliptical selection to define the spotlight. Select the Elliptical Marquee tool in Photoshop's toolbox **A**. Soften the edge of the selection by typing *4* in the Feather field in the Options bar **B**. Drag out an elliptical selection similar to the one in the illustration **C**. Without changing tools, drag the selection to the bottom-left corner of the image **D**.

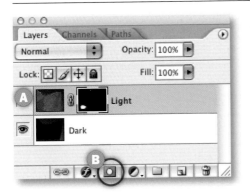

3. Add a Layer Mask

Select the Light layer in the Layers palette **A**. With the elliptical selection active, click the Add Layer Mask icon at the bottom of the Layers palette **B**. Press Command/Ctrl-D to deselect.

Photoshop adds a layer mask to the Light layer. The layer mask is filled with white inside the area you selected and with black everywhere else. The white pixels reveal the image on the Light layer, in the shape of a spotlight. The black pixels mask the Light layer so that you can see through to the Dark layer below.

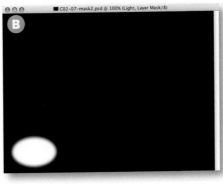

4. Display the Layer Mask

The layer mask is represented in the Layers palette by the grayscale thumbnail on the right side of the Light layer. Option/Alt-click the layer mask thumbnail **A** to view the layer mask in the document window **B**. You can see that the white hole in the black mask mirrors the spotlight effect in the image. Option/Alt-click again to return to normal view.

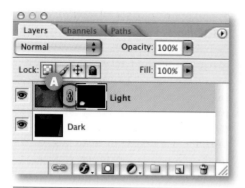

5. Unlink the Layer Mask

Click the link symbol between the layer mask thumbnail and the image thumbnail **A**. The link symbol disappears **B**, indicating that the layer and its layer mask are now unlinked. This makes it possible to move the layer mask independently of the image on the Light layer so that you can animate the layer mask without disturbing the image.

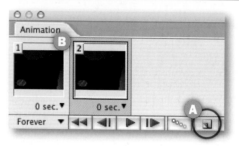

6. Create an Animation Frame

Choose Window>Animation to open the Animation palette with Frame 1 of the animation automatically displayed. Click the Duplicate Selected Frame button at the bottom of the Animation palette **A** to create Frame 2 **B**. Frame 2 is now a copy of Frame 1. Next, you'll make a change to Frame 2.

T I P

Managing Layer Masks. It's easier than ever to copy and move a layer mask between layers in Photoshop CS2. To copy a layer mask to another layer, Option/Alt-drag the layer mask thumbnail between layers. To move a layer mask to another layer just drag the layer mask thumbnail.

To temporarily disable a layer mask so you can see the whole image, Shift-click the layer mask thumbnail. A red X appears through the thumbnail.

To view a layer mask in the document window, Option/Alt-click the layer mask thumbnail in the Layers palette. You can modify the mask with grayscale painting tools, filters, and other editing tools.

To delete a layer mask without affecting the image, drag it to the trash can icon at the bottom of the Layers palette and click Delete at the prompt.

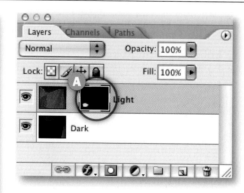

7. Select the Layer Mask Thumbnail

Click on the layer mask thumbnail **A** so that you're working on the layer mask, rather than on the Light image. If you look closely, you can tell the layer mask is selected because it's surrounded by a thin white border.

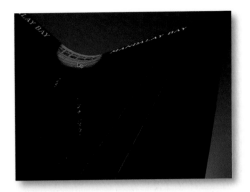

8. Move the Layer Mask on Frame 2

Select the Move tool in the toolbox. With Frame 2 selected, click in the image and drag the layer mask to the top of the building. This reinforces the illusion that there's a beam of light in the photograph. You're actually just rearranging the mask, hiding some areas of the Light layer with the black part of the mask and revealing other areas through the white part of the mask.

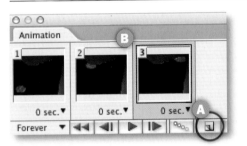

9. Create Frame 3

With Frame 2 selected, click the Duplicate Selected Frame button **A** in the Animation palette to create Frame 3 **B**. On Frame 3, with the layer mask still selected, use the Move tool to click and drag the spotlight to the top-right corner of the building.

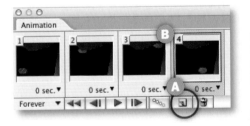

10. Create Frame 4

With Frame 3 selected, click the Duplicate Selected Frame button at the bottom of the Animation palette **A**, to create Frame 4. Check that the layer mask thumbnail is still selected on the Light layer in the Layers palette **B**. With the Move tool, click and drag in the image, moving the spotlight to the lower-right corner of the building.

T I P

Smoothing Out an Animation. If an animation isn't smooth enough for your taste, the solution usually is to add more frames. But the trade-off for more frames is larger file size.

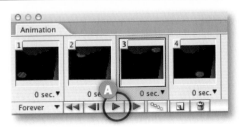

11. Play the Animation

Click the Play button on the Animation palette to view the animation. The spotlight jumps from one location to another. To smooth that transition, you'll add more frames in the next step. Click the same button to stop the animation.

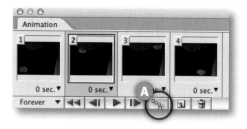

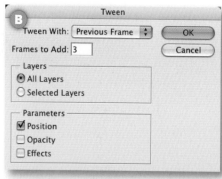

12. Tween Intermediate Frames

Now you'll have Photoshop create some additional, intermediate frames for you, adding gradual changes between the frames you made yourself. Select Frame 2 in the Animation palette **A**. Click the Tween button at the bottom of the Animation palette to open the Tween dialog box. Choose the following settings there **B**:

• Tween With: Previous Frame

• Frames to Add: 3

• Parameters: Position

Click OK. There are now seven frames. Photoshop made Frames 2, 3, and 4 automatically. Click the Next Selected Frame button to see that on those frames the spotlight in the image is located between the points you set at the bottom and top of the building **C**.

13. Tween Again

Select Frame 6 and repeat the preceding step. Then select Frame 10 and repeat again. The animation now has 13 frames. Expand the Animation palette to see all the frames by dragging the palette from its bottom-right corner.

14. Preview the Animation

Click the Play/Stop button at the bottom of the Animation palette **A** to watch the animation play in the document window. The spotlight moves around the building. Notice that there is a small jump at the bottom of the document window **B**. That's due to the sharp transition from the last frame to the first frame as the animation loops around. You'll fix that next.

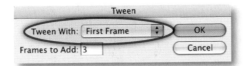

15. Tween Frame 13

Select Frame 13 and click the Tween button in the Animation palette again. In the Tween dialog box change Tween With to First Frame. Leave the other settings as they were and click OK.

16. Set the Timing

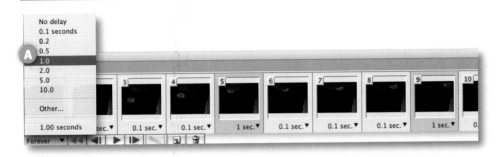

Choose Select All Frames from the Animation palette side menu. Click the Delay menu under any frame and choose 0.1 seconds. Command/Ctrl-click to select frames 1, 5, 9, and 13—the frames you made. Click the Delay menu on any of the selected frames and choose 1.0 second to pause the animation on some key spots **A**. Leave looping set to Forever.

17. Optimize the Animation

Choose File>Save for Web. Click the Optimized tab. Set format to GIF. Choose the maximum number of GIF colors (256), add dither (Diffusion 100%) to smooth the colors, and add lossy compression (10) to keep file size down. File size is still substantial, so click the Image Size tab, enter Width 300 px, leave Constrain checked, and click Apply. File size is now just 49.8K.

INSIGHT

Where Photoshop Is Weak. You must enter Photoshop's Save for Web window to preview an animation in a Web browser. If you then decide you want to change timing, looping, or number of frames, you have to exit Save for Web. ImageReady, which uses an easily accessible tabbed document window rather than a separate Save for Web Window, is easier to use in this regard.

18. Preview and Save

Click the Preview in Browser button in the Save for Web window. The animation starts playing when the page loads in a browser. If you're satisfied, click Save in the Save for Web window. In the Save Optimized As dialog box leave Format/Save as Type set to Images Only and click Save. Photoshop saves a single GIF file containing all the frames of the animation.

Finally, choose File>Save to resave the PSD source file to use for any changes in the future. ▥

Animating a Layer Style

Here's a quick and easy animation that gives the illusion of a moving light source. Once you get this down you'll be able to animate any layer style to produce animations in a heartbeat.

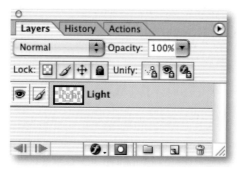

1. Start with a Layer of Text

Open C02-09-light.psd into ImageReady from Chapter 2-Animation>Ch2-9 or create your own file from scratch in ImageReady. Just use the Type tool to create text in a heavy font on a transparent layer. We rasterized our type layer, but this animation works fine if you leave your own type layer in its default state—as editable vector-based type.

2. Add a Background Layer

Select the Eyedropper tool and click in the text on the Light layer. This sets the Foreground Color in the toolbox to the same color as the text. Click the Create New Layer icon at the bottom of the Layers palette. Then press Option-Delete/Alt-Backspace to fill the new Layer 1 with the Foreground color. Drag Layer 1 beneath the Light layer in the Layers palette. Choose Layer>New>Background From Layer to make the bottom layer a non-editable **Background** layer. Your image now looks plain bluish/gray.

C A U T I O N

HTWWeb-Styles. If you don't see the HTWWeb-Styles in the Styles side menu, it means you haven't installed them properly from the CD at the back of this book. In that case, go back to the Introduction and follow the instructions there for installing the presets we provided on the CD.

3. Add a Style

Select the Light layer in the Layers palette. Open the Styles palette (Window>Styles). Click the arrow on the side of the Styles palette **A** and choose HTWWeb-Styles from the side menu. Click that arrow again and choose Large Thumbnail.

Click the **09_light** style to apply it to the text **B**. The Light layer in the Layers palette now displays a Drop Shadow and a Bevel and Emboss layer style.

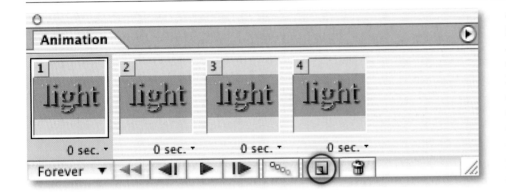

4. Start Building the Animation

Open the Animation palette (Window> Animation), which automatically displays Frame 1 of the animation. On Frame 1, the text displays the Drop Shadow and Bevel and Emboss layer styles you just applied. You'll make a simple change to those layer styles to create this animation.

First, you'll add a few more frames to the animation. Click the Duplicate Animation Frame icon at the bottom of the Animation palette three times, so that there are a total of four frames in the Animation palette. Each of the new frames is a copy of Frame 1. You'll change that in the next steps.

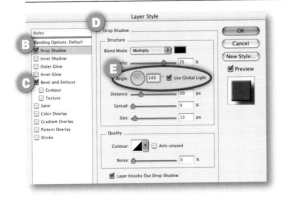

5. Open the Layer Style Dialog Box

Click on Frame 2 in the Animation palette. Then double-click Effects under the Light layer in the Layers palette **A** to open the Layer Style dialog box. It opens with the Drop Shadow style checked and highlighted on the left side of the dialog box **B**, the Bevel and Emboss style checked but not highlighted **C**, and and Drop Shadow options displayed on the right side of the dialog box **D**. Notice the Angle setting of **143°** **E**, which is the angle of the light source on the preceding frame—Frame 1.

INSIGHT

Layer Style Dialog Box. The checkmark and highlight on a style on the left side of the Layer Style dialog box mean two different things. The checkmark indicates that the style has been applied to and is visible (has an Eye icon) on the layer. The highlight means that that style's options are available to you on the right side of the dialog box. If you want to change a style option you must highlight the style in the Layer Style dialog box by clicking on it; the checkmark alone isn't sufficient.

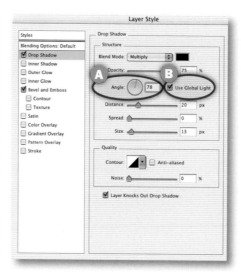

6. Change the Frame 2 Layer Style

With Drop Shadow highlighted (not just checked) on the left side of the Layer Style dialog box, go to the Drop Shadow settings on the right side of the dialog box and do two things:

- Change the Angle setting to *78°*. You can type 78 into the Angle field or spin the Angle wheel to that setting **A**.

- Make sure there's a checkmark in the Use Global Light check box **B**. This sets the light source angle globally so that it affects both the Drop Shadow and the Bevel and Emboss styles on the Light layer in Frame 2.

Click OK to close the Layer Style dialog box.

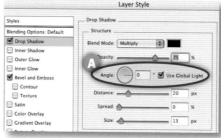

7. Change the Frame 3 Layer Style

Now you'll change the angle of the layer style on Frame 3 the same way. Select Frame 3 in the Animation palette. Double-click Effects under the Light layer in the Layers palette to open the Layer Style dialog box. In the Layer Style dialog box make sure the Drop Shadow style is highlighted.

Then change the Angle setting to *0°*, and make sure Use Global Light is checked **A**. Click OK to close the Layer Style dialog box.

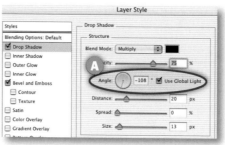

8. Change the Frame 4 Layer Style

Repeat the preceding Step 7 on Frame 4 **A**, this time changing the Angle setting to *–108°*. Click OK to close the Layer Style dialog box.

TIP

Smooth Animations. The more frames you include in an animation, the smoother the animation will appear when it plays. Of course, the downside of adding lots of frames is that file size will increase. The trick is to add just enough frames to make the animation look good, without inflating file size too much.

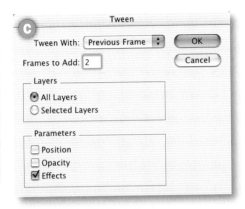

9. Tween Frame 2

You don't yet have enough frames to make the animation run smoothly. Rather than create all the frames by hand, let ImageReady do it for you with Tweening.

Select Frame 2 in the Animation palette **A**. Click the Tween button at the bottom of the Animation palette **B**. In the Tween dialog box **C**, set the following options and then click OK:

- Tween With: Previous Frame
- Frames to Add: 2
- Layers: All Layers
- Parameters: Effects

You now have a total of six frames. ImageReady added two frames, gradually changing the layer style angle across the tweened frames—current Frames 1 through 4. (The frames you made by hand are now Frames 1, 4, 5, and 6.)

10. Tween Two More Times

Repeat the preceding Step 10 twice more. The first time select Frame 5 and tween, adding two frames. The second time select Frame 8 and tween, adding another two frames. You now have a total of ten frames.

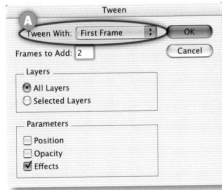

11. Tween the Last and First Frames

To make the animation run smoothly as it loops back from the last frame to the first frame, you'll do one more tween. Select the last frame—Frame 10. Click the Tween icon. This time, in the Tween dialog box choose Tween With: First Frame **A**. Leave the other settings as they were and click OK. ImageReady adds two frames to the end of the animation with gradual changes back to the layer style angle on Frame 1. You end up with 12 frames total. You're almost done with this project.

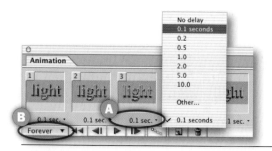

12. Set the Timing

Click the arrow on the side of the Animation palette, and choose Select All Frames from the side menu. Then click the Time Delay menu beneath any frame and choose 0.1 seconds **A**. Leave the looping option set to Forever so that the animation plays continuously **B**.

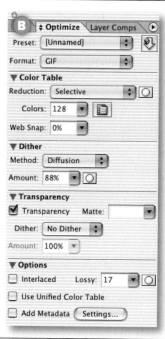

13. Optimize the Animation

Click the Optimized tab in the document window so you can see a preview of the image with the optimization settings you choose **A**. Open the Optimize palette and optimize the animation with GIF settings, as shown here **B**. Try 128 colors (to approximate the many tones in the bevel and shadow), add some Dither (to avoid banding), and add some lossy compression (to keep file size down). Leave Transparency checked (a prerequisite for the Redundant Pixel Removal method ImageReady applies by default), and uncheck Add Metadata. These settings affect all frames of the animation, so preview on several frames. You can reduce the image width and height (Image>Image Size) if you need a file that's smaller in file size.

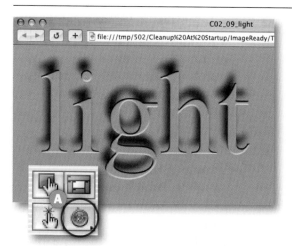

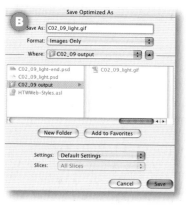

14. Preview and Save

Click the Preview in Browser button in the toolbox **A**. If you're happy with the browser preview, choose Save Optimized As to save the file as an animated GIF. In the Save Optimized As dialog box leave Format/Save as Type set to Images Only and click Save **B**. ImageReady produces a single GIF file with all of the frames you created. You can bring the GIF into a site-building program like GoLive to include it on a Web page.

Now that you've checked out all the animations in this chapter, try tweaking our recipes to come up with some unique variations of your own. ▥

Changing Layer Properties in an Animation

Normally any change you make to a layer in a particular frame of an animation affects that frame only. If you want a change in a layer's visibility, position, or style to affect all the other frames, you'll use Photoshop's or ImageReady's unify or match layer commands. Let's see how these commands work.

T I P

Photoshop Differences. The features addressed here are in slightly different locations in Photoshop CS2 and ImageReady CS2. The Unify buttons are always visible in the Layers palette in ImageReady; but in Photoshop by default they only appear in the Layers palette if the Animation palette is open. You can change that default by choosing Animation Options>Always Show or Always Hide from the Photoshop Layers palette side menu.

The Propagate Frame 1 Changes command is in the Layers palette side menu in ImageReady, but on the face of the Layers palette in Photoshop.

The Match feature is an item in the Layer menu in ImageReady; in Photoshop the equivalent command is Match Layer Across Frames in the Animation palette side menu.

Unifying Layer Properties

Assume that you're working on Frame 15 of an animation when you change your mind and decide that one of the layers in the image is extraneous and shouldn't be visible on any frame of the animation. You don't have to select each frame one by one, repeating the process of turning off the layer's Eye icon on every frame. Instead, select the layer in question and click the Unify Visibility button at the top of the Layers palette. Then turn off the Eye icon on that layer. Regardless of which frame is selected in the Animation palette, that change will ripple through all the frames of the animation. You can do the same thing with a layer's style or position. Select the layer, click the Unify Layer Style button or the Unify Layer Position button in the Layers palette, and then change a style or move the layer contents to affect the entire animation. Of course, if you want a layer's contents to move during an animation, don't use the Unify Layer Position button on that layer.

You don't have to bother with the Unify buttons if you have Frame 1 selected when you change a layer. By default, changes made on Frame 1 affect all layers of an animation. If you want to change that default behavior, turn off Propagate Frame 1 Changes in the Layers palette.

Matching Layers

There may be times when you've already made a change to a layer's visibility, position, or style and later realize that you want that change to apply to all frames of an animation. In that case the Unify buttons won't help you, because they are forward looking. A Unify button only applies to changes made after the button is activated.

To make a previous layer change ripple through the animation, select the frame on which you made the change in the Animation palette. Select the layer you changed in the Layers palette. Then choose Layer>Match in ImageReady or Match Layer Across Frames from Photoshop's Animation palette menu. The change will be applied throughout the animation.

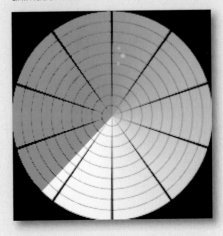

Vector-Based Flash Movie

You've heard of Flash. You've heard of ImageReady. But did you know you can create and export Flash format movies right in ImageReady? You'll make this homepage using vector-based text and shapes for fast Web download.

INSIGHT

Vector-Based Graphics. Vector-based graphics, unlike bitmap images (photographs or raster graphics), are not composed of pixels. Instead, they are defined by mathematical instructions. This gives vector graphics several advantages over bitmaps. They are scalable without negative effects on image quality. They have crisp edges that give a professional look to graphic art. And most important for our purposes, they are small in file size. Photoshop now has a full quiver of vector-based tools—vector type, vector shapes, paths, and even type on paths.

1. Have the Best of Both Worlds

The SWF format, popularized by Macromedia® Flash™, is reknowned for offering fast-downloading vector-based animations. The results are great, but the process of creating a movie in Flash is more complicated for many people than making an animation in ImageReady. Now you can have the best of both worlds. You can make vector artwork in Photoshop and export it in Flash (SWF) format from ImageReady.

In this project, you'll use vector-based Type and Shape tools in Photoshop to create this snappy homepage. Then you'll jump to ImageReady to animate your graphics, because you can't export SWFs from Photoshop. When you're done, you'll learn how to export the final product as an honest-to-goodness SWF movie, complete with an HTML file to display the movie on the Web.

In Photoshop, open C02-08-flash.psd from Chapter 2-Animation>Ch2-8.

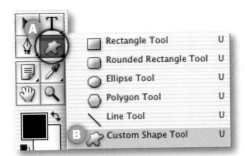

2. Prepare to Add Shapes

Start by adding some vector graphics to this page layout. Select the Shape 1 layer in the Layers palette so your next layer will be located above it. Click on the Shape tool slot in your toolbox **A** and choose the Custom Shape tool from the flyout menu **B**.

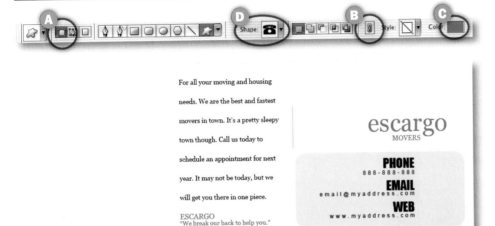

3. Set Custom Shape Tool Options

Do all of the following in the Custom Shape tool's Options bar:

- Make sure the Shape Layers icon **A** is selected (so you'll draw a shape rather than a path or a selection).

- If the Link icon is enabled (gray), click it to set properties for a new shape layer **B**.

- Click in the Color field **C** to open the Color Picker and choose red (R:204, G:0, B:0).

- Click the arrow on the Shape field to open the Shape Picker **D**.

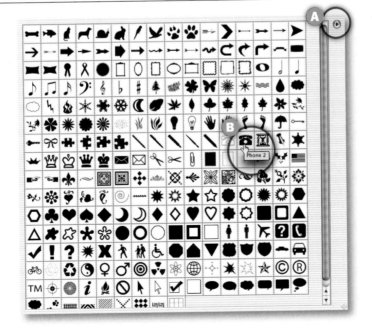

4. Select a Custom Shape

If your Shape Picker is not showing all the default shapes, like the illustration, click the arrow on the side of the Shape Picker **A** and choose All from the side menu. Locate the dark phone shape (Phone 2) **B**, and click on it. That shape will appear in the Shape field on the Options bar.

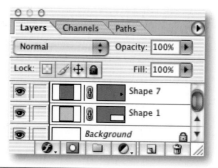

5. Draw a Phone Shape

Click and drag a small phone shape to the right of the phone number in the image **A**. There's now a new shape layer for the phone shape in the Layers palette. It has two thumbnails, one for the red color fill and another for the vector outline that defines this shape.

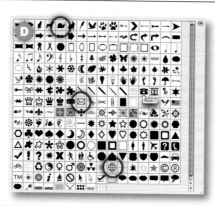

6. Draw More Shapes

Repeat Steps 3–5 to draw a green envelope to the right of the email address **A** and a blue wireframe globe to the right of the Web address **B**.

Then finish off the logo by drawing a large red snail shape above the red logo text **C**. (A shape can be drawn to any size because it's vector based.) You'll find custom shapes for all these shapes in the Shape Picker **D**.

7. Make Contact Info Invisible

You used the contact information to position the shapes. Now make the contact information invisible so it's ready to fade in as part of the animation you'll make later. Select the Contact layer set **A** and reduce the Opacity to 0% in the Layers palette **B**.

8. Add the Address

Type is another vector-based element. Select the topmost shape layer. Select the Horizontal Type tool in the toolbox. In the Options bar choose Arial, Regular, 14 pt, black **A**. In the Character palette (Window>Character) set Leading to 30 pt. Type three lines of text, pressing Return/Enter between each line: **_20 Snail Way, Sleepy Hollow, Slowville, TX 56457_**. Click the checkmark on the Options bar to commit the type. Use the Move tool to drag the type into place to the right of the gray bar.

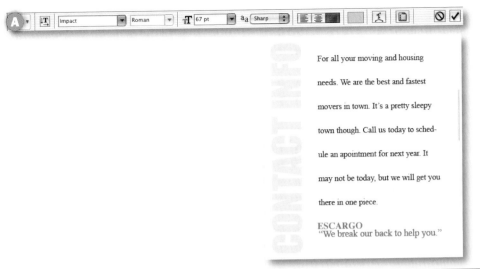

9. Add Decorative Text

Click in the image with the Horizontal Type tool and in the Options bar choose Impact, 67 pt, and gray (R:236, G: 236, B: 236) **A**. Type **CONTACT INFO** in uppercase letters. Then choose Edit>Transform>Rotate 90° CCW. Use the Move tool to position the text along the left edge of the page.

10. Jump to ImageReady

Now you'll move to ImageReady to create the animation. Click the Edit in ImageReady button at the bottom of Photoshop's toolbox to open this file in ImageReady.

11. Begin the Animation

First you'll make a block of text fly in from off screen when the page opens in a Web browser. Click the bottom right of the document window and drag to expand the window so you can see the gray area outside the document window. Open the Animation palette (Window>Animation), which displays Frame 1 automatically.

12. Change Timing and Looping

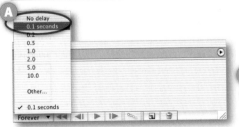
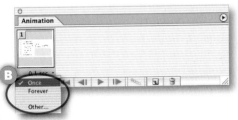

Now you'll change the timing on Frame 1. All subsequent frames will inherit this time delay. Click the Time Delay menu under Frame 1 and choose 0.1 seconds **A**.

You only want the animation to play once. So click the looping option and choose Once **B**.

13. Create Frame 2

Click the Duplicate Animation Frame button at the bottom of the Layers palette to create Frame 2. Frame 2 is currently a copy of Frame 1. You'll change that in the next step.

14. Change Position on Frame 2

Select the Move tool in the toolbox. Select the FlyIn layer in the Layers palette. With Frame 2 selected, hold the Shift key (to move ten pixels at a time) and click the left arrow on your keyboard to move the block of text to the left until it is just outside your document window. You won't see the text at this point.

15. Reverse Frames 1 and 2

Now you'll reverse the frames so the frame with the text off-screen becomes Frame 1. Just click the arrow on the right side of the Animation palette and choose Reverse Frames.

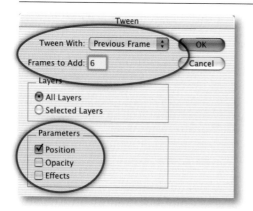

16. Tween Position

Next, you'll use tweening to add six frames in-between the two existing frames. ImageReady will gradually change the position of the text block across the additional frames. Select Frame 2 and click the Tween button at the bottom of the Animation palette **A**. In the Tween dialog box set the following options and click OK:

- Tween With: Previous Frame
- Frames to Add: 6
- Parameters: Position

17. Play the Animation

Click the Play/Stop button in the Animation palette to watch the animation play. The text block should fly into position from off-screen.

18. Add Frame 9

You now have eight frames. Click the Duplicate Animation Frame icon at the bottom of the Animation palette to add Frame 9.

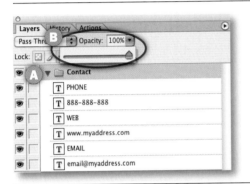

19. Change Opacity on Frame 9

With Frame 9 selected, go to the Layers palette and select the Contact layer set A. The Opacity field at the top of the Layers palette reads 0%. Change the Opacity to 100% B so that the layers in the set become fully visible in the image.

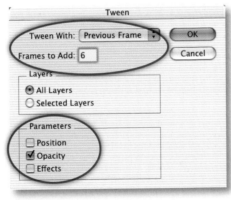

20. Tween Opacity on Frame 9

Now you'll use tweening to fade in the contact information. With Frame 9 selected, click the Tween button on the Animation palette A. In the Tween dialog box set the following options and click OK:

- Tween With: Previous Frame
- Frames to Add: 6
- Parameters: Opacity

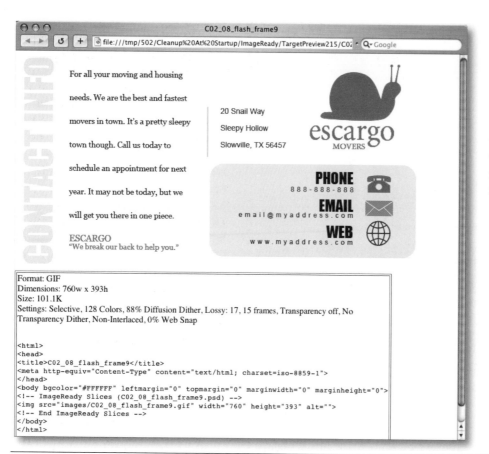

21. Preview in a Browser

Click the Preview in Browser icon in the toolbox to watch your animation play in your default browser. The text block flies in from the left, and then the contact information fades in. The temporary HTML code in the Browser window tells you that this file is currently a GIF with a file size of about 100K. In the next steps you'll turn it into a Flash movie that will be 1/5 of this file size!

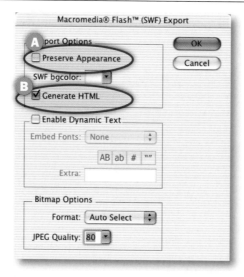

22. Export as SWF

Choose File>Export>Macromedia® Flash™ SWF. In the Macromedia® Flash™ (SWF) Export dialog box, choose the following settings and click OK:

- Make sure that Preserve Appearance is **_unchecked_** A. Leaving this setting off ensures that your graphics will remain vector-based for fast download.

- Check Generate HTML B. This tells ImageReady to create an HTML file with code to display your SWF in a Web browser.

- Leave the other options at their defaults, as shown here. They are not relevant because you are not including bitmap images in your SWF.

23. Save.

In the Export As Macromedia™ SWF dialog box choose a location for your files and click Save. ImageReady makes a SWF file and an HTML file to display it. You could bring the files into a site-building program for inclusion in a full site, post them on the page as a single page, or bring the SWF into Flash for inclusion in work you're doing there.

Choose File>Save to resave the original PSD file with the graphics you added to it. The SWF is not editable so it's important to save the editable PSD file.

24. View the Flash Movie in a Browser

Open the HTML file directly from your Web browser to see the SWF play there.

25. Check Out the File Size

Find the SWF file on your hard drive and check its file size. It comes in at only 20K, a file size significantly lower than that of the animated GIF format. That's because SWF does a terrific job of compressing vector-based images like those you used in this page layout. If you had incorporated bitmap images the SWF file size would be larger. ▥

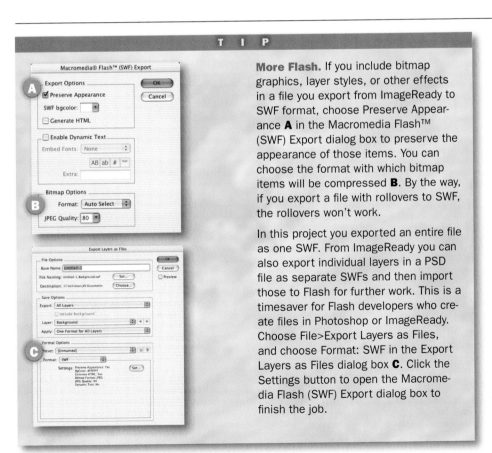

T I P

More Flash. If you include bitmap graphics, layer styles, or other effects in a file you export from ImageReady to SWF format, choose Preserve Appearance **A** in the Macromedia Flash™ (SWF) Export dialog box to preserve the appearance of those items. You can choose the format with which bitmap items will be compressed **B**. By the way, if you export a file with rollovers to SWF, the rollovers won't work.

In this project you exported an entire file as one SWF. From ImageReady you can also export individual layers in a PSD file as separate SWFs and then import those to Flash for further work. This is a timesaver for Flash developers who create files in Photoshop or ImageReady. Choose File>Export Layers as Files, and choose Format: SWF in the Export Layers as Files dialog box **C**. Click the Settings button to open the Macromedia Flash (SWF) Export dialog box to finish the job.

3

AUTOMATION

Putting Photoshop and ImageReady to Work for You

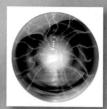

D O YOU EVER FEEL LIKE A SLAVE to your computer? Then it's time you focused on getting your computer to work for you. Automating repetitive tasks, like resizing photographs, can increase your productivity, standardize your output, and brighten your day. Automation also helps you accomplish more complex tasks, like working with data sets, that may have seemed too daunting to take on from scratch.

In this chapter we explore ways that Photoshop and ImageReady can help you automate your Web graphics workflow. These techniques are not only useful. Some of them, like building actions and droplets, encourage you to look under the hood of your favorite graphics programs to understand how they work. This kind of deep understanding is bound to make you a better, more knowledgeable Photoshop user.

We start out this chapter with a good look at Photoshop's actions and batch processing features, in Batch Processing Photos for the Web. This lesson runs from the practical (making small versions of photos for use on the Web)

to the artistic (automatically sepia-toning and building professional-looking frames around your thumbnails). Once you understand the principles of constructing actions and running them on multiple images, you'll be able to record your own timesaving actions.

Next, in Batch Processing with the Image Processor, we show you the hassle-free way to resize and format photo thumbnails for the Web using the automatic Image Processor script that's built into Photoshop CS2.

If you think Photoshop actions are useful, you'll be amazed to learn what ImageReady can do with conditional actions in Preparing Photos for the Web with Conditional Actions. You'll instruct ImageReady to resize images only if they meet your conditions. You'll also get the program to automatically distinguish between text graphics and photographs, optimizing the fomer as GIFs and the latter as JPEGs.

In Making Multiple Web Graphics you'll try out two automatic features. You'll use Photoshop's Crop and Straighten Photos command to break a single file into individual graphics. Then you'll optimize those graphics automatically with a droplet in ImageReady.

This chapter includes two projects devoted to creating multiple web page layouts—Designing Multiple Web Pages in a Single File, and Outputting Multiple Linked Web Pages. The first focuses on using layer comps and slice sets to efficiently produce multiple pages for a Web site. The second covers a hidden export feature that automatically links pages that contain the Selected rollover state, allowing you to create a complete Web-ready site in ImageReady.

This chapter ends with a bang. You'll learn how to use variables and datasets to create a collection of data-driven Flash Web banners in ImageReady in Creating Dynamic Flash Web Banners. Then you'll use similar features in Photoshop CS2 to generate multiple product descriptions in Making Product Pages for an Online Catalog.

Get ready to dig into a very meaty chapter. You'll increase your productivity and your creativity by putting Photoshop and ImageReady to work for you. And just think. Once you get this automation thing down, you can set up your computer to do your bidding, and take off for the beach.

Batch Processing Photos for the Web

If you have a life away from your computer, you'll love actions. They seriously reduce the time you spend in front of your screen. Here you'll create an action in Photoshop to make a small, sepia-toned, framed photo. You'll use that action to batch process a group of photos, creating images that look great on a Web page.

INSIGHT

What Are Actions? Actions are macros that record the steps you take as you process an image. Once an action is recorded, you can apply it to a single image or to multiple images using a batch process command to maximize efficiency.

Actions are great for automating any series of repetitive tasks. You can record many things you might do to prepare an image for the Web—renaming, resizing, correcting color, sharpening, applying special effects, optimizing, adding copyright information, and more. After you've worked through this project, try recording an action to fit your own Web workflow.

1. Open a Photo in Photoshop

Small copies of photographs come in handy as links to larger images in an online portfolio or as a way to display a large collection of photographs on the Web. You can imagine what a chore it would be to reduce multiple photos to thumbnail size, add a toning effect, sharpen, add a frame, and optimize each image in Web format if you had to make all those changes to one photo at a time.

Fortunately, you only have to do the work once, recording your steps as an action. Then you can play the action on a batch of photos, letting Photoshop do the bulk of the work for you. Open C03-01-001.tif from the Chapter 3-Automation>Ch3-1 folder.

T I P

Premade Actions. Photoshop comes with some premade sets of actions, including commands, frames, image effects, and more. You can load any of those sets by clicking the arrow on the side of the Actions palette and choosing a set from the side menu. Click the arrow to the left of any set to see the actions it contains.

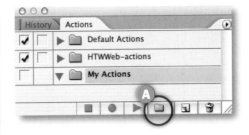

2. Create an Action Set

Open the Actions palette (Window>Actions). You'll see the Default Actions set that ships with Photoshop. You should also see the HTWWeb-Actions set. If you don't, take a minute to install the HTW Presets following the instructions in the Introduction. You'll create a new action set to hold the action you're about to make.

Click the Create New Set icon at the bottom of the Actions palette **A**. In the New Set dialog box that opens, name the set **My Actions** and click OK **B**.

I N S I G H T

Adjustment Layers. In the next step you use an adjustment layer. Adjustment layers, which are non-pixel-based instructions for adjusting underlying layers, are almost always preferable to direct adjustments for several reasons: An adjustment layer doesn't directly change or destroy image pixels. It can be edited at any time by clicking the left thumbnail on its layer. Its opacity and blending mode can be varied. Its application can be limited by a selection, and it has a minimal impact on file size.

3. Create a New Action

Click the Create New Action icon at the bottom of the Actions palette **A**. In the New Action dialog box that opens, name the action **Photo Thumbnail** and choose My Actions from the Set menu **B** to put the action in that set.

Click Record in the New Action palette **C**. Most everything you do while the red button **D** is active in the Actions palette is recorded as part of the Photo Thumbnail action, so try not to make mistakes. As you add steps, they will appear beneath the Photo Thumbnail action in the Actions palette.

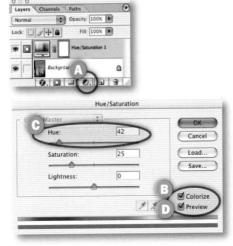

4. Sepia Tone the Photo

Your Photo Thumbnail action will contain a series of commands. The first command colorizes a photo with a sepia tone. Click the Create New Adjustment Layer icon at the bottom of the Layers palette **A** and choose Hue/Saturation from the pop-up menu. In the Hue/Saturation dialog box, check the Colorize checkbox **B**. Then move the Hue slider to 42 **C**. Leave Preview checked **D** to see a live preview of the sepia-toned image in the document window. Click OK. You'll see the Make adjustment layer command in the Actions palette.

INSIGHT

Other Resizing Methods. Alternatively, you could resize multiple images using the Image Size command in the Image>Image Size dialog box or in the Save for Web window, but you'd have to choose whether to set either height *or* width (the other dimension is set automatically to keep the image proportions when you check Constrain Proportions). Fit Image, by contrast, allows you to specify a maximum height *and* width and automatically fits your images within both specified dimensions.

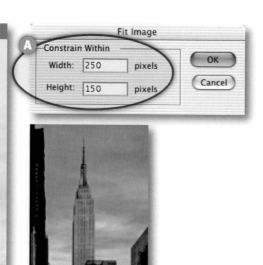

5. Resize the Image

Now you'll add another command to this action to reduce the image to thumbnail size. Choose File>Automate>Fit Image. In the Fit Image dialog box, set Width to 250 pixels and Height to 150 pixels **A** and click OK.

Fit Image is a useful way to resize when you're creating an action to run on images of different sizes or orientations. All the photos to which this action is applied will be resized so that they are proportional and don't exceed 250 pixels wide and 150 pixels high.

6. Sharpen

Reducing the size of an image often makes the image look soft. So the next step in this ongoing action is to sharpen the resized image.

Move the selection down one layer in the layer stack **A** by pressing Option/Alt-[, because you want to run the Unsharp Mask filter on the layer that contains image content, not on the adjustment layer. Use this shortcut so the action will work regardless of the name of the content layer.

Choose Filter>Sharpen>Unsharp Mask. In the Unsharp Mask dialog box, choose these settings, which are typical of settings for small, low-resolution Web images: Amount: 100, Radius: 0.5 pixels, Threshold: 3 **B**. Check Preview **C**. Click OK.

Choose Edit>Fade Unsharp Mask. (If you do something else first, this command will be unavailable.) In the Fade Unsharp Mask dialog box choose Luminosity from the Blending Mode pop-up menu **D**. Click OK. This reduces the chance that sharpening will change the color of photos during batch processing.

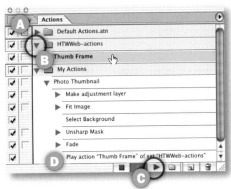

7. Include a Nested Action

We've created another action for you that automatically draws a professional-looking frame around a small image. In this step you'll nest that Thumb Frame action inside the Photo Thumbnail action you're building. Nesting actions gets extra mileage out of an action that also can stand on its own.

With your Photo Thumbnail action still recording, click the arrow on the HTWWeb-actions action set to open that action set **A**. Select the Thumb Frame action in that set **B**; then click the Play Action button at the bottom of the Actions palette **C**. You'll see a frame being created around your photo, and a step labeled Play action "Thumb Frame" of "HTWWeb-actions" is added to your Photo Thumbnail action **D**.

INSIGHT

Transparency. The frame is transparent in the original view and white in the optimized view. That's because JPEG does not support transparency. In the JPEG, the transparent pixels are filled with the Matte color.

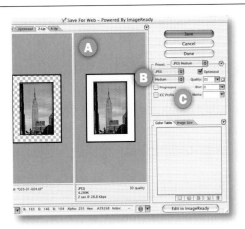

8. Save for Web

To complete your Photo Thumbnail action you'll optimize and save a copy of the file as a Web-ready JPEG. Choose File>Save for Web. In the Save for Web dialog box, click on the 2-up tab and select the right pane **A**. Set Format to JPEG and Quality to Medium **B**. Leave Matte set to White **C**. Leave the other settings at their defaults. Click Save. In the Save Optimized As dialog box that opens, leave Format/Save as Type set to Images Only, make a destination folder, and click Save. This saves a copy of one thumbnail-sized photo with sepia toning, sharpening, and a frame in JPEG format, ready to be added to a Web page.

9. Stop the Recording

Click on the Stop button at the bottom of the Actions palette to stop the Photo Thumbnail action recording. Then close the original image, 03-01-001.tif, without saving.

10. Test the Action on a Single File

Open Bridge by clicking the Bridge icon in the Options bar **A** or choosing File>Browse. In Bridge, navigate to the Chapter 3-Automation>Ch3-1 project files. Double-click on one of the images of Central Park to open it **B**. In Photoshop's Actions palette, select the Photo Thumbnail action, and click the Play button **C**.

The action plays on the selected image, saving a JPEG to the destination you recorded in the action and leaving a TIFF with a transparent frame on your desktop **D**. Close the TIFF without saving. Open the JPEG to check it. If the action works, pat yourself on the back and skip the next step.

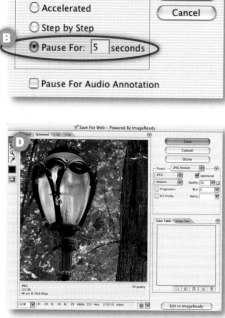

11. Troubleshoot the Action

If your action doesn't run as expected, troubleshoot one step at a time. Click the arrow at the side of the Actions palette **A** and choose Playback Options. In the Playback Options palette, click Pause For, type in 5 seconds, and click OK **B**. Open an image. Select the Photo Thumbnail action and click the Play button at the bottom of the Actions palette **C** to move slowly through the steps.

When you find the step with the problem, double-click the step to open its command and try to fix what's wrong. (For example, if you saved to the wrong folder, double-click the Export step to reopen the Save for Web dialog box **D**, click Save, and change the destination folder in the Save Optimized As dialog box.) Or drag the step to the Trash icon at the bottom of the Actions palette to delete it, select the step just above the former step, and re-record the deleted step. If all else fails, drag the entire action to the trash and re-record, keeping in mind that a file must be open before you begin recording this action.

TIP

Save Action Sets, Not Actions. You cannot save individual actions. You have to save the entire action set in which an action is located.

12. Save your Action Set

Select the My Actions set **A**. Click the side arrow on the Actions palette, choose Save Actions, navigate to Photoshop CS2>Presets>Photoshop Actions, and click Save. The set will be available from the Actions palette side menu when you relaunch Photoshop

13. Batch Process

Now you reap your reward for building the action. In Bridge, Command/Ctrl-click the remaining four images of Central Park to select them, leaving the night shots deselected. Choose Tools>Photoshop>Batch from the menu at the top of Bridge.

Choose the following settings in the Batch dialog box:

- Set: My Actions

- Action: Photo Thumbnail

- Source: Bridge (The action will run on the files you selected in Bridge.)

- Override Action "Open" Commands: Unchecked (see Insight)

- Include All Subfolders: Unchecked

- Suppress File Open Options Dialog: Checked

- Suppress Color Profile Warnings: Checked (to avoid a warning if a file's color profile differs from your working space)

- Destination: None (because the action contains the destination for the JPEGs)

INSIGHT

Override Action Open Commands. This batch setting can be confusing. The upshot is that when you have no Open step in an action, as in this case, this box must be unchecked or no files will open. When you do have an Open step in an action, this box should be unchecked if you want your batched files to open, rather than just the original file.

Now click OK and kick back to let Photoshop apply your Thumbnail Photo action to each of the selected images. When it's done, close the TIFFs without saving and open the JPEGs from your destination folder to admire them. You can bring these thumbnail photos into a site-building program like GoLive or Dreamweaver to include in a Web site.

Making the Most of Actions

Actions have lots of wrinkles. Here are some tips that will keep you on track as you create and apply actions. If you're serious about working with actions, take a look at some of the action exchanges on the Web, like the Adobe Studio Exchange (http://share.studio.adobe.com) or Actionfx.com.

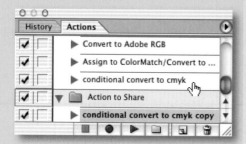

Sharing Actions

You can share your best actions with friends by saving them. Unfortunately, you can't save just one action from Photoshop, but you can save an action set. So if you want to share a single action, make a new action set in the Actions palette by clicking the palette's side arrow and choosing New Set. With the original action set open, Option/Alt-drag a copy of the action to the new action set. Select the new action set, click the Actions palette's side arrow, and choose Save Actions. Save the file with an .atn extension to a location other than the Photoshop default location (which is Presets>Photoshop Actions), and transfer the .atn file to a friend.

Loading Actions

If you're the recipient of an action file, it's easy to load it into your Actions palette. Just click the Actions palette's side arrow and choose Load Actions from the side menu. Navigate to the .atn file you want to add and click Load. A new action set will appear in your Actions palette. Click the arrow to the left of the new action set to access its contents. The new action set will be saved automatically when you exit Photoshop. If you want the action to appear in the Actions palette's side menu the next time you open Photoshop, save it to the Presets>Photoshop Actions folder inside the Photoshop application folder by choosing Save Actions from the Actions palette's side menu.

Assigning Function Keys to Actions

To streamline the playback process, you can assign one of the function keys on your keyboard to an action. Then just click that function key and the action will play, even if the Actions palette is closed. You can assign a function key when you create an action in the New Action dialog box. Or assign a function key later by selecting the existing action in the Actions palette, clicking the palette's side arrow, and choosing Action Options. When you assign a function key to an action, choose from any of the F keys on your keyboard. If most of those are being used for other commands, add a checkmark next to the Shift or Command/Ctrl modifier in the New Action or Action Options dialog box to expand the available choices. If you forget which function key you've assigned to an action, select that action and choose Action Options. By the way, on Windows you can't assign the F1 key because it's reserved. Function keys are most handy when you're viewing your actions in Button Mode (described on the next page), because the function key appears right on the face of an action's button.

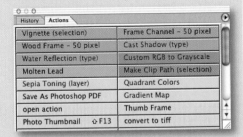

Playing Actions from Button Mode

Button Mode offers a simplified view of your actions. Each action appears as a big push button, complete with any colors and function keys that you've assigned to the action. Action sets and steps are invisible in Button Mode, making the landscape simpler to negotiate. Switch into Button Mode by clicking the Actions palette's side arrow and choosing Button Mode. Feel free to stretch the button bar across the bottom or side of your screen by clicking on its bottom-right corner and dragging. Keep in mind that although you can play actions from Button Mode, you can't create or edit actions in that view. For those purposes, you'll toggle back to the list view of the Actions palette, by choosing Button Mode again from the Actions palette's side menu.

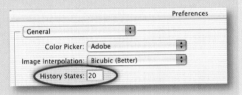

Working with Only One Undo

One of the challenges of creating actions is that you can only use Undo on the last step you made. Fortunately, Photoshop's History palette records most of your steps. To return to a previous step you recorded in an action, you can select that step in the History palette. But keep in mind that actions often contain lots of steps, and the History palette is set to record only 20 steps by default. To increase that number, go to Photoshop/Edit>Preferences>General and type a higher number into the History States field.

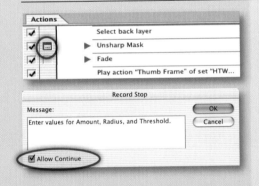

Pausing an Action for Input

If an action includes a command that has a dialog box, like the Unsharp Mask filter you worked with in the preceding project, you can program the action to pause at that step and open the command's dialog box so that the user can enter values of her choice. Otherwise dialog boxes do not appear in actions, and commands are applied with default values. To pause an action at a step for user input, click in the Modal Control column just to the left of the step to display a dialog box icon. Click there again if you want to remove this icon. You can also add a message to users explaining what the user should do on a particular step by clicking the side arrow on the Actions palette and choosing Insert Stop. Type your message in the Record Stop dialog box that opens. Add a checkmark to the Allow Continue box to offer users the option of continuing to play the action.

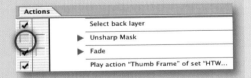

Customizing an Action for Playback

If there's a particular step you want to skip when you play an action on a file, just click in the far left column of the step to delete the checkmark before running the action.

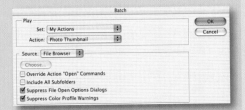

Batch Processing

We can't emphasize enough that the beauty of actions is their ability to run automatically on a collection of files. You can batch process a folder of files with an action from Photoshop's File menu (File>Automate>Batch). Alternatively, you can batch process a collection of files displayed in Adobe Bridge by choosing Tools>Photoshop>Batch from Bridge's menu bar. ▥

Batch Processing with the Image Processor

The quickest, easiest way to resize and reformat photos for the Web is to run them through the automatic Image Processor that's built into Photoshop CS2.

TIP

Two Locations. You can access the Image Processor from either Bridge (Tools>Photoshop>Image Processor) or Photoshop (File>Scripts>Image Processor). Accessing it from Bridge allows you to visually select the files you want to process and to do other work in Photoshop while the processing is occurring.

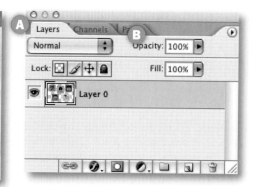

TIP

Batch Renaming in Bridge. You can automatically rename large batches of photos with successive filenames in Bridge. Select photos to rename and choose Tools>Batch Rename. Choose Copy to other folder to avoid overwriting originals **A**, include the Sequence Number as part of the file name, and set the starting file number **B**. Preview your filenaming convention **C**. Then click Rename.

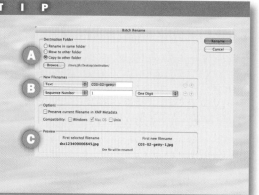

1. Prepare a Single Image

Photoshop CS2 has a built-in Image Processor that takes the pain out of the initial processing of multiple photographs. There's no need to spend time creating an action and setting up the Batch command if your goal is simply to reduce the size of multiple photos and save them in Web-ready JPEG format. The Image Processor makes those tasks quick and easy to accomplish.

This project starts in Adobe Bridge, a separate application for viewing and managing files across the Creative Suite 2 applications. Right-click in the Preview panel, choose New Folder, and make a destination folder for the processed files. Use the Folders panel **A** to navigate to the Chapter 3-Automation>Ch3-2 folder. In the Preview panel, click on C03-02-getty-001, press and hold down the Shift key, and click on C03-06-getty-006 to select only those images for processing **B**.

T I P

Multiprocessing. The Image Processor can simultaneously save multiple copies of a file in more than one file format (JPEG, PSD, and TIFF), with size varying by format. Use this feature to scale down a photo to thumbnail size and save it as a JPEG, to save a larger version as a PSD for future editing, and to save a large TIFF for your commerically printed promo cards—all at the same time.

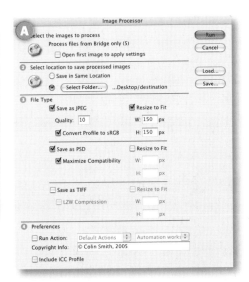

T I P

Multitasking. If you have lots of files to process, you don't have to sit idly by. The Image Processor will continue to run even if you're doing other work in Photoshop.

T I P

Running an Action. If you want the Image Processor to do something more to your images, like frame or colorize each photo, record those commands as an Action, and trigger that action to play on multiple images from the Preferences area of the Image Procesor.

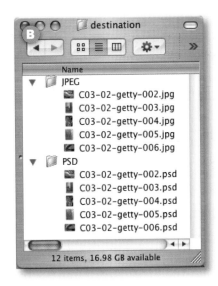

2. Choose Settings

The Image Processor window is intuitive, with clear labels and tooltips that appear when you mouse over a field. This makes the Image Processor easier to use than the Batch dialog box used in conjunction with Actions (see Batch Processing Photos for the Web earlier in this chapter.) Choose these settings in the Image Processor **A**:

- Leave Save in Same location unchecked to avoid overwriting your originals.

- Click Select Folder and browse to a location for the processed images.

- Check Save as JPEG and set Quality to around 5.

- To the right of Save as JPEG, set Resize to Fit to 150 px by 150 px. This doesn't make every photo exactly 150x150 pixels, as you might think. It resizes all selected photos, whether horizontal or vertical, to fit within a space of that size.

- Check Convert Profile to sRGB to approximate color appearance in a typical Web browser.

- Check Save as PSD. Leave the related Resize to Fit field unchecked to save a large master of each file for future editing. The PSDs will be saved to a separate folder by default.

- Enter copyright info: Option+G/ Alt=0169 for the copyright symbol, along with the photographer's name and the year. Leave Include ICC Profile unchecked to keep file size down.

Click Run to run the Image Processor script on your selected photos. When processing is done, open your destination folder to find a folder of small JPEGs and a folder of larger PSD files **B**.

© Ali Sabet: sabet.com

Making Multiple Web Graphics

This project uses two timesaving automation techniques. Break a file into individual graphics with Photoshop's Crop and Straighten Photos command. Then optimize those graphics all at once as Web-ready GIFs using an ImageReady droplet.

TIP

Background Layer Restrictions.
A Background layer cannot have transparent pixels. Erasing on a Background layer displays the Background color from the toolbox. You can't move the layer's content or drag another layer beneath it. So you'll often want to change a Background layer to a regular layer.

1. Prepare a Single Image

Open C03-03-graphics.tif into Photoshop. This document has several graphics on a single layer. In the steps that follow you'll automatically separate these graphics into individual files and optimize them all as GIFs.

Start by changing the single Background layer into a regular layer so you can make some of its pixels transparent. Double-click the Background layer **A**, and click OK in the New Layer dialog box to convert this layer to a regular layer. Select the Magic Wand tool in the toolbox. Control/right-click the tool icon at the far left of the Options bar and choose Reset Tool **B** to return the tool to its default settings. Click on the white background to select everything except the graphics **C**, and press Command/Ctrl-X to delete the selected area. The checkerboard represents transparency **D**.

T I P

Clean Up the Crop. Sometimes the Crop and Straighten Photos command doesn't do a perfect job of cropping the individual images it produces. Try using the Crop tool or other editing tools on the individual images to tidy up the edges of the files.

2. Crop the Image Automatically

Next you'll separate the graphics in this image into individual files. You could do this with the Slice tool, but there's a faster way. Use Photoshop's Crop and Straighten Photos command, which was designed to allow photos to be scanned together and then quickly separated and straightened. This feature works just as well on graphics like these, which were created in a drawing program on a single layer. Choose File>Automate>Crop and Straighten Photos from Photoshop's menu bar. Wait just a second, and you'll have five separate images, each closely cropped to one of the graphics.

Close C03-03-graphics.tif without saving. Make a new folder on your hard drive—C03-03-tiffs. Save each of the individual graphics into that folder. Leave Format/Save as Type set to TIFF, and click OK in the TIFF Options dialog box to accept its defaults. Close all but one of the individual graphics, the cat, which you'll use to create an optimization droplet.

3. Jump to ImageReady

With the cat graphic open, click the Edit in ImageReady button at the bottom of the Photoshop toolbox. That image opens in ImageReady, ready for further editing there.

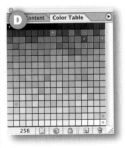

4. Set Up an Optimizing Workspace

In ImageReady, click the 2-Up tab in the document window to see and compare the original graphic and a preview of the optimized graphic **A**. Open the Optimize palette (Window>Optimize). Click the double-pointed arrow on the Optimize tab to see all the palette's settings **B**. Click the Color Table icon on the Optimize palette **C** to open the Color Table palette **D**.

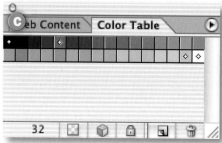

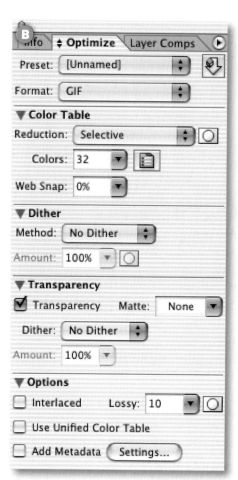

5. Optimize the Graphic as a GIF

Click in the preview pane of the document window **A** and choose the following settings in the Optimize palette **B**. (For further explanation of these settings see *GIF Optimization Settings* in Chapter 1.)

- Format: GIF
- Reduction: Selective
- Colors: 32 (This setting has the most impact on file size and appearance. These colors are visible in the Color Table palette **C**.)
- Dither Method: No Dither
- Transparency: Checked (to maintain the transparent background pixels)
- Matte: None (This creates a hard-edged graphic with no halo; but if you know the color of the page background on which you plan to place these graphics, choose that color.)
- Lossy: 10 (to further reduce file size)
- Add Metadata: Unchecked (to avoid inflating file size)

The GIF preview looks like the original image and is small in file size.

INSIGHT

What Is a Droplet? A droplet is a small application that you can run on a single file or on a collection of files. A droplet generated from ImageReady's Optimize palette is used to optimize other files with the same settings. A droplet can also be created from ImageReady's or Photoshop's Actions palette and used to run that action on multiple files.

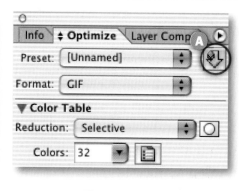

Make GIF (32 colors, Selective, 0% dither)

6. Create a Droplet

Creating a droplet is as easy as clicking the Droplet icon on the Optimize palette **A** and dragging to your desktop. The droplet appears on your desktop automatically named with the optimization settings **B**.

Alternatively, if you want the chance to choose the name or location of the droplet, click the side arrow on the Optimize palette and choose Create Droplet. In the Save Optimized Settings as Droplet dialog box, give the droplet a name and location, and click OK. Close the graphic without saving.

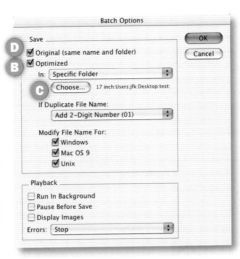

7. Edit the Droplet

Create a new C03-03-gifs folder on your hard drive. By default the droplet will save the optimized GIFs to the same folder as the original TIFF files—C03-03-tiffs. To save the optimized GIFs to the C03-03-gifs folder instead, double-click the droplet. In the droplet window that opens, double-click Batch Options **A**. In the Batch Options dialog box that opens, leave Optimized checked, choose In: Specific Folder **B**, click the Choose button, and navigate to your C03-03-gifs folder **C**.

It's a good idea to also save a copy of the small source graphics. If you need to make a change to the files in the future, these will be the files to use. Image-Ready will save a copy of each as a PSD file in the same folder as the original TIFFs if you check Original (same name and folder) **D**. Click OK to close the Batch Options dialog box. Then close the droplet window and click Save at the prompt to save your batch processing changes along with the droplet.

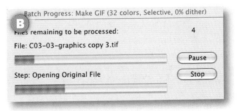

8. Apply the Droplet

Now you'll use the droplet to automatically optimize all the small graphics you created earlier. Close the cat graphic so that it will be included in the files optimized by the droplet. Click and drag the folder into which you saved the small TIFFs, C03-03-tiffs, on top of the droplet on your desktop **A**. You can see the progress of the files as they process in the Batch Progress window **B**.

9. View the Results

Open C03-03-gifs, the folder you made earlier for GIFs. You'll see five optimized GIFs ready to be brought into a Web-building program for inclusion on a Web page. ▦

Demystifying Droplets

Droplets are mini-applications you can create from ImageReady or Photoshop and apply to a single file or use to batch process a collection of files. Here are some tips for understanding and using droplets.

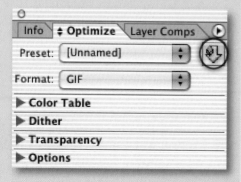

Optimization Droplets

The simplest droplet is one created from the Optimize palette in ImageReady. This kind of droplet contains only optimization settings and is used to optimize one or more files by applying the same optimization settings, as you did in the third project in this chapter, **Making Multiple Web Graphics.**

To create a droplet from ImageReady's Optimize palette, drag the droplet icon from that palette onto your desktop. Alternatively, click the droplet icon in the Optimize palette and choose a droplet name and location, or click the side arrow on the Optimize palette and choose Create Droplet.

Action Droplets

The other kind of droplet is one created from an action in either Photoshop or Image-Ready. This kind of droplet can contain any action you create in the corresponding program. It is used to batch process multiple files with that action. In ImageReady, a droplet is the only way to batch process an action. In Photoshop, you can batch process an action by dragging a folder of files onto a droplet, by using the File>Automate>Batch command, or by using the Tools>Photoshop>Batch command from Adobe Bridge, as you did in the first project in this chapter, **Batch Processing Photos for the Web.**

To create a droplet from an action in ImageReady, click the side arrow on ImageReady's Actions palette and choose Create Droplet. To create a droplet from an action in Photoshop, choose File>Automate>Create Droplet and specify the action set and action in the Create Droplet dialog box that opens.

Including a Droplet in an Action

When you create an action in ImageReady, you can specify optimization settings to be applied along with the other steps in the action by choosing optimization settings in the Optimize palette and then dragging the droplet icon from the Optimize palette into the action in the Actions palette. Set Optimization To [the format you chose in the Optimize palette] will appear as a step in the action, just above the selected step. You cannot drag a droplet from your hard drive into the Actions palette.

Cross-Platform Droplets

Droplets can be used across Windows and Macintosh platforms. To use a Photoshop droplet created in Windows on a Mac, drag the droplet onto the Photoshop icon in your OS X dock (or drag an ImageReady droplet onto the ImageReady icon in your dock).

To use a droplet created on a Mac in Windows, change the extension on the droplet file name to .exe, because it is an executable mini-program.

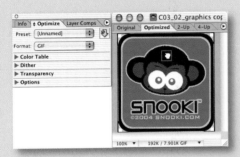

Applying a Droplet to a Slice

In ImageReady, a droplet containing optimization settings can be applied to optimize an entire image, or alternatively to optimize selected slices in an image. To apply an optimization droplet to a slice, choose settings in ImageReady's Optimize palette, and then drag the Droplet icon from the Optimize palette onto the slice in the document window. You cannot drag a droplet from your hard drive onto a slice.

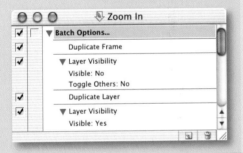

Editing a Droplet

In ImageReady you can edit a droplet directly. Double-click an ImageReady droplet to open the droplet window. That window contains a list of all the steps in the action. In the droplet window, you can delete a step by dragging it to the Trash icon at the bottom of the window, or you can click and drag steps to rearrange them. In Photoshop you edit the underlying action and create a new droplet.

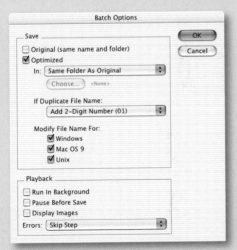

Droplet Batch Options

In ImageReady, you can set options for how a droplet will be applied to a batch of files by double-clicking the droplet to open the droplet window, and then double-clicking Batch Options at the top of the droplet window. This opens the Batch Options dialog box. In that dialog box you can choose whether to save original files in addition to optimized files, and where to save the optimized files. You can specify how to name any duplicate files to avoid overwriting files, and you can instruct ImageReady to create filenames that are appropriate for various operating systems. Among the Playback settings are options to display images while they are being processed and to pause before saving each image. In Photoshop, batch processing options are located in the Create Droplet dialog box and are the same as the batch options covered in the **Batch Processing Photos for the Web** project earlier in this chapter.

Preparing Photos for the Web with Conditional Actions

Kick your actions up a notch by adding conditions. This action uses conditional logic to automatically resize photographs to a uniform height and to optimize photos and related text graphics in different formats for display on the Web.

INSIGHT

Conditional Actions Simplified.
You don't have to be a programmer to understand and use conditional actions in ImageReady. A conditional action is just like a regular action except that it only takes place if a particular condition is met. Image-Ready accomplishes this by applying simple conditional logic: if X is true then do Y. The conditional commands are easy to apply because they're simplified and built into one dialog box, as you'll see in this project.

TIP

Font Warning. When you open this text file, you may get a warning about substituting fonts. Allow the font substitution and change the font later if you have one that looks better to you.

1. Open a Photo and a Text Graphic

You can make actions more useful by including logic that triggers a step only if a certain condition is met. In this project you'll create a "smart" action that identifies vertical and horizontal photos that are taller than a certain size and resizes them for display on a Web page. The action also distinguishes between photographs and text graphics, and optimizes the former as JPEGs and the latter as GIFs.

Start by opening a vertical photo, C03-04-004.tif, and a related text graphic, C03-o4-citylife.psd, in Image-Ready. You'll use these files to set up the action. Later you'll apply the action to a batch of photos using a droplet. Conditional logic is an ImageReady-only feature, so this project takes place in ImageReady.

TIP

No Action Sets in ImageReady.
Actions made in ImageReady, unlike those in Photoshop, are not arranged in action sets.

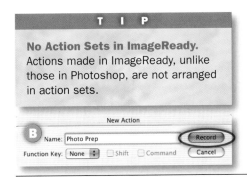

INSIGHT

Bicubic Sharper Interpolation.
This is the interpolation method the program will use to downsample (reduce the number of pixels in) the resized images. The Bicubic Sharper method is designed to be used when you're reducing image size. It keeps images relatively sharp so that further sharpening with the Unsharp Mask filter is often unnecessary.

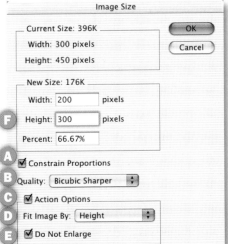

2. Create a New Action

Click on the photo and open the Actions palette (Window>Actions). Click the Create New Action icon at the bottom of the ImageReady Actions palette **A**. In the New Action dialog box, name the action Photo Prep and click Record **B**. The red button at the bottom of the Actions palette means the action is recording **C**.

3. Choose Resizing Options

The first step you'll record comes with a built-in condition. This step tells ImageReady to resize every image on which the action is run to a height of 300 pixels, but only if the image is taller than 300 pixels to begin with.

Choose Image>Image size to open the Image Size dialog box, and set the options in the dialog box *in this order*:

- Constrain Proportions: Checked **A**.
  (to maintain the proportionality of the resized photos)

- Quality: Bicubic Sharper **B**.
  (see sidebar)

- Action Options: Checked **C**.
  (to turn on the following options that are designed for batch processing)

- Fit Image By: Height **D**.
  (to make the reduced photographs the same height. The width of each resized photo will vary based on the proportions of the original.)

- Do Not Enlarge: Checked **E**.
  (to ensure that no image will be up-sampled, which protects the quality of your photos.)

- Height: 300 pixels **F**.
  (to set the height to which each image taller than 300 pixels will be resized. Width changes automatically and will be different than the 200 pixels you see here for photos that are different proportions than this one.)

4. Complete the Resize Step

Click OK to close the Image Size dialog box and resize the open photograph to a height of 300 pixels. There's now a Resize Image step in the Photo Prep action. Click the arrow to the left of the step to see its parameters.

5. Select the Top Layer

Now you'll begin building steps that optimize text graphics as GIFs and photographs as JPEGs. You'll add a command to make sure the action selects the top layer of every file, because the text graphics on which you'll be running this action contain type on their top layers and pixel-based graphics on their other layers.

Click on the open text graphic, C03-04-citylife.psd. Press Shift+Option/Alt-] (the right bracket key on your keyboard). This is the shortcut for selecting the top layer in a file. You'll see a new step in the action labeled Select Front Layer.

INSIGHT

Interpreting the Statement. In this project step you inserted a conditional statement based on if/then logic. The statement tells ImageReady that **if** a particular condition is met (if the selected layer is a text layer) **then** the action should include the next step (which will be to optimize the image as a GIF). If that condition is not met, the action will skip that next step.

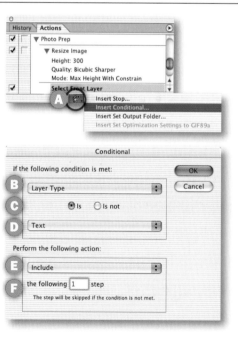

6. Insert a Conditional Statement

In this step you'll insert a conditional statement to ensure that your text graphics are optimized as GIFs. Click the Insert Step icon at the bottom of the Actions palette and choose Insert Conditional from the pop-up menu **A**. In the Conditional dialog box, choose the following settings and then click OK:

- Choose Layer Type from the top pop-up menu **B**.

- Choose the button labeled **is C**.

- Choose Text from the second pop-up menu **D**.

- Choose Include from the third pop-up menu **E**.

- Enter **1** in the field at the bottom of the dialog box **F**.

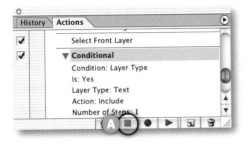

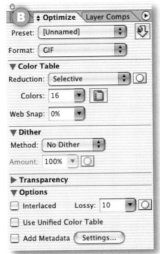

7. Choose GIF Optimization Settings

Click the Stop button at the bottom of the Actions palette **A** to stop recording the action. Otherwise, every change you now make to the optimization settings will be recorded as a separate step in the action, which is unnecessary.

Click the Optimized tab in the document window, and open the Optimize palette (Window>Optimize). Choose the following optimization settings for this image in the Optimize palette—Format: GIF, Reduction: Selective, Colors: 16, Dither: No Dither, Lossy: 10; Add Metadata, unchecked **B**. Leave the other settings at their defaults.

8. Insert a GIF Optimization Step

With Record still off, click the Insert Step button at the bottom of the Actions palette and choose Insert Set Optimization Settings to GIF89A (a fancy name for GIF) **A**. This adds a step to the action that contains the GIF optimization settings you chose in the last step **B**.

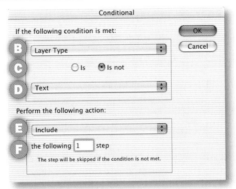

9. Add Another Condition

Now you'll insert a conditional statement that ensures your photographs will be optimized as JPEGs. Leave Record off. (It doesn't have to be on when you use the Insert Step commands). Click the Insert Step icon **A** and choose Insert Conditional from the pop-up menu. In the Conditional dialog box, choose the following settings and click OK:

- Choose Layer Type from the top pop-up menu **B**.
- Choose the button labeled **is not** **C**.
- Choose Text from the second pop-up menu **D**.
- Choose Include from the third pop-up menu **E**.
- Enter **1** in the field at the bottom of the dialog box **F**.

INSIGHT

Interpreting this Statement. This conditional statement is similar to the one on the preceding page. It tells ImageReady that **if** the selected layer is not a text layer **then** the action should include the next step (which will be to optimize the image as a JPEG). The combination of these two conditional actions will cause each image on which the action is played to be optimized to the appropriate Web file format.

10. Choose JPEG Settings

Click on the Optimized tab in the document window of the open photograph, C03-04-004.tif **A**. With Record still off, choose the following optimization settings in the Optimize palette **B**: Format: JPEG, Quality: Medium. Leave the other settings at their defaults.

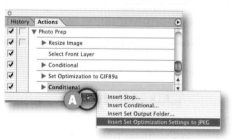

11. Insert a JPEG Optimization Step

With Record still off, click the Insert Step button at the bottom of the Actions palette **A** and choose Insert Set Optimization Settings to JPEG. This adds a step to the action that contains the JPEG optimization settings you chose in the last step **B**.

12. Test the Action on Individual Files

Choose File>Revert to return the open photograph to its original, larger state. In the Actions palette, select the Photo Prep action and click the Play button **A**. The photograph should become smaller. Click the Information box at the bottom of the photograph's document window and choose Optimized Information. The Information box should indicate that the image is now a JPEG **B**. Repeat this step on the open text graphic. The text graphic should stay the same size (because it was shorter than 300 pixels to start with) and become a GIF **C**. If all went as expected, move to the next step.

If the action doesn't work as expected, troubleshoot by selecting each step in the action one by one, clicking the side arrow on the Actions palette **D**, and choosing Play [name of step]. If you find a faulty step, double-click it to try to open its command, where you can fix the settings. Or drag the step to the Trash icon in the Actions palette and re-record. If all else fails, start all over.

> **TIP**
>
> **Information Box.** ImageReady offers two identical Information boxes at the bottom of every document window. (You only see one in the open photograph because its window is narrow.) The Information menus contain lots of valuable information about an image. Explore them when you get a chance.

13. Insert Output Folder

Click the Insert Step icon at the bottom of the Actions palette and choose Insert Set Output Folder **A**. In the dialog box that opens, click New Folder and name it *C03-04-output* to make an output folder for the files generated by this action. Click Choose. Be aware that if you move your output folder, the action won't be able to find it. In that case, create a new output folder as explained in the tip.

TIP

Changing the Output Folder. You can change the output folder any time by double-clicking the droplet icon on your hard drive to open a list of the droplet's steps. Double-click the Set Output Folder step. In the dialog box that opens, create a new output folder and click Choose. Close the droplet list and click Save. The new output location is saved as part of the droplet.

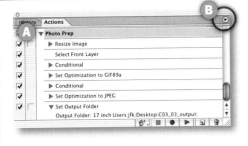

14. Create a Droplet

The real advantage of recording a conditional action is that you can use it to process a whole folder of images. Select the Photo Prep action in the Actions palette **A**. Click the palette's side arrow **B** and choose Create Droplet from the bottom of the menu. Navigate to your desktop and click Save. The named droplet icon **C** will appear on your desktop.

15. Process a Folder of Photographs

Now comes the best part! Drag the C03-04-images project files folder onto the Photo Prep droplet on your desktop **A**. Then sit back while ImageReady runs the action on all the files in the folder. Check the results by opening your output folder C03-04-output **B**. It will be filled with vertical and horizontal photographs optimized as JPEGs and resized to 300 pixels high, along with the two text graphics files optimized as GIFs. These files are all ready to be brought into a Web site–building program. Try running this droplet on your own images to save processing time. ▥

Designing Multiple Pages in a Single File

Here's an efficient way to design a whole site full of pages in a single file. Use layer comps to create multiple page designs in one file. Then save time by using slice sets to slice pages that are similar.

INSIGHT

Using Layer Comps in Web Design.

A layer comp is a snapshot of the state of a file's layers. A file can have multiple layer comps, each of which records layers' visibility, position, and appearance at a point in time.

In this project, you'll use layer comps to design multiple pages for a Web site within a single file. The home page has one navigation scheme, and the three inner pages share another navigation scheme. The resulting pages offer several advantages over designing a site's pages one by one:

- The pages are visually consistent, which is a hallmark of good Web design.
- You don't have to slice each page separately. Instead, similarly structured pages can share a slice set.
- You can present all the page designs to a client in one PSD file.

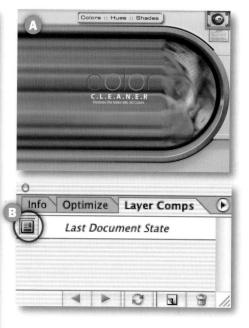

1. Open the Layer Comps Palette

Before you start, take a look at the sidebar on this page to learn how you'll use layer comps in this project. Begin by opening C03-05-cleaner.psd in Image-Ready **A**. Notice that there are some layers in the Layers palette that don't have an Eye icon to their left. These layers are currently not visible in the document window. They'll be used later in the project as you create content for the individual pages in this Web site and record the state of each page as a separate layer comp.

Open ImageReady's Layer Comps palette by choosing Window>Layer Comps. The Last Document State at the top of the palette is a snapshot of the most recent state of the layers in the image. You can return to that state at any time by clicking in the Apply Layer Comp field to the left of the Last Document State **B**.

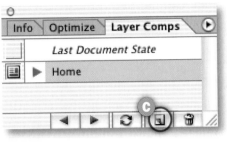

2. Make the Home Page Layer Comp

The home page of the site you're creating will include the artwork that's currently visible in the document window, plus some text links. Click the Eye icon to the left of the TextLinks layer set in the Layers palette **A** to make the text links visible **B**.

Now you'll make a layer comp that is a snapshot of this home page design. Click the Create New Layer Comp button at the bottom of the Layer Comps palette **C**. In the New Layer Comp dialog box that opens, name this layer comp *Home* **D**. Check Visibility and Position—the two properties of this layer that you want the program to keep track of. You can type some notes into the Comment field about this layer comp if you wish **E**. Click OK to create the Home layer comp in the Layer Comps palette.

3. Design the Colors Page

This site has three inner pages—the colors page, the hues page, and the shades page. In this step you'll design the colors page by changing the visibility and position of some of the layers.

Click in the Visibility field of the Buttons layer set in the Layers palette **A** to display an Eye icon. A set of navigation buttons appears on the left side of the image **B**. Click the arrow to the left of the TopNav layer set **C** to open that layer set, and click in the Visibility field of the ColorsMarker layer to add an Eye icon there **D**. A marker appears on the Colors link in the navigation bar at the top of the image **E**. Finally, select the Move tool in the toolbox and click the Move tool icon in the Options bar **F**. Select the TextLinks layer set in the Layers palette **G**. Hold down the Shift key to constrain vertical movement, and drag the text links to the left until they are on top of the buttons **B**.

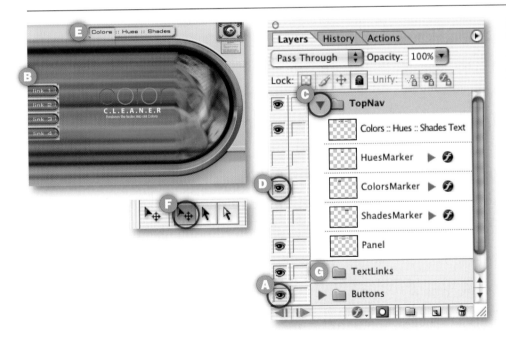

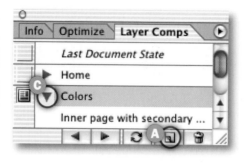

4. Create the Colors Layer Comp

Now you'll make a second layer comp—a snapshot of layer visibility, position, and appearance in the colors page you just designed.

Click the Create New Layer Comp button at the bottom of the Layer Comps palette **A**. In the New Layer Comp dialog box **B**, name this layer comp *Colors.* Check Visibility, Position, and Appearance. (Appearance includes layer styles, layer blending modes, and layer opacity.) You can type notes into the Comment field if you wish. Then click OK. You'll see a new Colors layer comp in the Layer Comps palette. If you click the arrow to the left of the layer comp **C** you'll see the comments you entered in the New Layer Comp dialog box.

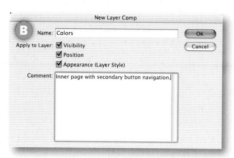

T I P

Layer Comp Properties. We often leave all three layer properties—Visibility, Position, and Appearance—checked in the New Layer Comps dialog box, even if we're not sure we need to include all of these properties in a layer comp. That way our bases are always covered.

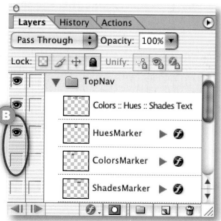

5. Design the Hues Page

The hues page is another inner page of this site. It is similar in structure and content to the colors page. The only difference is that the Hues marker is visible and the Colors marker is not visible on the hues page **A**.

To set up the hues page, click in the Visibility field of the HuesMarker layer in the Layers palette to add an Eye icon there. Then click in the Visibility field of the ColorsMarker layer to turn off that Eye icon **B**.

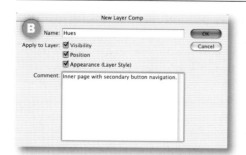

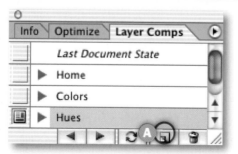

6. Create the Hues Page Layer Comp

Now you'll make a layer comp of the hues page you designed in the last step. Click the Create New Layer Comp button at the bottom of the Layer Comps palette **A**. In the New Layer Comp dialog box **B**, name this layer comp *Hues.* Check Visibility, Position, and Appearance, and add a comment if you wish. Click OK to create the Hues layer comp in the Layer Comps palette.

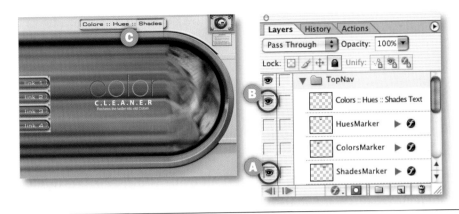

7. Design the Shades Page

Now you'll design the final page—the shades page, which is another inner page with the same structure as the colors and hues pages. In the Layers palette, click in the Visibility field of the ShadesMarker layer to add an Eye icon there **A**. Then click in the Visibility field of the HuesMarker layer to turn off its Eye icon **B**. There's now a marker on the Shades link in the navigation bar at the top of the image **C**.

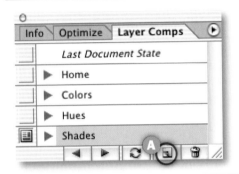

8. Create the Shades Layer Comp

To create a layer comp for the shades page, click the Create New Layer Comp button at the bottom of the Layer Comps palette **A**. In the New Layer Comp dialog box **B**, name this layer comp **Shades**. Check Visibility, Position, and Appearance, and add a comment if you wish. Click OK to create the Shades layer comp in the Layer Comps palette.

> **CAUTION**
>
> **Viewing Layer Comps.** Don't make the mistake of trying to view a layer comp by clicking on the layer comp in the Layer Comps palette. That just selects the layer comp for editing. To view a layer comp in the document window, click in the Apply Layer Comp field to the left of the layer comp.

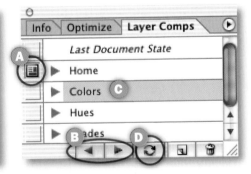

9. View the Layer Comps

View each of the layer comps by clicking in the Apply Layer Comp field to the left of each layer comp **A**. Alternatively, click the Previous and Next icons at the bottom of the Layer Comps palette to cycle through the layer comps **B**. (This is a good way to quickly show a client all of your page designs in a single file.)

If one of the designs does not look as expected, click on its layer comp in the Layer Comps palette to select that layer comp **C**. Edit the image. Then click the Update Layer Comp icon at the bottom of the Layer Comps palette **D**. When you're satisfied, choose File>Save As to save the image with all of its layer comps.

> **CAUTION**
>
> **Nonreversible Edits.** If you make a nonreversible change to an image (like deleting a layer, merging layers, or changing image modes) you'll see a yellow triangle in the layer comps affected by that change. You have three options:
> - Update the layer comps by selecting each one and clicking the Update Layer Comp icon at the bottom of the Layer Comps palette.
> - Control/right-click the warning icons and choose a removal option. This deletes the warnings. However, it can result in unexpected changes to the layer comps.
> - Open the History palette (Window>History) and choose a previous history state to undo the nonreversible changes.

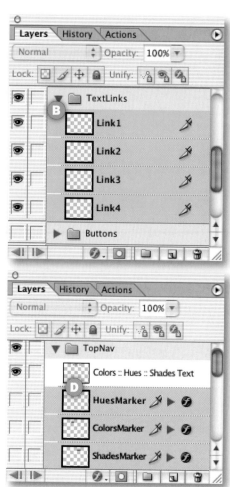

10. Slice the Home Page Layer Comp

Now you'll begin slicing up the image, so that each of the navigation graphics (the text links, markers, and buttons) can be saved as a separate GIF or JPEG. This will allow you to assign a separate URL link to each navigation graphic in a Web site–building program like Dreamweaver or GoLive. You'll start by slicing the home page, which has different navigation graphics than the other three pages.

Click in the Apply Layer Comp field to the left of the Home layer comp **A** to display that layer comp in the document window. In the Layers palette, click the arrow to the left of the TextLinks layer set to open that layer set. Click on the Link1 layer; then hold down the Shift key and click on the Link4 layer to select all the text link layers **B**. Choose Layer>New Layer Based Slices from the menu bar at the top of the screen to create a separate slice around each of the text links **C**.

Now select the HuesMarker layer in the Layers palette. Hold down the Shift key and click on the ShadesMarker layer. This selects the three marker layers **D**. Choose Layer>New Layer Based Slices from the menu bar to create slices around each of the navigation markers in the top navigation bar **E**.

INSIGHT

Slice Sets and Layer Comps. A slice set is a collection of slices that can be applied to multiple layer comps. This means that if you have several layer comps that have the same structure (like the three inner pages In this project) you can slice just one of those layer comps, save the result as a slice set, and use that same slice set to automatically slice the other similar pages.

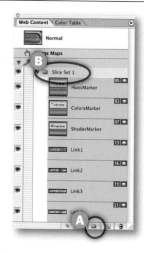

11. Create Slice Set 1

Open the Web Content palette (Window>Web Content), where you'll see all of the slices you just made. Click on the top slice in the palette; then hold the Shift key and click on the bottom slice to select all the slices. Click the Create New Slice Set button at the bottom of the Web Content palette **A**. This creates Slice Set 1 **B** which contains all of the slices indented beneath it.

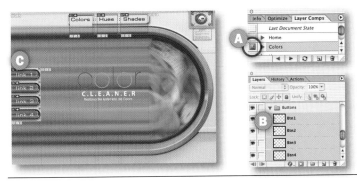

12. Slice the Colors Layer Comp

Now you'll slice the buttons that appear only on the inner pages. Click in the Apply Layer Comp field to the left of the Colors layer comp **A**. In the Layers palette, open the Buttons layer set. Shift-click to select the four button layers **B**. Choose Layer>New Layer Based Slices from the menu bar at the top of the screen to create four button slices **C**.

13. Make Another Slice Set

In the Web Content palette, Shift-click to select all the button slices. Click the Create New Slice Set icon at the bottom of the Web Content palette to create Slice Set 2 **A**, which contains only the button slices. You don't have to slice any of the other pages you've designed!

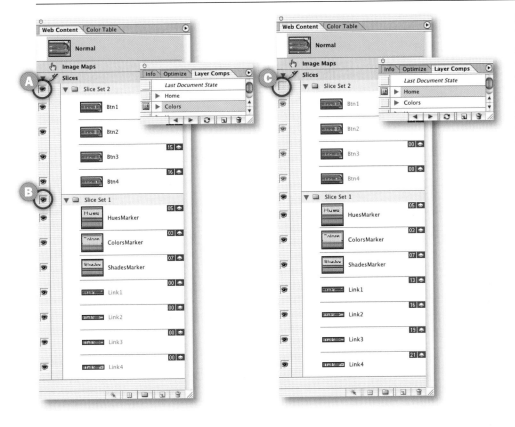

14. Save Each Page

We've already optimized for you, so you can go ahead and save each layer comp using the relevant slice sets. You'll start by saving the Colors layer comp. Make sure both slice sets display an Eye icon in the Web Content palette **A**, **B**. Click the Apply Layer Comp icon on the Colors layer comp. Choose File/Save Optimized As. Then set Format/Save As Type to HTML and Images. Make a new folder for the colors page output, and click Save. Repeat this step for the Hues and the Shades layer comps, making a separate output folder for each.

Turn off the Eye icon on Slice Set 2 **C** (because the home page doesn't need the button slices) and repeat this step on the Home layer comp. Choose File>Save to resave the PSD file with its slice sets.

In the output folders on your hard drive you'll find an HTML file for each page and a folder of images generated by only the slices that relate to that page. Open each HTML page in a Web browser to admire your work. ▥

Linking HTML Pages from Layer Comps

The previous project, *Designing Multiple Pages in a Single File*, explained how to produce multiple Web pages using layer comps and slice sets. But the pages ImageReady generates from layer comps are not automatically linked together. If you want to link the resulting pages to one another you have to do some advance planning, as we explain here.

T I P

.HTML vs. .HTM. When you're naming HTML files for the Web you can append either of two extensions—*.html* or *.htm*. Both mean the same thing. However, you must use the same extension on your page names and in the links to those page names. Photoshop and ImageReady apply the *.html* extension by default.

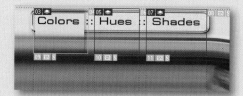

In order to create links between the HTML pages generated by the layer comps you made in the last project you have to know two things in advance—the name of each HTML file and where it will be saved. This will allow you to create relative links between the files. (To review relative links take a look at **Image Map Navigation** in Chapter 1).

First let's talk about filenames. In the previous project you saved each HTML file with its default filename. If you look in your output folders you'll see that ImageReady named each HTML file with the same name, C03-05-cleaner.html, which it took from the name of the PSD source file. If you're going to link the pages together, each page will have to have a unique name. You can take care of that by typing a unique name into the Name field of the Save Optimized As dialog box when you save each file. But you'll have to know the names you're going to give each file in advance so you can create links before saving. Let's say you'll name the files **hues.html**, **colors.html**, **shades.html**, and **home.html**.

Now let's plan where you're going to save each file. Assume you'll save each HTML page into a separate folder, each of which is located in the same folder/directory on your hard drive, and that those folders will be named **hues** folder, **colors** folder, **shades** folder, and **home** folder.

Now you have the information you need to create the links. Click in the Apply Layer Comp field to the left of the Colors layer comp. In the Web Content palette, select the Colors-Marker slice in Slice Set 1. Choose Window>Slice to open the Slice palette. In the URL field of the Slice palette, type **../colors/colors.html**. This means go up one level, look for the colors folder, and then go down one level to find the file colors.html. Repeat this on the HuesMarker slice (../hues/hues.html) and on the ShadesMarker slice (../shades/shades.html). If you want to link back to the home page, you'll have to add an extra slice to the image (perhaps around the silver button at the top right of the image), and type **../home/home.html** in the URL field for that slice. Now save each layer comp as an HTML file as you did in the last project, but give each file its unique name and save it to the planned folder. ▥

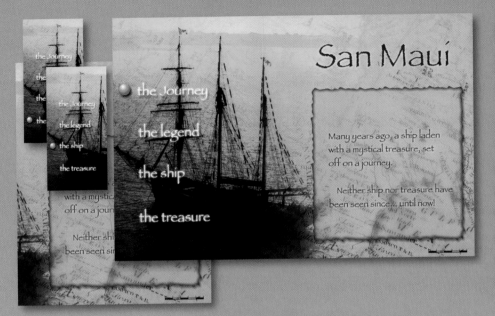

Outputting Multiple Linked Web Pages

Take advantage of a hidden output feature in ImageReady that allows you to generate multiple page layouts that are automatically linked together, complete with rollovers, and ready to put on line.

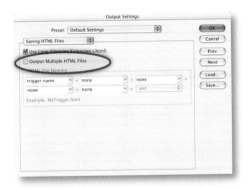

T I P

Automatic Palette Arrangement.
ImageReady comes with some default palette arrangements. A quick way to open and arrange the palettes you'll use when you're making rollovers is to choose Window>Workspace>Inter-activity Palette Locations. This opens the Web Content palette, the Layers palette, and the Slice palette all neatly arranged on your screen.

1. Open a Layered File in ImageReady

Buried deep in ImageReady's Output Settings is a little-known checkbox labeled Output Multiple HTML Files. This feature works in conjunction with the Selected rollover state to create multiple linked files with rollover navigation. In this project you'll use these features to make four pages for a Web site in a single file. Each page has rollover buttons programmed with the Selected state and remote rollovers that change the content of the page. If you want to learn more about making remote rollovers, review **Pointers and Remote Rollovers** in Chapter 1. If you're eager to see what we have in store for you here, dig right in.

Open C03-06-treasure.psd from Chapter 3-Automation>C3-6. We made this file in Photoshop, including lots of layers with the artwork for four Web pages. Choose View>Show>Layer Edges to turn off the distracting blue box that identifies the boundaries of a selected layer's contents.

TIP

Custom Slice Naming. If you change ImageReady's slice-naming convention, you can save your changes for future use by clicking the Save button in the Output Settings dialog box and giving your custom setup a name. That name will appear in the Preset menu at the top of the dialog box the next time you choose File>Output Settings>Slices.

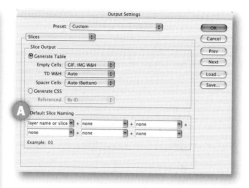

2. Change the Slice-Naming Default

You'll be using lots of slices in this project, so take a minute to make the automatic slice names shorter and more meaningful. Choose File>Output Settings>Slices. In the Default Slice Naming area of the Output Settings dialog box **A**, click the arrow on the first menu and choose Layer Name or Slice No. Click the arrow on the second menu and choose None. Click the arrow on the third menu and choose None. Click OK.

3. Slice the Markers

First, you'll slice the navigation markers that will tell your audience which page they're viewing. In the Layers palette, click the arrow to the left of the Markers layer set to open that layer set. Click in the Visibility field of each of the layers in the set **A** to make all the markers visible in the document window. Select all the marker layers by clicking on the JourneyMarker layer, holding down the Shift key, and clicking on the Treasure-Marker layer **B**. Now choose Layer>New Layer Based Slices from the menu bar at the top of the page. This makes a slice around each marker **C**.

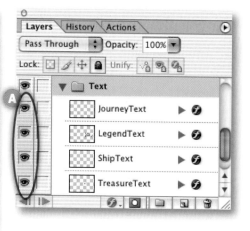

4. Slice the Page Text

Now you'll add one big slice around the area that will contain different text on each page. This area must be sliced because it will be a target of the remote rollovers you'll be creating. In the Layers palette, click the arrow to the left of the Text layer set to open that layer set. Click in the Visibility field of each layer in that layer set **A** to make all the text layers visible, one on top of the other. Select the Slice tool in the toolbox and draw a slice that's big enough to encompass all of the text **B**.

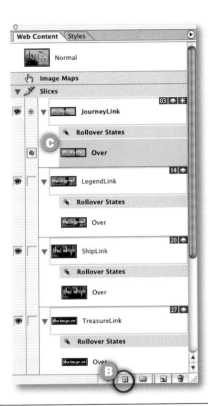

5. Slice the Text Links

Now you'll add a slice and add a roll-over state to each of the text links—all in one step. In the Layers palette, click the arrow to the left of the Links layer set to open that layer set. Click on the JourneyLink layer, hold down the Shift key, and click on the TreasureLink layer to select all the layers in the layer set **A**. Open the Web Content palette (Window>Web Content), and click on the Create Layer-Based Rollover icon at the bottom of the Web Content palette **B**. The Web Content palette now lists each of the text link slices with an Over state indented beneath it **C**. You'll change each of the Over states to a Selected state later in this project.

6. Set Up the Normal State

Now that you've finished slicing, you'll set up the Normal state of the document—the way it will look when it first loads in a viewer's Web browser. In the Layers palette, make sure the Eye icons on each of the following layers is turned off to make those layers invisible in the Normal state **A**, **B**:

- LegendMarker
- ShipMarker
- TreasureMarker
- LegendText
- ShipText
- TreasureText

INSIGHT

Selected State. The Selected state of a rollover link is triggered by a click. It keeps the current image in view until the viewer clicks another link that's programmed with a Selected state. The Selected state is useful for rollover buttons, where it can be applied to keep one button differentiated from the others so a viewer knows which page he is on.

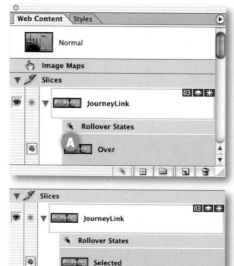

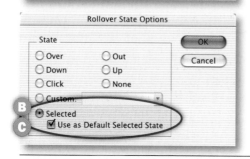

7. Set Up the Selected States

Now you'll change the Over state of each text link slice to a Selected state. Double-click on the Over state of the JourneyLink slice in the Web Content palette **A**. In the Rollover State Options dialog box that opens, choose Selected **B**. Then check Use as Default Selected State **C**, so that the journey link is in the Selected state when the site loads in a viewer's Web browser.

Repeat this step on each of the other text link slices—the LegendLink slice, the ShipLink slice, and the TreasureLink slice—except that for these three slices be sure to **uncheck** Use as Default Selected State in the Rollover State Options dialog box.

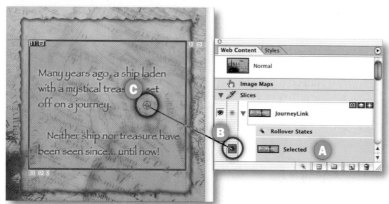

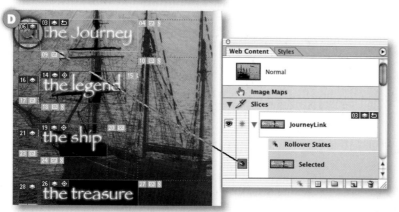

8. Complete the Journey Page

Each of the four pages in the site you're building will appear on the Selected state of one of the four text links. In the following steps you'll construct each page by changing its appearance on the Selected state of the corresponding text link. There are no changes to be made to the appearance of the journey page, which loads first into a viewer's browser. However, there is one small, but important technical change to be made to the Selected state of the JourneyLink slice.

Click on the Selected state of the JourneyLink slice in the Web Content palette **A**. Then click on the spiral icon to the left of that Selected state **B** and drag to the slice around the remote text in the image **C**. Do this again, dragging to the slice around the journey marker in the image **D**. This step is necessary to make the remote changes work when a viewer is on another page in the site and clicks on the journey link.

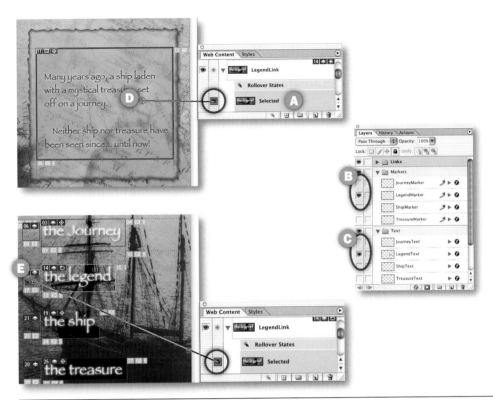

9. Create the Legend Page

Now you'll change the appearance of the legend page. Click on the Selected state of the LegendLink slice in the Web Content palette **A**. In the Layers palette, click in the Visibility field of the JourneyMarker layer to turn off its Eye icon. Click in the Visibility field of the LegendMarker layer to add an Eye icon **B**.

In addition, click in the Visibility field of the JourneyText layer to turn off its Eye icon and click in the Visibility field of the LegendText layer to add an Eye icon there **C**. In the Web Content palette, click on the Selected state of the LegendLink slice, click on the spiral icon to its left and drag to the remote text slice in the image **D**. Do this again, dragging to the slice around the Legend marker in the image **E**. In the image, a marker appears to the left of the legend text link and text about the legend appears in the remote slice.

10. Create the Ship Page

Next you'll change the appearance of the ship page. Click on the Selected state of the ShipLink slice in the Web Content palette **A**. In the Layers palette, click in the Visibility field of the JourneyMarker layer to turn off its Eye icon and click in the Visibility field of the ShipMarker layer to add an Eye icon **B**.

Then click in the Visibility field of the JourneyText layer to turn off its Eye icon and click in the Visibility field of the ShipText layer to add an Eye icon **C**. In the Web Content palette, click on the Selected state of the ShipLink slice, click on the spiral icon to its left and drag to the remote text slice in the image **D**. Repeat this, dragging to the slice around the ship marker in the image **E**. In the image, a marker appears to the left of the ship text link and text about the ship appears in the remote slice.

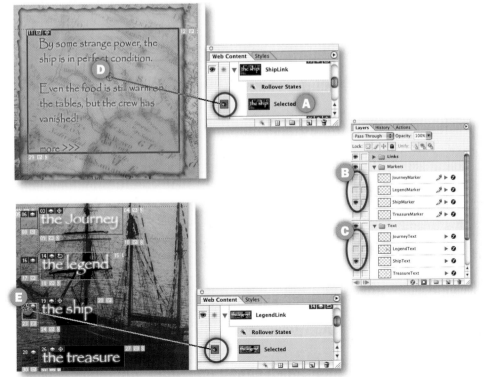

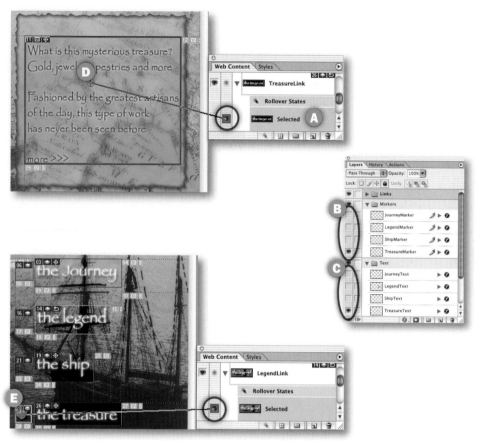

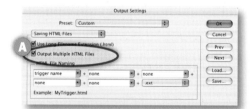

11. Create the Treasure Page

Now you'll change the appearance of the treasure page on the selected state of the TreasureLink slice. Click on the Selected state of the TreasureLink slice in the Web Content palette **A**. In the Layers palette, click in the Visibility field of the JourneyMarker layer to turn off its Eye icon and click in the Visibility field of the TreasureMarker layer to add an Eye icon **B**.

Click in the Visibility field of the JourneyText layer to turn off its Eye icon and click in the Visibility field of the TreasureText layer to add an Eye icon there **C**. In the Web Content palette, click on the Selected state of the TreasureLink slice, click on the spiral icon to its left, and drag to the remote text slice in the image **D**. Do this again, dragging to the slice around the treasure marker **E**. In the document window, a marker appears to the left of the treasure text link and text about the treasure appears in the remote slice. You've now finished creating the pages. Click the Preview in Browser button in the toolbox and try out each text link in the browser.

12. Save Multiple Linked Pages

This is the secret to saving multiple pages with automatically created links. Choose File>Output Settings>Saving HTML Files. In the Output Settings dialog box, check Output Multiple HTML Files **A** and click OK.

We optimized the image for you. So just choose File>Save Optimized As. In the Save Optimized As dialog box **B**, set Format/Save as type to HTML and Images, create a new folder, and click Save. Click OK at the filename warning. The output folder on your hard drive contains four HTML pages and a folder of images. You have a whole site of linked pages ready to upload to a Web server! ▥

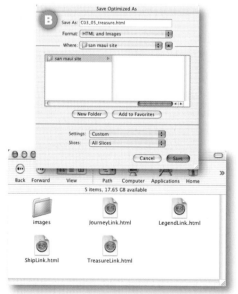

CAUTION

File Structure. The links between the HTML pages ImageReady created depend on the relative location of the HTML files and image files. You can move all the files together (for example to upload them to a server), but don't move the individual files or put them into different folders or the links will break.

Creating Dynamic Flash Web Banners

In this advanced project you'll automatically create variations on a Flash Web banner using data sets and dynamic text variables. You can use the resulting Web banners to spice up individual pages in a Web site.

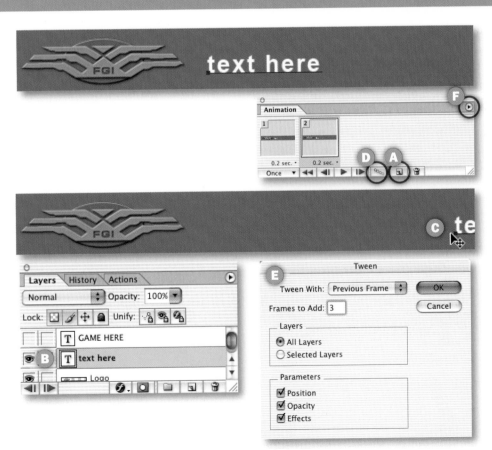

1. Create a Fly-In Animation

Open 03-07-dynamic.psd from Chapter 3-Automation>Ch3-7 into ImageReady. First, you'll make a simple tweened animation in ImageReady. We'll walk you through the process, but if you have any questions about animations review Chapter 2, **Animation**. Choose Window>Animation to open the Animation palette. Click the Duplicate Animation Frame icon at the bottom of the Animation palette **A** to create Frame 2. In the Layers palette, select the **text here** layer **B**. Select the Move tool in the toolbox, and press the right arrow key on your keyboard several times to move the text to the right until it is outside the document window and no longer visible in the image **C**.

With Frame 2 selected, click the Tween icon at the bottom of the Animation palette **D**. In the Tween dialog box **E**, choose Tween With: Previous Frame, and Frames to Add: 3. Leave all three Parameters checked and click OK. Click the side arrow on the Animation palette **F** and choose Reverse Frames.

2. Add a Fade-In Animation

Select Frame 5 in the Animation palette. In the Layers palette, select the GAME HERE layer and click in the Visibility field to the left of the GAME HERE layer to add an Eye icon **A**, making the words GAME HERE visible in the image. Change the Opacity field at the top of the Layers palette to 0% **B**. Click the Duplicate Animation Frame icon at the bottom of the Animation palette **C** to create Frame 6. With Frame 6 selected, change the Opacity field in the Layers palette back to 100%. Then click the Tween icon **D**. Leave the options in the Tween dialog box as you set them in the previous step and click OK. You now have nine frames in the animation.

Click the Play button at the bottom of the Animation palette **E** to see the words *text here* fly in from the right, followed by the words GAME HERE fading into view. Select Frame 9 in the Animation palette so all of the elements are visible in the document window.

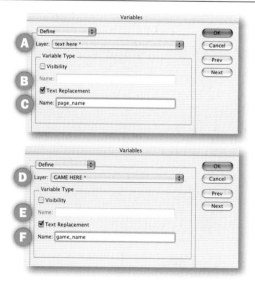

3. Define Text Variables

Now things get really interesting. You'll define two variables, one for each of the text layers. Choose Image>Variables>Define. In the Variables dialog box, choose *text here* from the Layer menu **A** to define the source of the first variable. Check Text Replacement to establish that this is a text variable **B**. Type *page_name* as the name of this variable, being careful not to include spaces or unusual characters in the variable name **C**. Don't click OK yet.

To define the second variable, choose GAME HERE from the Layer menu **D** in the Variables dialog box, check Text Replacement **E**, and type *game_name* as the name of this variable **F**.

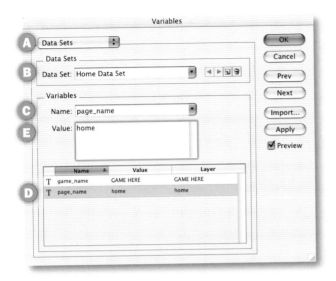

4. Create the Home Banner Data Set

In the next two steps you'll create a set of data that will be used to replace the words **text here** and GAME HERE on one of the Web banners you're creating—a banner for a home page.

First you'll create the data for the page_name variable (the data that will replace the words **text here** on the home Web banner). Choose Data Sets from the menu at the top of the Variables dialog box **A**. Set the fields in the Data Sets panel of the Variables dialog box as follows:

- Type **Home Data Set** in the Data Set field **B**. This names the set of data that will be used for the home Web banner. This data set will have two variables—the page_name variable and the game_name variable.

- Choose page_name from the Name menu **C**. This is the name of the variable you're working on. You'll see this variable highlighted in the variables list at the bottom of the dialog box **D**.

- In the Value field, type **home E**. This is the text that will appear in place of the words **text here** on the home Web banner.

T I P

Understanding What You've Done.
This is pretty advanced stuff, but if you understand what you've done so far, making the rest of the data sets will be easy. You may want to reread Steps 3 through 5 to make sure you understand how you made the variables and the home data set before moving on to Step 6.

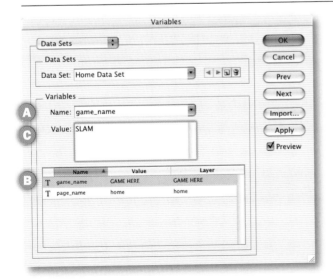

5. Add to the Home Banner Data Set

Now you'll create the data for the game_name variable (the data that will replace the words GAME HERE on the home Web banner). Choose game_name from the Name menu **A**. You'll see this variable highlighted in the variables list at the bottom of the dialog box **B**. In the Value field type **SLAM**—the name of a fictitious game **C**. This is the text that will appear in place of the words GAME HERE on your home Web banner. Leave this dialog box open for the next steps.

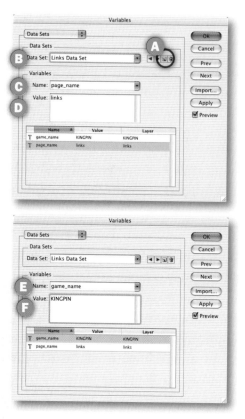

6. Create the Links Banner Data Set

Now you'll make another data set that will replace the page_name and game_name variables on another Web banner—a banner for a links page. In the Variables dialog box, make a new data set by clicking the New Data Set icon **A**. Then set the rest of the fields as follows to create data for the page_name variable in this data set:

- Type **Links Data Set** in the Data Set field to name this new data set **B**.

- Choose page_name from the Name menu **C**.

- Type **links** in the Value field. This is the text that will appear in place of the words **text here** on the links Web banner **D**.

Now choose game_name from the Name menu **E** to create data for the second variable in this data set. In the Value field type **KINGPIN**—the name of another game **F**. This is the text that will appear in place of the words GAME HERE on your links Web banner.

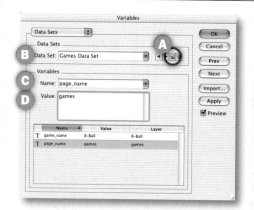

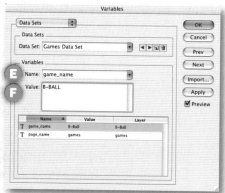

7. Create the Games Data Set

Now make a third data set for another Web banner, this one for a games page. There's nothing new here, so relax. Make a new data set by clicking the New Data Set icon in the Variables dialog box **A**. Set the rest of the fields as follows to create data for the page_name variable in this data set:

- Type **Games Data Set** in the Data Set field **B**.

- Choose page_name from the Name menu **C**.

- Type **games** in the Value field **D**.

- Now choose game_name from the Name menu **E**.

- And in the Value field type **B-BALL**, the name of another game **F**.

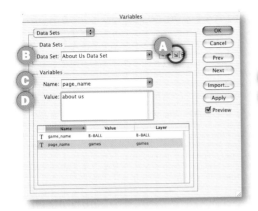

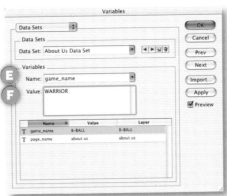

8. Create the About Us Data Set

Now you'll make the last data set, this one for a Web banner to use on an about us page. This step is just like the last two steps. Are you starting to get the picture?

Make a new data set by clicking the New Data Set icon in the Variables dialog box **A**. Set the rest of the fields as follows to create data for the page_name variable in this data set:

- Type *About Us Data Set* in the Data Set field **B**.

- Choose page_name from the Name menu **C**.

- Type *about us* in the Value field **D**.

- Now choose game_name from the Name menu **E**.

- And in the Value field type *WARRIOR,* the name of another game **F**.

9. Preview the Web Banners

Click the forward arrow in the Variables dialog box **A** to cycle through the data sets you created. Leave Preview checked **B** to see a live preview of each of the data sets. If you notice any errors, correct them by editing the fields in the Variables dialog box. When you're satisfied, click OK. Choose File>Save to save the PSD file with its data sets.

10. Export the Banners as a Flash File

Each of the four data sets you've made will generate a separate Web banner. You can export them all together as a Flash movie (SWF format). This allows you to check that all the banners export correctly and gives you a quick reference file. Choose File>Export>Macromedia®Flash™ SWF. This opens the Macromedia Flash (SWF) Export dialog box, where you'll set export options in the next step.

C A U T I O N

Truncated Text. Occasionally, the text in a dynamic text file will look truncated in the exported file. Use the Flash movie you exported in this step to check for truncated text. If some text is cut off, go back to your original PSD file and try substituting a different font. Make sure the original text layer (text here, GAMES HERE) is longer than the text in each of your data sets.

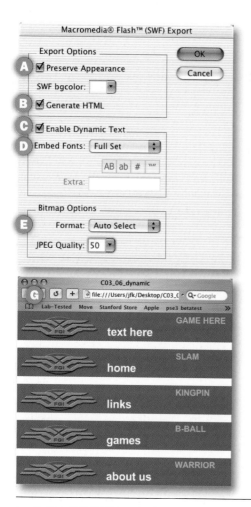

11. Set SWF Export Options

In the Macromedia Flash (SWF) Export dialog box, set the following options:

- Check Preserve Appearance **A**. This ensures that the text retains its appearance.

- Check Generate HTML **B**. This creates an HTML file to display the SWF in a Web browser.

- Check Enable Dynamic Text **C**. This is necessary to make your dynamic text variables work.

- Choose Full Set from the Embed Fonts menu **D**. This embeds a full set of fonts in your Flash movie.

- Under Bitmap Options, leave Format set to Auto Select, and set JPEG Quality to 50 **E**. This controls how the logo and background are optimized.

Click OK to open the Export as Macromedia™ SWF dialog box **F**. Create a new output folder, and click OK. Open the resulting HTML file in a Web browser to view all four of your Web banners and the original template in a Flash movie **G**.

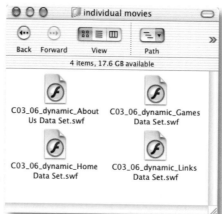

12. Export Individual Flash Banners

You can also export the Web banners generated by your data sets as individual Flash movies so that you can add each of them to a different page in a Web site. Choose File>Export>Data Sets as Files. Click Choose to choose an output folder **A**. Leave Data Set set to All Data Sets **B**. Choose Macromedia®Flash™ (.swf) from the Save As menu **C**. Leave the SWF settings as they were in the last step. Otherwise you'd click Set **D** to open the SWF Export dialog box. Click OK. You'll find four SWF and HTML files on your hard drive. Each SWF is a separate Web banner ready to be added to individual pages. █

Creating and Importing External Data Sets

The previous project, *Creating Dynamic Flash Web Banners*, covered how to create data sets in ImageReady's Variables dialog box for use with variables in a PSD file. Another way to make data sets for that purpose is to enter data into an external spreadsheet and then import data sets from the spreadsheet into ImageReady. You can also use an external data sheet when you're working with variables in Photoshop CS2. This is the easier way to go if you're working with preexisting data sets, or if you have lots of data or variables.

Create a Data Set

Let's take a look at how to make an external data set instead of the data set we created in ImageReady in the previous project, *Creating Dynamic Flash Web Banners*. We'll use Microsoft Excel here, but you can use any spreadsheet editor that saves files in tab-delimited text format.

In the first row of the spreadsheet, type the names of the two variables that will change in each version of your Web banners: **page_name** and **game_name**. Don't use spaces or unusual text characters.

In the page_name column enter each of the text values that will replace the words **text here** in the Web banners you plan to make: **home**, **links**, **games**, and **about us**, in that order. In the **game_name** column enter the text value of each game that will replace the words **GAME HERE** in your Web banners: **SLAM, KINGPIN, B-BALL**, and **WARRIOR**, in that order. Each row of the spreadsheet now contains a data set made up of the two values that appear together in a Web banner. Save the spreadsheet in a tab-delimited format. In Excel, choose Format: Text (tab delimited) in the Save dialog box.

Import a Data Set

To import your external data sets, choose Image>Variables to open the Variables dialog box **A**. In that dialog box, choose Define from the top menu. To define the first variable, choose **text here** from the Layer menu, check Text Replacement, and type **page_name** in the Name field. Then choose **GAME HERE** from the Layer menu, check Text Replacement, and type **game_name** in the Name field.

Choose Data Sets from the top menu. Click the Import button **B**. In the Import Variable Data Sets dialog box **C**, check Use First Column For Data Set Names, and Replace Existing Data Sets. Click the Choose button and navigate to your spreadsheet file. Click OK. Click the forward arrow in the Variables dialog box to view each of your data sets in action. ▥

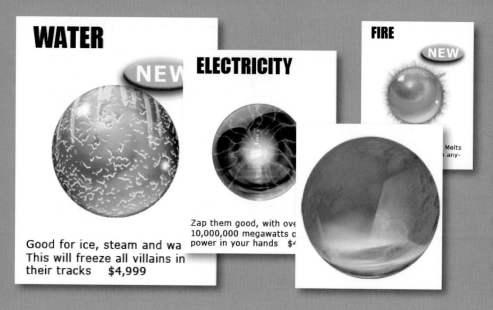

Making Product Pages for an Online Catalog

Online catalogs display lots of items in the same design. There's no need to lay out each catalog entry by hand. Photoshop will do it for you dynamically with variables and data sets.

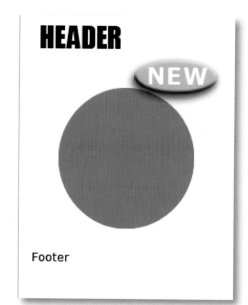

1. A Practical Use for Variables

A practical use for variables and data sets is to generate entries for an online catalog. It's typical for a catalog to display each product in the same layout. Although the design template is the same, the information is different for each product. It would be tedious to put together each item by hand. Fortunately, you don't have to. Photoshop CS2, for the first time, can dynamically populate variables with image and text data to produce a variety of results from one file. If you worked through the previous project, *Creating Dynamic Flash Web Banners,* in ImageReady, this project will be a snap. The variables features in Photoshop and ImageReady are similar, although only ImageReady can output the results in animated formats.

Open 03-08-orb.psd from Chapter 3-Automation>Ch3-8 into Photoshop. You'll use this file as a template for a series of catalog items—each with a different product name, illustration, and description.

T I P

Asterisks Mark Variables. The asterisks in the Layer menu in the Variables dialog box identify layers you've defined as variables.

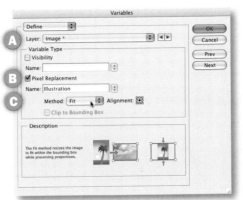

2. Define a Pixel Replacement Variable

Your first task is to define the variables. You'll tell Photoshop which layers in this file you plan to vary. Choose Image>Variables>Define. In the Variables dialog box, click the Layer menu to see a list of the file's layers. Choose the image layer from this menu **A**.

Check Pixel Replacement to set the variable type **B**. A pixel replacement variable is one that can be replaced by an external image file. Type *Illustration* as the name of this variable **C**. This name does not appear in your image; it's for internal purposes only. Choose Method: Fit to set the way that replacement images will be resized to fit the template. Moving your mouse over each method in this menu displays an explanation of the method.

I N S I G H T

Types of Variables. Photoshop recognizes three kinds of variables: pixel replacement variables for replacing images, text replacement variables for replacing strings of text, and visibility variables for hiding or showing variable layers.

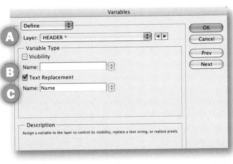

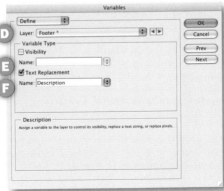

3. Define Text Variables

Now you'll define two text variables—the product name and description. Choose HEADER from the Layer menu **A** in the Variables dialog box, check Text Replacement to set the variable type **B**, and type *Name* as the name of this variable **C**. A text replacement variable is one that can be replaced by a string of text.

Choose Footer the Layer menu **D**, check Text Replacement again **E**, and type *Description* as the name of this variable **F**.

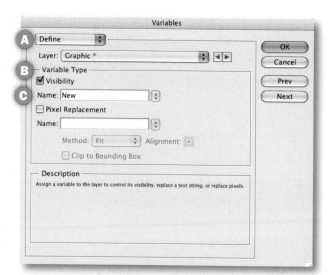

4. Define a Visibility Variable

The last variable you'll define is a visibility variable, which allows you to control whether a layer is visible or invisible in a data set. This is useful for graphics or text, like a New or For Sale icon, that will appear on some of your catalog entries, but not on others.

Choose Graphic from the Layer menu **A** in the Variables dialog box, check Visibility to set the variable type **B**, and type **New** as the name of this variable **C**.

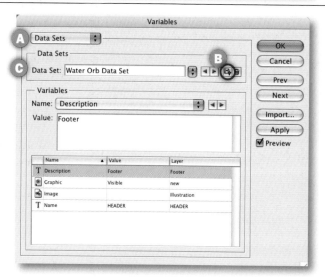

5. Create a Data Set

Now you'll create and input a set of data that will replace the variables you just defined. This data set is the source of one of the four catalog items that will be dynamically created for you.

Choose Data Sets from the menu at the top of the Variables dialog box **A**. If the fields in the Data Sets panel of the Variables dialog box are blank, click the Create New Data Set button **B**.

Type **Water Orb Data Set** over Data Set 1 in the Data Set field **C**. This names the set of data that will be used to generate the first catalog item. Each data set will contain the four variables you just created—Description, Illustration, Name, and New.

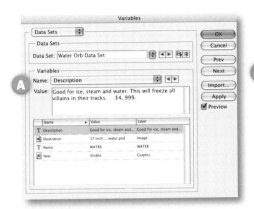

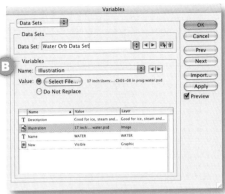

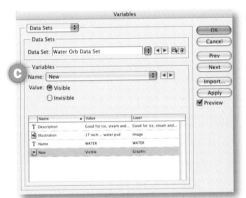

INSIGHT

Entering Data Values. If, as here, you have only a few variables, it's fast to enter the values of the variables into the Variables>DataSets dialog box. But if you're working with lots of variables, it's more efficient to create a spreadsheet of values and import them into Photoshop. Learn more in the preceding section, *Creating and Importing External Data Sets.*

WATER

NEW

Good for ice, steam and water. This will freeze all villains in their tracks $4,999

6. Enter Values for the Data Set

You'll specify values for each of the four variables in the Water Orb Data Set. Photoshop will use these values to generate a catalog entry for a magical water orb:

- Choose Description from the Name menu **A**. This identifies the variable you're defining now. You'll see this variable highlighted in the variables list at the bottom of the dialog box. In the Value field, type *Good for ice, steam and water. This will freeze all villains in their tracks $4,999*. This is the text that will appear in place of the word *Footer* in the catalog entry for the water orb product.

- Choose New from the Name menu, and click the Visible button **B**. This will make the New Graphic visible in the water orb catalog entry.

- Choose Illustration from the Name menu **C**. Click Select File, and navigate to Chapter 3-Automation>Ch3-8>water.psd. This identifies the external image file that will replace the gray circular placeholder in the water orb catalog entry.

- Choose Name from the Name menu, and enter *WATER* **D**. This is the text that will replace the word HEADER in the water orb catalog entry.

All the values you just entered are reflected in the variables list at the bottom of the dialog box **E**. Don't click OK yet. You still have to enter data for three more data sets, each of which will produce a separate catalog entry for a different magical orb.

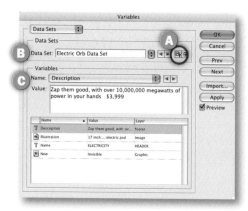

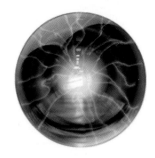

ELECTRICITY

Zap them good, with over 10,000,000 megawatts of power in your hands $4,999

7. Create the Electric Orb Data Set

Make another data set, this one for a catalog entry for another magic orb—an electric orb.

Create a new data set by clicking the New Data Set icon in the Variables dialog box **A**. Set the rest of the fields as follows:

• Type *Electric Orb Data Set* in the Data Set field **B**.

• Choose Description in the Name menu and type in the Value menu: *Zap them good, with over 10,000,000 megawatts of power in your hands $3,999* **C**.

• Choose New in the Name field and choose Invisible.

• Choose Illustration in the Name field and navigate to electric.psd.

• Choose Name in the Name field and enter *ELECTRICITY* in the Value field.

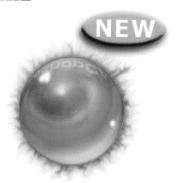

FIRE

Good old fashioned fire. Melts or burns its way through anything $4,999

8. Create the Fire Orb Data Set

Create a third data set by clicking the New Data Set icon in the Variables dialog box **A**. Set the rest of the fields as follows:

• Type *Fire Orb Data Set* in the Data Set field **B**.

• Choose Description in the Name menu and type in the Value menu: *Good old fashioned fire. Melts or burns its way through anything $4,999* **C**.

• Choose New in the Name field and choose Visible.

• Choose Illustration in the Name field and navigate to fire.psd.

• Choose Name in the Name field and enter *FIRE* in the Value field.

Time travel made easy. Quantum emitter sold separately
$4,999

9. Create the Time Orb Data Set

Create a fourth data set by clicking the New Data Set icon in the Variables dialog box **A**. Set the rest of the fields as follows:

- Type *Time Orb Data Set* in the Data Set field **B**.

- Choose Description in the Name menu and type in the Value menu: *Time travel made easy. Quantum emitter sold separately $4,999* **C**.

- Choose New in the Name field and choose Invisible.

- Choose Illustration in the Name field and navigate to time.psd.

- Choose Name in the Name field and enter *TIME* in the Value field.

Good old-fashioned fire. Melts or burns its way through any-thing. $4, 999.

10. Preview the Catalog Entries

Click the forward arrow in the Variables dialog box **A** to cycle through the data sets. With Preview checked, you'll see a live preview of each of the data sets in the open document. If anything looks wrong, reopen the Variables dialog box and make changes there. Click OK to close the Variables dialog box.

11. Export Individual Catalog Entries

With the template file still open, choose File>Export>Data Sets as Files. Click Select Folder to choose an output folder **A**. Leave Data Set set to All Data Sets **B**. To avoid long filenames, in the File Naming section, change the first field to Data Set Name and all other fields to None **C**. Click OK **D**. Photoshop saves four PSD files—one for each data entry. (Unlike ImageReady, Photoshop can't save data sets in JPEG, GIF, or SWF format.) You could slice and then optimize each of the PSD files in Photoshop, or use the PSD files with the site-building program Adobe GoLive. Choose File>Save to resave the template file. ▥

4

SITES THAT WOW!

Pulling It All Together to Make Eye-Popping Web Sites and Home Pages

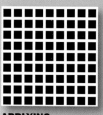

THIS IS THE BIG PAYOFF. Bring together all you've learned and mix in more new techniques to build these exciting and practical home pages and sites. In this chapter you get a real-world sense of how to use what you know to design eye-popping, useful Web pages with that Wow quality that will keep viewers coming back for more. By the time you've finished this chapter, you'll be confident that you've mastered the graphic techniques, tips, and tricks you need to make some of the best-looking sites on the Web.

Getting in the Game

This chapter starts with a bang with the Wow Game Site. We show you how to construct the home page of a portal site for gamers. This page is the gateway to everything from a chat room to a forum. You'll learn how to pack in lots of diverse items on a home page using a modular design that pulls everything together. The beauty of this design is that it's easy to update. Substituting new graphics can give the page a whole new look without the need for a complete redesign. As you build this design, you'll learn the secrets to creating those sexy interface graphics you've seen on other sites with high-end graphics. We give you some easy recipes for creating cool, lightweight patterns in

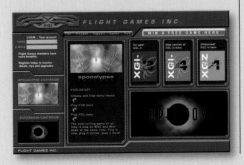

the section called *Web Pattern Recipes*. You learn how to make scan lines, grids, diagonal lines, boxes, and frames. Along with the recipes come instructions on how to use these patterns as repeating page background graphics and as pattern presets for filling foreground graphics. All that is found in the section *Applying Patterns to Web Graphics*.

Showing Off

The Web is the perfect venue for exhibiting your photographs and artwork. We've put together a couple of projects that will help you do that efficiently and with style. You'll be amazed at how easy it is to automatically make complete, interactive Web sites in Photoshop. Try it out in Web Photo Galleries with Viewer Feedback and the new Flash Web Photo Gallery. We weren't content to stop with Photoshop's built-in gallery templates. We show you how to personalize your galleries in the sections *Customizing a Web Photo Gallery* and *Adding File Information to Images*. Then we take things a step further with the *Wow Portfolio Site* project. There you'll learn how to build a stunning three-dimensional portfolio interface and use it to repurpose images generated by Photoshop's Web Photo Gallery.

Getting Serious

You'll switch gears from image to information as you work through the Wow Information Site project. This project offers two ways to position text and graphics on a page. You'll learn how to create tables in ImageReady to hold everything in place, and how to export a page with CSS (Cascading Style Sheet) positioning. And you may be surprised to learn that you can add HTML text to a page right in ImageReady.

We're sure you can't wait to dive into the last project, the *Wow Flash Splash Page*. We'll walk you through an Image-Ready workaround for making a site splash page with a Flash movie that tests whether your viewers have the Flash Player installed on their systems. So jump right in and try out all these exciting projects.

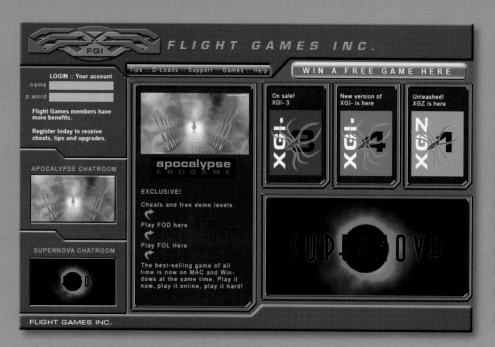

Wow Game Site

This home page for a game site is ultra-cool. You'll learn how to create its modular elements in Photoshop, and output the results as a full HTML page that's all ready to be included in a Web site for gamers. After you practice these techniques with our files, try them on a site of your own.

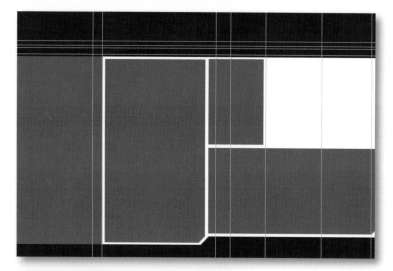

C A U T I O N

Turn Off Guides. We've added some guides to this layout to help you along. If they're in your way, you can turn them off temporarily by choosing View>Show>Guides.

1. Design with Modules

This page layout has lots of information. Its modular design pulls together the diverse elements on the page and makes it easy to update separate pieces of information to keep the page current. You'll begin this project by finishing up the page layout we've started for you. In Photoshop, open C04-01-games.psd from Chapter4-Sites That Wow. The gray boxes establish the location of each module. In the steps to come you'll shape and style these rectangles to become cool-looking frames.

If you're ever working on a site that offers lots of diverse items on the home page—like games, chat rooms, tutorials, and forums—try this modular approach. When you're working on your own designs, make some plain filled rectangular selections to begin laying out the modular elements of your design. If you make the rectangles on separate layers, you can move them around as you develop the layout.

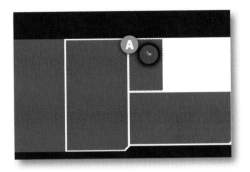

2. Move a Box to a Separate Layer

The gray boxes are located on the Frames layer. You'll start by moving the small gray box on the upper-right to its own layer. Select the Frames layer in the Layers palette. Select the Magic Wand tool and check Contiguous in the Options bar. Click on the upper-right gray box to select it **A**. Then press the Shift and Command/Ctrl-J keys to cut the selected box from the Frames layer and move it to an automatically created new layer—Layer 1.

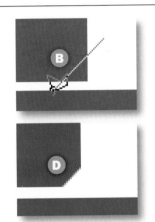

3. Use a Selection to Shape the Box

Now you'll cut off a diagonal corner of the Layer 1 box. Select the Polygonal Lasso from the toolbox **A**. Click on one side of the bottom-right corner of the box, press Shift, then click on the other side of the corner to create a 45° selection edge **B**. Release the Shift key and click twice more to make the other two legs of a triangular selection **C**. Then press Delete/Backspace to delete the selected corner **D**. Press Command/Ctrl-D to deselect.

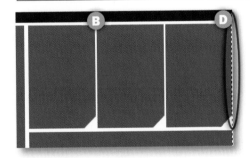

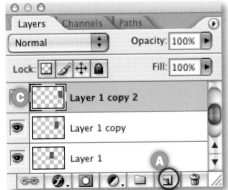

4. Make Two More Boxes

Make a copy of Layer 1 by dragging it to the Create New Layer icon at the bottom of the Layers palette **A**. Select the Move tool and press the arrow keys on your keyboard to move the copy to the right. Repeat to create and position the second copy, spacing the three boxes evenly **B**.

Next you'll cut out a narrow space between the third box and the edge of the document window to accommodate the style you'll be adding to the box later. Select Layer 1 copy 2 in the Layers palette **C**. Select the Rectangular Marquee tool and draw a narrow vertical selection at the right side of the third box **D**. Press Delete/Backspace to delete. If you get a warning that no pixels were selected, try again, moving the selection slightly.

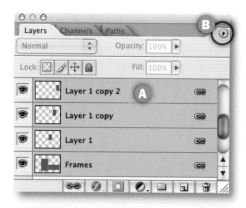

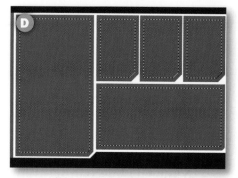

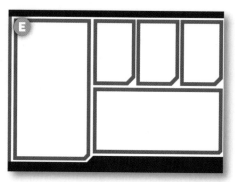

5. Turn the Boxes into Frames

Now you'll merge all the lighter gray box layers into one layer. Select the Frames layer, press Shift, and select the Layer 1 copy 2 layer to select all three Layer 1 copy layers and the Frames layer **A**. Click the Layers palette side arrow and choose Merge Layers from the side menu **B**. Rename the resulting merged layer My Frames.

Next you'll select and delete the center of each box. Hold the Command/Ctrl key as you click directly on the thumbnail on the My Frames layer in the Layers palette **C** to load a selection of each of the boxes on that layer **D**. (This method of loading a selection is new in CS2.) Choose Select>Modify>Contract. Type **10** (pixels) into the Contract Selection dialog box that opens, and click OK. Then press Delete/Backspace to delete the selected area of each of the boxes **E**. Press Command/Ctrl-D to deselect.

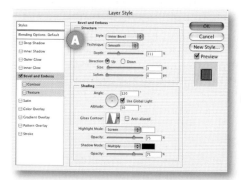

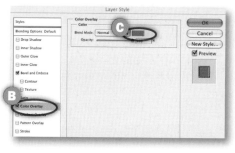

6. Style the Frames

With the My Frames layer selected, click the *f* icon at the bottom of the Layers palette and choose Bevel & Emboss. In the Layer Style dialog box that opens, choose the following Bevel and Emboss settings: Style: Inner Bevel, Technique: Smooth, Depth: 311, Direction: Up, Size: 3 px, Soften: 0 px, Gloss Contour: Ring **A**. Leave the other settings at their defaults.

Add another style by highlighting the Color Overlay style in the Layer Style dialog box **B**. Click in the Color field on the right side of the Layer Style dialog box **C** to open the Color Picker, and choose gray-green (R: 120, G: 124, B: 112). Click OK to close the Color Picker. Click OK again to close the Layer Style dialog box.

> ### CAUTION
>
> **Customizing a Layer Style.** If you want to change the default settings of a layer style, that style must be highlighted on the left side of the Layer Style dialog box. It isn't enough to just put a checkmark next to the style.

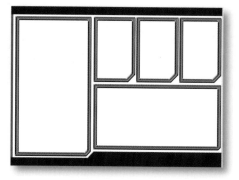

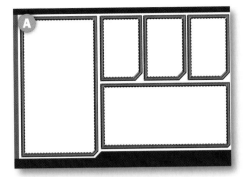

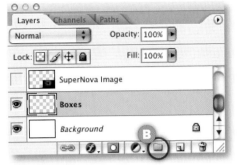

7. Create Boxes Inside the Frames

Now you'll create some dark gray boxes to fill the inner area of each frame. Select the Magic Wand tool with Contiguous checked in the Options bar. Hold the Shift key as you click in the white center of each of the five frames to select their centers **A**.

Make a new layer for all the boxes by clicking the Create New Layer icon at the bottom of the Layers palette **B**. Rename this new layer ***Boxes.*** Drag the Boxes layer just above the Background layer in the Layers palette.

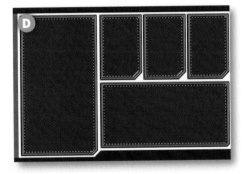

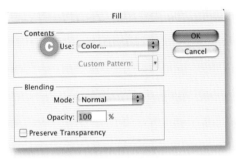

Choose Edit>Fill. In the Fill dialog box, choose Color from the Use menu **C**. In the Color Picker that opens, choose dark gray (R: 66, G: 66, B: 66). Click OK to close the Color Picker. Click OK again to fill the boxes with gray **D**. Press Command/Ctrl-D to deselect.

8. Style the Shapes on the Left

Expand the ShapesLeft layer set by clicking its arrow in the Layers palette **A**. Select the FramesLeft1 layer in that layer set. Click the *f* icon at the bottom of the Layers palette **B** and choose Bevel and Emboss. In the Layer Style dialog box, choose the following Bevel and Emboss settings: Style: Pillow Emboss, Technique: Smooth, Depth: 100, Direction: Up, Size: 5 px, Soften: 0 px **C**. Leave the other settings at their defaults and click OK.

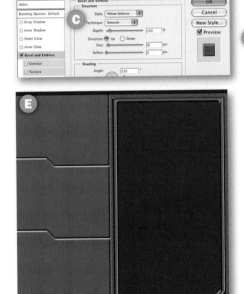

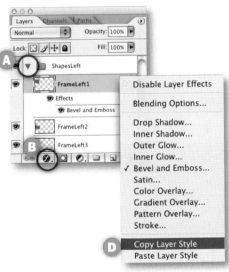

Now you'll use the same layer style on the other two layers in this layer set. Control/right-click on the FrameLeft1 layer in the Layers palette, and choose Copy Layer Style from the pop-up menu **D**. Control/right-click on the FrameLeft2 layer, and choose Paste Layer Style from the menu. Control/right-click on the FrameLeft3 layer and choose Paste Layer Style again. Beveled edges now separate the three shapes on the left **E**.

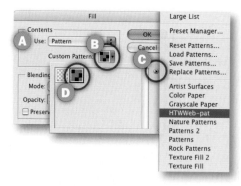

9. Add a Patterned Background

Select the Background layer in the Layers palette. Choose Edit>Fill. In the Fill dialog box, choose Use: Pattern **A**. Click in the Custom Pattern field **B** to open the Pattern picker. Click the arrow on the right side of the Pattern picker **C**. Choose HTWWeb-Pat from the side menu and click OK at the prompt. (If you don't see HTWWeb-Pat in this menu, you probably haven't installed the HTWWeb Presets from the CD. Go ahead and do that now following the instructions in the Introduction. You'll use several items from those presets in this project.)

Double-click the diagonal bg pattern that appears in the Pattern picker **D**. Click OK to close the Fill dialog box. The background of the image, which is visible around the frames, is filled with a diagonal pattern **E**.

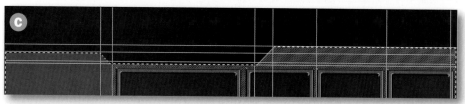

10. Cut Out the Top Bar

Next you'll use a selection to shape the black bar at the top. Select the BarTop layer that is inside the Bars layer set in the Layers palette. If blue guides are not showing, choose View>Show>Guides. Click on the bottom-right corner of the document window and drag outward to display gray around the image.

Select the Polygonal Lasso tool, and click on the left edge of the second guide from the top **A**. Following the illustration, click at the intersections of horizontal and vertical guides to create this tab-shaped selection. When you reach the right edge of the image **B**, click around the top of the document window until you arrive back at the beginning of the selection. Choose Select>Inverse. Then press Delete/Backspace to delete the selected portions of the bar, creating a unique shape **C**. Press Command/Ctrl-D to deselect.

> **T I P**
>
> **Try the Prebuilt Selection.** If you don't feel like making your own selection of the top bar, use the one we made for you. Choose Select>Load Selection and in the Load Selection dialog box choose bar top from the Channel menu. Click OK.

11. Style the Top and Bottom Bars

In this step you'll add pattern, color and dimension to the top and bottom bars. Hide the guides by choosing View>Show>Guides. Open the Styles palette (Window>Styles). Click the arrow on the right side of the Styles palette **A** and choose HTWWeb-Styles from the pop-up menu. (You won't see this style set unless you've installed the HTWWeb Presets, as explained in the Introduction.)

Drag the Blue Grid style from the Styles palette **B** onto the top bar **C** in the document window. The style is immediately applied to the top bar. Drag the same style from the Styles palette onto the bottom bar **D**.

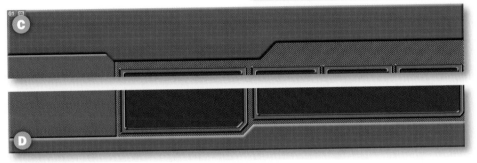

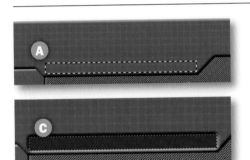

12. Create a Navigation Bar

Select the Rectangular Marquee tool and make a short, wide rectangular selection in the tab area of the top bar **A**. Select the BarTop layer in the Layers palette, and press Delete/Backspace to delete the selected area from the top bar **B**. The beveled edges of the deleted area come from the style you applied to the top bar in the last step.

Make a new layer above the BarTop layer by clicking the Create New Layer icon at the bottom of the Layers palette. Name the layer *NavBar*. Use the Eyedropper tool to sample the dark gray color (R: 66, G: 66, B:66) in one of the other boxes on the page. If your rectangular selection is gone, choose Select>Reselect. Choose Option/Alt-Delete to fill the selection with gray **C**. Press Command/Ctrl-D.

Choose the Type tool. In the Options bar choose a small sans serif font (try Arial, 12 px) and type some navigation labels separated by decorative colons (Tips :: D-Loads :: Support :: Games :: Help) **D**.

INSIGHT

Blue Grid Style. If you're wondering how we made the Blue Grid style you applied to the top and bottom bars, it's a combination of three layer styles—Bevel and Emboss, Color Overlay, and Pattern Overlay. We chose options for each in the Layer Style palette and made them into a reusable style by clicking the New Style button in the Layer Style palette.

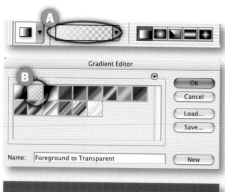

CAUTION

Loading a Selection. In Photoshop CS2, you must Command/Ctrl-click directly on a layer thumbnail to load a selection around the contents of the layer. This is a change from previous versions of the program. Don't let it trip you up.

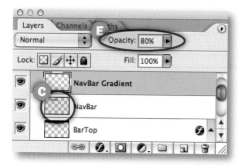

13. Add a Gradient

Now you'll add a gradient to the navigation to make it look rounded. Make a new layer above the NavBar layer and name it **NavBar Gradient**. Press D, X to set the Foreground Color box to white.

Select the Gradient tool in the toolbox. Click the Gradient field in the Options bar **A**. In the Gradient Editor that opens, select the White to Transparent gradient **B** and click OK. Command/Ctrl-click directly on the layer thumbnail in the NavBar layer **C** to load a selection of the navigation bar. With the NavBar Gradient layer selected, drag a short vertical line in the top one-third of the navigation bar **D** to make a gradient. In the Layers palette, lower the opacity of the NavBar Gradient layer to 80% **E**. Press Command/Ctrl-D.

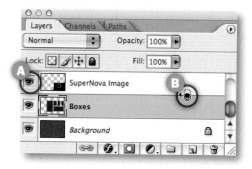

14. Make a Clipping Mask

Click in the Visibility field to the left of the Supernova Image layer in the Layers palette **A**. In this step you'll link this layer to the Frames layer below it in the Layers palette so that the Supernova image appears to be inside the frame. Hold the Option/Alt key and move your cursor over the border between the Supernova Image layer and the Boxes layer. When you see a double-circle icon **B**, click to make a clipping mask of the two layers. The Supernova image now appears in the image only where it overlaps content (one of the boxes) on the layer below **C**.

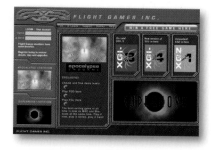

15. Make Content Layers Visible

Now you're all set to turn on the layers of content that we made for you. Click in the Visibility field to the left of the Skin layer set and the Free Game layer set in the Layers palette. The content of the layers on those layer sets is now visible in the image.

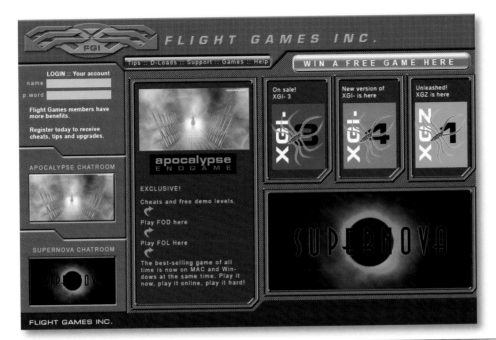

16. Slice

Select the Slice tool in the toolbox and draw slices around each of the text buttons in the small navigation bar so that you can give each button a separate link in a site-building program. Slice each content module too so that each module outputs as a separate GIF or JPEG. This will facilitate updating individual parts of the page later on. For more on slicing and optimizing, take another look at Chapter 1, *Navigation*.

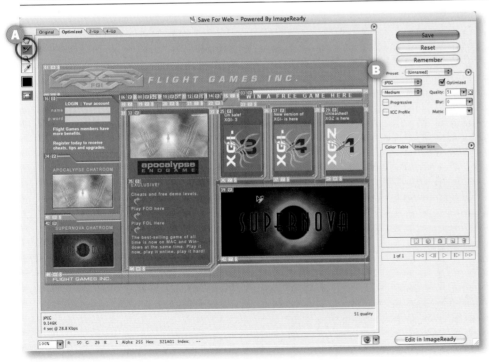

17. Optimize and Save

Choose File>Save for Web. In the Save for Web dialog box, optimize individual slices, selecting them with the Slice Select tool **A** and choosing Optimization settings on the right side of the dialog box **B**. Optimize each slice so that it is as small as possible, but still looks good. Some slices, like the slice around the Supernova image, will optimize best as JPEGs. Others, like the slice around the Login area, will optimize best as GIFs.

When you're done, click Save. In the Save Optimized As dialog box that appears choose Format/Save As Type: HTML and Images. This will generate a separate GIF or JPEG file for each slice, along with an HTML file with a table that holds the sliced images in place on the Web page. You can bring the HTML file and images into a site-building program like Dreamweaver to incorporate this cool page into a complete game site. ▧

Applying Patterns to Web Graphics

You can use custom-made patterns as tiling Web page backgrounds or as pattern presets for filling foreground objects. Let's review how to do both.

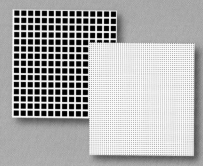

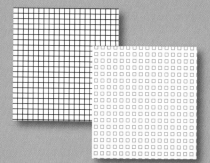

Tiling Background Patterns

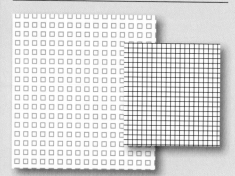

To make a tiling background pattern, start with a small pattern file like those described in the next section, **Web Pattern Recipes**. Save the file as an optimized GIF or JPEG. With a Web page layout open, specify the small file as the background in the Output Settings>Background dialog box. To access that dialog box in Photoshop, choose File>Save for Web, click the arrow on the top right of the Save for Web dialog box, choose Edit Output Settings from the side menu, and choose Background from the second menu in the Output Settings dialog box. To access the Background dialog box in ImageReady, choose File>Output Settings>Background. In the Output Settings dialog box, click the Choose button on the Path field **A** and navigate to the small pattern file. When you save the page layout, choose Format/ Save as Type: HTML and Images so that the program generates an HTML file with a background tag that causes the small pattern to repeat itself horizontally and vertically in a viewer's Web browser.

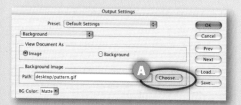

Pattern Presets

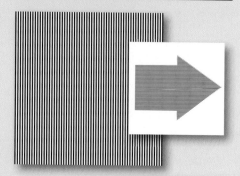

Another way to use a custom pattern is to define it as a pattern preset, and then use it to fill a layer or a selection in a Web graphic. To define a pattern, open a small file, like those in the following section, in Photoshop or ImageReady. Press Command/Ctrl-A to select all, or use the Rectangular Marquee tool to select an area of a larger image. Choose Edit>Define Pattern, and give the pattern a name. The pattern will be added to the currently active pattern set. To fill a layer or selection of a Web graphic with the pattern, choose Edit>Fill. In Photoshop's Fill dialog box choose Pattern from the Use pop-up menu. Then click in the Custom Pattern field to open the Pattern picker and select your newly defined pattern from the active pattern set that's displayed there **A**. Click OK to fill with the pattern. In ImageReady's Fill dialog box just choose Pattern from the Use menu to fill with the last defined pattern. ▥

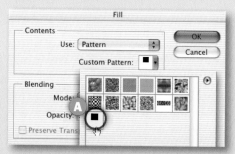

Web Pattern Recipes

Use these pattern recipes to make tiling backgrounds for your Web pages or to fill your Web graphics, using the techniques explained in the last section, *Applying Patterns to Web Graphics.* You can make these patterns in Photoshop or ImageReady.

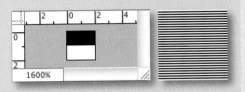

Scan Lines

Make a new white image 2 x 2 pixels. Zoom in to 1600%. Select the Pencil tool and choose a 1–pixel hard round tip from the Brush pop-up palette. Set the Foreground Color box to black. Draw a horizontal line across the top of the image. Optimize and save as a GIF for use as a page background, or define as a pattern for filling foreground images.

Grid

Make a new white image 8 pixels x 8 pixels. Zoom in to 1600%. Select the Pencil tool and choose a 1–pixel hard round tip. Set the Foreground Color box to black. Draw a horizontal line across the top of the image and a vertical line along the left side of the image. Optimize and save as a GIF with two colors, or define as a pattern.

Diagonal Lines

Make a new medium gray image 3 pixels x 3 pixels. Zoom in to 1600%. Select the Pencil tool and choose a 1–pixel hard round tip. Set the Foreground Color to dark gray. Draw a horizontal line across the top of the image from the right edge of the document window to the 1–pixel mark on the horizontal ruler. Click in the center of the image to draw a 1–pixel square. Draw a vertical line along the left edge of the image from the bottom of the document window up to the 1–pixel mark on the vertical ruler. Click in the bottom-right corner of the image to draw a 1-pixel square. Optimize as a GIF or define as a pattern.

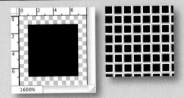

Boxes

Make a new transparent gray image 7 pixels x 7 pixels. Zoom in to 1600%. Select the Pencil tool and choose a 3–pixel hard round tip. Set the Foreground Color box to black. Click in the center of the image to draw a 3–pixel square. Optimize and save as a GIF with two colors, or define as a pattern.

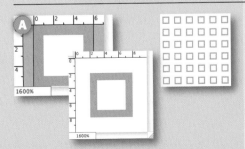

Frames

Make a new white image 6 pixels x 6 pixels. Zoom in to 1600%. Select the Pencil tool and choose a 1–pixel hard round tip. Set the Foreground Color box to medium gray. Make a new layer. Draw a 1–pixel border touching all sides of the document window A. Choose Image>Canvas size. In the Canvas size dialog box, check Relative and enter 4 pixels in both the width and height boxes. Click OK. Optimize and save as a GIF with two colors, or define as a pattern. 🖐

Gallery Site with Viewer Feedback

This complete site gives your viewers a way to communicate with you. Use it to show proofs or design comps to your clients and solicit their feedback. It's a snap to make using Photoshop's new and improved Web Photo Gallery.

1. Let Photoshop Do the Work for You

In this project you'll use Photoshop's Web Photo Gallery feature to create a multipage Web site, ready for upload to a Web server. This site displays thumbnails and larger versions of image files. Each large image has two pop-up areas. One gives viewers information about the image **A**. The other gathers Web viewers' feedback about your images **B** and incorporates the feedback in an email message to you.

Creating this site is a completely automatic process. You don't have to know a thing about Web design or writing code. And you don't have to do anything special to prepare image files for inclusion in the site, other than attaching whatever file information you want to appear in the Image Info portion of the site (see sidebar). Read on to learn how to set up Photoshop to make this gallery site for you automatically.

T I P

Adding File Information. The project files you'll be using are Colin's award-winning Photoshop illustrations. They already contain copyright and other file information. Read the topic that follows this project to learn how to attach file information to your own files for use in a site like this one.

2. Select the Site Images

Click the shell icon on the right side of Photoshop's Options bar to open Adobe Bridge. Use the Folders panel **A** on the top left of Bridge to navigate to the C04-02-art folder in Chapter 4-Sites That Wow>Ch4-2. The thumbnails in the content area on the right side of Bridge represent the files in that folder. To select some of these files for inclusion in the Web Photo Gallery, Command/Ctrl-click on the following six thumbnails: butterfly.tif, camera.tif, gameboy.jpg, guitar.psd, tentacles.jpg, and watch.tif.

Use Bridge's label and filter functions to isolate these thumbnails so you can see how they look as a group. Choose Label>Red from Bridge's menu bar, and click OK at the prompt. This adds a red label to each of the selected thumbnails **B**. Click the arrow next to Unfiltered at the top right, and choose Show Labeled Items Only from the Filter menu **C**. The only items now visible in the Bridge content area are those you labeled. Decide on the order in which you want the images to be displayed in the Web Photo Gallery site, and click and drag the thumbnails around Bridge's preview pane to reflect that order.

TIP

Using Bridge Labels. The meaning of Bridge labels is up to you. Use them to categorize by subject matter, author, quality, or any criteria you like. You can give labels meaningful names by typing over the default color names in Bridge/Edit>Preferences>Labels.

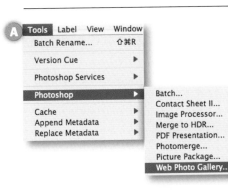

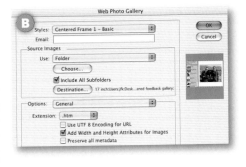

3. Open the Web Gallery Dialog Box

Choose Tools>Photoshop>Web Photo Gallery from the Bridge menu bar **A**. This opens Photoshop's Web Photo Gallery dialog box **B**, displaying the last settings you chose there. Alternatively, the Web Photo Gallery dialog box can be opened from Photoshop's File>Automate menu.

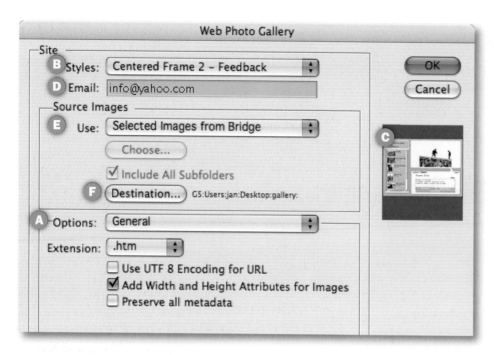

TIP

Image File Format. The source images you include in a Web Photo Gallery can be in any color mode (RGB, CMYK, Grayscale) and format (PSD, TIFF, JPEG, GIF, PDF, AI, EPS, etc.) that can be compressed as a JPEG.

4. Choose General Settings

The Web Photo Gallery dialog box has several panels, each accessed from the Options pop-up menu **A**. The first is the General panel. Choose the following settings in that panel:

- Styles: Centered Frame 2 - Feedback **B**

  This is one of Photoshop's prebuilt Web Photo Gallery style templates. You'll see a small preview of this style on the right side of the dialog box **C**. The rest of the settings vary depending on which style you choose.

- Email: Enter your email address **D**.

  Your Web audience will use this address to send you email feedback about the images you display. Use any email box or alias you own.

- Use: Selected Images from Bridge **E**.

  The advantage of this choice is that it allows you to include images from anywhere on your hard drive, as long as they are currently displayed in Bridge. If you choose Folder instead, you would have to prepare by putting all the images you plan to include in one folder.

- Destination: Click the Destination button **F** to open a destination dialog box. Create a new gallery folder to hold all the site files Photoshop will create for you, and click Choose.

Leave the other settings in the General panel at their defaults, and leave the Web Photo Gallery dialog box open for the next step.

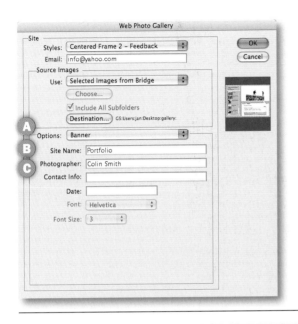

5. Set Banner Options

Choose Banner **A** from the Options menu in the Web Photo Gallery dialog box. These settings determine the information that will appear in the small space at the top of the thumbnails in this design. Enter **Portfolio** in the Site Name field **B** and **Colin Smith** in the Photographer field **C**. Leave the Contact Info and Date fields blank if you want white space in your design. You don't have to comply with the labels on the Banner fields; they are only suggestions. You can type in anything that fits in the available space. Don't click OK yet.

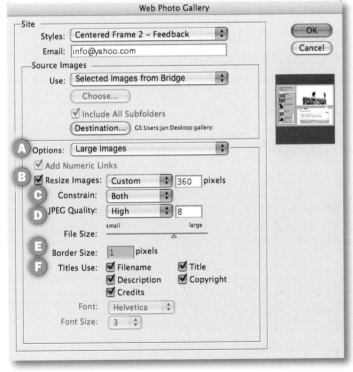

6. Choose Large Image Settings

Choose Large Images **A** from the Options menu to open more settings. These settings govern the display of the large images on the right side of the design. Set these fields as follows:

- Resize Images **B**: With this field checked, enter **360** in the pixel size box. This sets the largest dimension of the images. The menu label automatically changes to Custom.

- Constrain **C**: Leave this set to Both to maintain the proportions of the images.

- JPEG Quality **D**: High (8) to ensure that each image looks its best when the program compresses the image as a JPEG. The File Size slider automatically changes. The trade-off for higher JPEG Quality is larger file size.

- Border Size: 1 **E**. This adds a narrow black border around each image to set it off from the background.

- Titles Use **F**: Check all. These appear in the Image Info pop-up window for each image. The information is taken from the File Info dialog box.

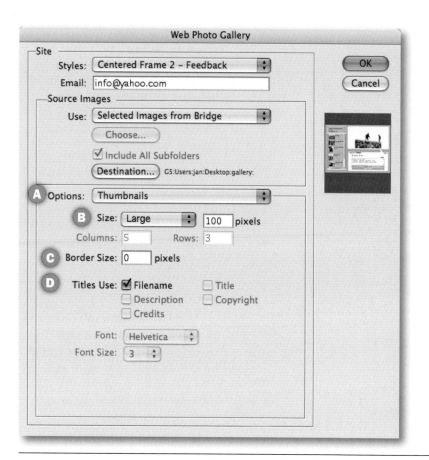

7. Set Thumbnail Options

Choose Thumbnails from the Options menu **A**. These settings determine how the thumbnails in the lefthand vertical bar will be displayed.

- Size **B**: Large. This sizes each thumbnail to fit proportionally within a 100–pixel square area.

- Border Size **C**: Leave this set to 0 so there will be no border around the thumbnails in the site.

- Titles Use **D**: Leave Filename checked to add the filename of each image next to its thumbnail.

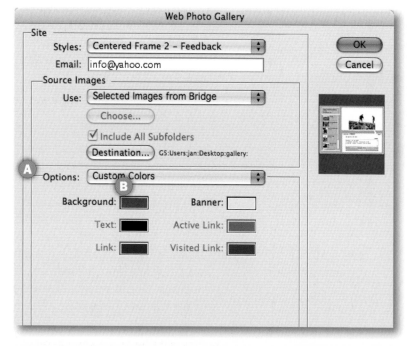

8. Choose Custom Colors

Choose Custom Colors from the Options menu **A**. Click in the Background field **B** to open the Color Picker. Check Only Web Colors, choose dark gray (R: 102, G: 102, B: 102), and click OK. This determines the background color of each page in the site. Leave the other options at their defaults, as in this illustration.

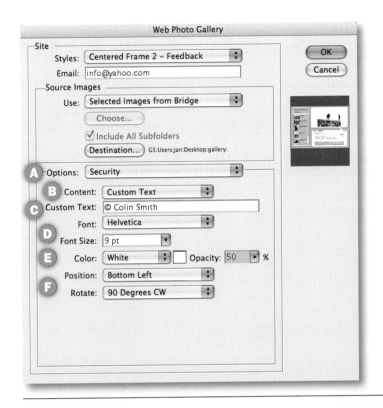

9. Set Security Options

Choose Security from the Options menu **A**. Here you can specify text that will appear on top of each large image to protect it from unauthorized use. We'll apply a custom copyright message. Set the options as follows:

- Content **B**: Custom Text.

- Custom Text **C**: Type © *Colin Smith* (pressing Option-G/typing *Alt-0169* for the © symbol).

- Font: Helvetica and Font Size: 9 pt **D**.

- Color: White and Opacity: 50% **E**. This will give the copyright message a ghosted look so it doesn't interfere with the view of the image.

- Position: Bottom Right, and Rotate: 90 Degrees CW **F** to locate the copyright vertically along the right edge of each image.

10. Complete the Site

Click OK in the Web Photo Gallery dialog box to set Photoshop in motion creating your site. It resizes each image as a thumbnail and a large image, compresses the images as JPEGs, and writes the code for a complete Web site. In a few seconds a Web browser opens to the first page of the site.

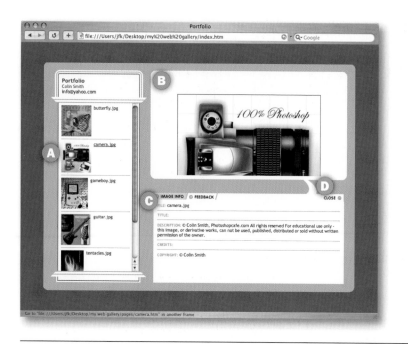

11. Preview the Site as a User

Put yourself in the shoes of your Web audience for the steps that follow. In the Web browser, click on a thumbnail on the left **A** to see a large version of the corresponding image on the right **B**. Use the vertical scrollbar to scroll down to more thumbnails.

Click on the Image Info tab **C** to open a pop-up window displaying information about the selected image, including the filename and copyright information. This is information that we attached to each image in Photoshop's File Info dialog box. Learn how to prepare your own images with similar information in the topic that follows this project—*Adding File Information to Images.* Click Close **D** to close this pop-up window.

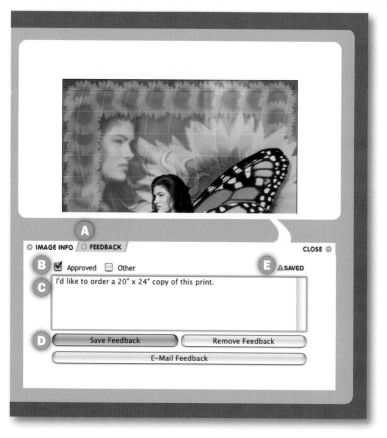

12. Prepare Image Feedback

In the Web browser, click on the Feedback tab **A** to open the Feedback pop-up window. Your Web viewers can use this window to approve and correspond with you about the images. Put a checkmark next to Approved **B** and type a message ordering a print in the box **C**. Then click Save Feedback **D**. This stores the message so that it can be combined with feedback on the other images before being automatically emailed to the site owner. You'll see a Saved notation in the Feedback window **E**.

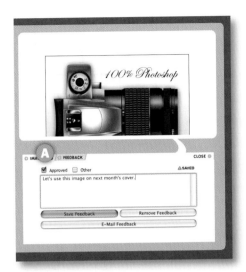

13. Prepare Feedback on other Images

Select another thumbnail in the Web browser and click the Feedback tab to provide feedback on that image **A**. Put a checkmark next to Other and write a message in the box. Click Save Feedback.

Select a third thumbnail and prepare feedback the same way. This time click E-mail Feedback **B**. Type the name of a fictitious viewer in the JavaScript dialog box that opens and click OK.

CAUTION

Save Your Gallery Site. Keep the site Photoshop made for you in a safe place. Later in this chapter, in the *Wow Portfolio Site* project, you'll repurpose the site images, displaying them in a unique, custom-built interface.

14. Email Feedback to the Site Owner

The default mail program automatically opens with a message **A** from the viewer **B** addressed to the email address you entered earlier into the Web Photo Gallery dialog box. The message contains all of the viewer's feedback on the site images. The viewer can add to the message or send it as-is to you—the site owner—by simply clicking his mail program's Send button. As you can see, this built-in feedback makes it easy for viewers to communicate with you about the site and its images.

Adding File Information to Images

The last project, *Gallery Site with Viewer Feedback*, covered how to make a Web site that can display file information along with images. There are two ways to attach nondefault file information to an image—in Photoshop's File Info dialog box or in the Metadata panel of Adobe Bridge. Give either of these methods a try on your own images before making a gallery site of your own.

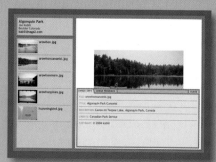

File Info Dialog Box

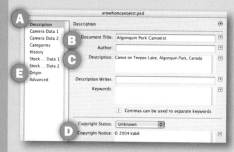

Choose File>Open to open an image in Photoshop. Then choose File>File Info to open the File Info dialog box. Leave Description highlighted on the left side of the dialog box **A**. Type a caption for the image in the Document Title field **B** and a short description of the image in the Description field **C**. In the Copyright Notice field **D** press Option-G (type *Alt-0169* on Windows) to enter a copyright symbol. Type the year and your name after the copyright symbol. Click Origin **E** on the left side of the dialog box and enter any relevant information into the Credits field. Click OK. Then save the file. You can choose to display any of these items in your site in the Web Photo Gallery template (Centered Frame 2 - Feedback) used in the preceding project. The other File Info fields are not reflected in that template.

To attach the same information to multiple files, record an action as you enter this file information and apply it with batch processing. Or click the side arrow on the File Info dialog box and choose Save Metadata Template. To apply the template, open another file, click the arrow at the top of its File Info dialog box, and choose the template by name.

Jan Kabili

Adobe Bridge Metadata Panel

In Adobe Bridge, select the thumbnail of an image you plan to include in your Web Photo Gallery site **A**. In the Metadata panel on the bottom left of Bridge **B**, scroll to the area labeled IPTC Core (an acronym for a press organization) and click the pencil icon **C** next to the Title field, which is one of the fields that can be edited in the Metadata panel

FIll in the Title and Description fields. In the Copyright Notice field press Option-G (type *Alt-0169* on Windows) to enter a copyright symbol. Type the year and your name after the copyright symbol **D**. You can ignore the other fields because they're not reflected in the Centered Frame 2 - Feedback template for the Web Photo Gallery that you used in the previous project. You can add Credits, which are in that template, in the File Info dialog box as explained to the left. ▦

Jan Kabili

Customizing a Web Photo Gallery

A Web site produced by the Photoshop Web Photo Gallery command is just like any other Web site. It consists of HTML pages and images. This means that you can change the look of a finished Web Photo Gallery site by modifying the image files in Photoshop or editing the HTML code in a site-building program. Here are some ideas for making changes to the gallery site you built in the previous project, **Gallery Site with Viewer Feedback**. We used Dreamweaver in these examples, but you can do the same using GoLive or any site-building program. Use these ideas as a starting point for customizing your own site.

INSIGHT

Web Photo Gallery Tokens. You can also modify Web Photo Gallery templates to create a new, reusable gallery style. Frankly, this is not something we often do, because it requires too much hands-on coding for our tastes, using a token system proprietary to Photoshop along with HTML. If you're interested in learning more, take a look at the topic Creating New Web Photo Gallery Styles in the Photoshop Help files.

Add a Background Image

Colin Smith

Find the folder that contains all of the HTML and image files Photoshop made for you in the previous project. This is the root folder of your Web Photo Gallery site. Take one of the background patterns we showed you how to make earlier in this chapter in the section on **Web Pattern Recipes** (we used the diagonal pattern bg.gif) and put it into the Images folder **A** inside your Web Photo Gallery root folder. In Dreamweaver, open the index.htm page from that root folder. Choose Modify>Page Properties from Dreamweaver's main menu bar. In the Page Properties dialog box, click the Browse button next to the Background Image field **B**, navigate to the file bg.gif in your root folder, and click OK. Then resave the index.htm page into the root folder. Open index.htm in a Web browser to see the repeating striped background.

Change Navigation Graphics

The inner pages of the Web Photo Gallery site you made in the previous project are located in that site's pages folder **A**. Open one of those inner pages—butterfly.htm—in Dreamweaver. Use Dreamweaver's split view to see the page design and its HTML code. Click on the three pieces of the navigation bar **B** to see the names of those graphics in code view **C** (PopClosed.gif, popClosedFeed.gif, and popClosedImage.gif). Now that you know the names of these navigation graphics, open each one from the root folder into Photoshop, change them as you like, and resave them as GIFs back into the pages folder in the root folder. The images will change on each page in the site, because these graphics are used on every page. Open index.htm in a Web browser to see your site with its new buttons. ▥

Colin Smith

Wow Portfolio Site

Make this eye-popping interface for displaying a portfolio on the Web. It's easier than it looks if you follow our lead. After you build this 3-D interface, you'll use it to display Web-ready images generated automatically by the Web Photo Gallery.

1. Focus on Efficiency

In this project you'll create a three-dimensional portfolio interface that looks good enough to eat. The focus here is on efficiency. We'll teach you techniques that simplify and save effort. For example, you'll make only one thumbnail frame from scratch, and then apply a useful step and repeat technique to create the others. And you'll learn how easy it really is to make custom-built 3-D effects with alpha channels.

This portfolio interface is specially designed for repurposing images generated by the Web Photo Gallery template you used in the previous project, *Gallery Site with Viewer Feedback*. You won't have to resize and optimize individual images, write an action for batch processing, or set up the Image Processor. Just run your own images through the Web Photo Gallery with the same settings you used before, and the resulting Web-ready images will fit perfectly into this interface.

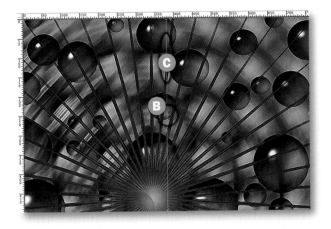

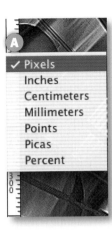

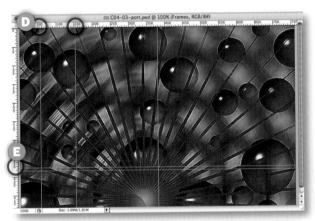

2. Create Some Guides

In Photoshop, open C04-03-port.psd from the Chapter 4-Sites That Wow>Ch4-3 folder. This is the background for an interface you'll build that will display six thumbnail-sized images and one larger image inside a three-dimensional bell shape.

Start by setting up some positioning guides. Choose View>Rulers to display horizontal and vertical rulers in the document window. If your rulers are not displaying pixels, Control/right-click in one of them and choose pixels from the pop-up menu **A**.

First you'll place a vertical guide at the center of the document. To find the center, press Command/Ctrl-A and then Command/Ctrl-T. An anchor point appears at the document's center **B**. Click in the vertical ruler and drag out a vertical guide to that point. Click the Cancel icon on the Options bar to exit transform mode and view the guide **C**. Press Command/Ctrl-D to deselect. Drag out two more vertical guides, placing them at about 55 and 153 pixels on the horizontal ruler **D**. Drag two horizontal guides from the top ruler and place them at about 375 and 383 pixels **E**. Use the Move tool to tweak the position of the guides if necessary.

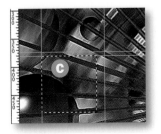

3. Create a Thumbnail Placeholder

Now you'll make a selection for a square thumbnail placeholder. Select the Rectangular Marquee tool in the Toolbox. In the Options bar, choose Fixed Size from the Style menu **A**, and type *101 px* into both the Width and Height fields **B**. Click in the document to create a square selection. With the Rectangular Marquee tool, drag the selection to the intersection of the first vertical and horizontal guides **C**.

4. Step and Repeat

Now you'll learn a great way to make evenly spaced copies of selections. You'll use this technique to create and distribute selections for the rest of the thumbnail placeholders. We love this technique because it's automatic and doesn't require doing math.

The square selection you made in the preceding step should still be active. Press Q to enter Quick Mask mode. This mode is just another way of viewing a selection. The selection is clear, and the non-selected area has a red mask **A**.

With the Rectangular Marquee tool selected, change the Style setting in the Options bar to Normal **B**. Click and drag a rough selection around the clear square **C**. Hold the Option/Alt key and choose Edit>Free Transform. This creates a copy of the clear selection. You can't see the copy yet because it's on top of the original. Still in transform mode, click the right arrow key on your keyboard to move the clear selection copy to the right until its left edge is aligned with the second vertical guide from the left **D**. Click the big checkmark in the Options bar to exit transform mode. Leave the selection active.

Now you'll step and repeat in Quick Mask mode to make and position the other thumbnail selections. Holding the Option/Alt key, press Command/Ctrl-Shift-T four times. You'll see a total of six clear boxes, evenly spaced horizontally and aligned vertically **E**. Press Q to exit Quick Mask mode. The boxes now look like regular selections **F**.

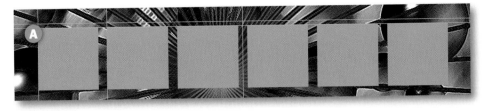

5. Fill the Thumbnail Selections

In the Layers palette, select the Design layer, click the side arrow, and choose New Layer. Name the layer *Frames*, and click OK. Click the Foreground Color box to open the Color Picker. Choose gray (R: 153, G: 153, B: 153). Press Option-Delete/Alt-Backspace to fill the selections with the foreground color **A**. Press Command/Ctrl-D to deselect.

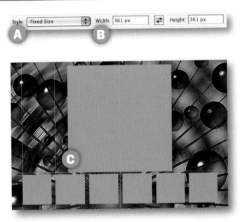

6. Make the Large Image Placeholder

Select the Rectangular Marquee tool. In the Options bar set Style to Fixed Size **A** and type *361 px* in both the Width and Height fields **B**. Click to create a large square selection. With the Rectangular Marquee tool still selected, drag the large selection so that its bottom rests on the top horizontal guide and is centered horizontally **C**.

With the Frames layer selected in the Layers palette, press Option-Delete/Alt-Backspace to fill the large square selection with the gray foreground color. Press Command/Ctrl-D to deselect.

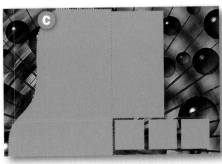

7. Create Half a Bell Shape

Now you'll work on the 3-D bell shape that surrounds the images in this interface. We made things easier for you by creating a path that outlines half of a bell shape. (If you'd rather draw the path yourself, click and drag with the Pen tool.) In the Paths palette (Window>Paths), select the half bell path **A** and click the Load Path as Selection icon at the bottom of the palette **B**. This creates a half bell-shaped selection.

Click the side arrow on the Layers palette, and choose New Layer. Name the layer *Bell*. Choose Option-Delete/Alt-Backspace to fill the selection with the gray foreground color **C**. Press Command/Ctrl-D to deselect.

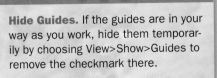

TIP

Hide Guides. If the guides are in your way as you work, hide them temporarily by choosing View>Show>Guides to remove the checkmark there.

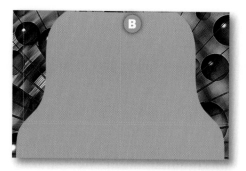

8. Complete the Bell Shape

Duplicate the Bell layer by dragging it to the Create New Layer icon at the bottom of the Layers palette **A**. With the new layer selected, choose Edit>Transform>Flip Horizontal. Select the Move tool in the toolbox. Hold the Shift key to constrain vertical movement and drag the second half of the bell to the right so that its left edge joins the right edge of the other half **B**. Press Command/Ctrl-D to deselect. Click the side arrow on the Layers palette **C** and choose Merge Down to merge the two halves of the bell into one Bell layer.

INSIGHT

What Is an Alpha Channel? An alpha channel is a special grayscale channel that describes image transparency. The black part of an alpha channel represents transparent pixels in an image. The white part of an alpha channel represents opaque pixels in the image, and gray areas in an alpha channel correspond to semitransparent pixels in the image.

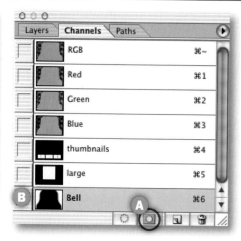

9. Make an Alpha Channel for the Bell

In this step you'll begin to add dimensionality to the bell shape by creating an alpha channel. Command/Ctrl-click directly on the thumbnail on the Bell layer to load a selection around the bell shape. Choose Select>Inverse to select everything but the bell.

Click the Channels tab to bring that palette forward. Click the Save Selection as Channel icon at the bottom of the Channels palette **A**. This creates an alpha channel in which the opaque bell shape is represented as black **B**. Double-click the new Alpha 1 channel and name it *Bell*. Press Command/Ctrl-D to deselect.

INSIGHT

Why Blur an Alpha Channel? Blurring an alpha channel adds gradually changing shades of gray to the alpha channel. The shades of gray translate into semitransparent pixels in the image that shade the image, giving it a 3-D look.

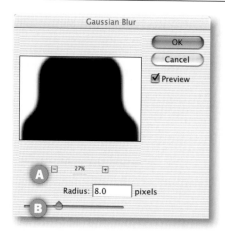

10. Blur the Alpha Channel

With the Bell channel highlighted in the Channels palette, choose Filter>Blur>Gaussian Blur. In the Gaussian Blur dialog box click the minus sign several times **A**, and set Radius to 8.0 pixels **B**. Click OK. This blurs the edges of the bell shape in the alpha channel, which adds grays to the alpha channel and shape to the image. Select the RGB channel in the Channels palette to view the image in its normal state.

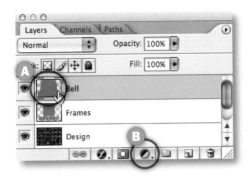

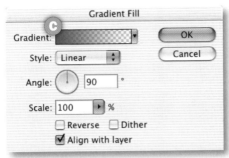

INSIGHT

Gradient Tools. Another way to make a gradient is with the Gradient tool in the toolbox. We prefer using a Gradient Fill layer, as you did in this project, because unlike the Gradient tool, a Gradient Fill does not alter the underlying image pixels (it comes in on its own layer) and it remains editable. You can modify a Gradient Fill at any time by double-clicking the gradient thumbnail on its layer to reopen the Gradient Editor.

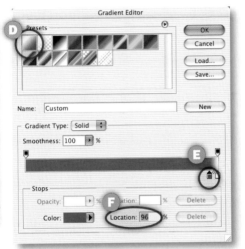

11. Add a Gradient to the Bell

In this step you'll add a small gradient to the bell shape to increase the illusion of dimensionality. Command/Ctrl-click directly on the thumbnail on the Bell layer in the Layers palette **A** to load a selection around the bell shape.

Press D on your keyboard to set the Background Color box in the toolbox to white. Click the Foreground Color box, choose a medium gray (R: 102, G: 102, B: 102) from the Color Picker that opens, and click OK.

With the Bell layer selected in the Layers palette, click the New Fill or Adjustment layer icon (a black and white circle) at the bottom of the Layers palette **B** and choose Gradient from the pop-up menu. In the Gradient dialog box that opens, click in the Gradient field **C** to open the Gradient Editor. In the Gradient Editor, select the Foreground to Background gradient thumbnail **D**. Then drag the lefthand gray color stop under the gradient bar **E** to the right until the Location field **F** reads about 96%. This will make the white area at the top of the gradient in the image very short. Click OK in both gradient dialog boxes. The top edge of the bell now looks rounded. Press Command/Ctrl-D to deselect.

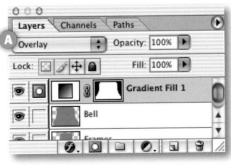

12. Change Gradient Blending Mode

With the new Gradient Fill 1 layer selected in the Layers palette, choose Overlay from the Blending Mode field at the top of the Layers palette **A**. This blends the colors in the gradient layer with the underlying colors, softening the gradient shading on the bell.

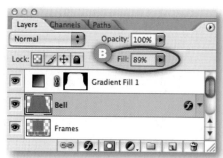

13. Style the Bell

With the Bell layer selected, click the Portfolio Iface style in the Styles palette (Window>Styles) to give the bell a custom bevel and emboss style **A**. Decrease the Fill field at the top of the Layers palette to 89% to lower the opacity of the bell, without affecting its layer style **B**.

You won't see the Portfolio Iface style in the Styles palette if you didn't install and load the HTWWeb Presets as instructed in the Introduction. Go back and do that now; then try this step.

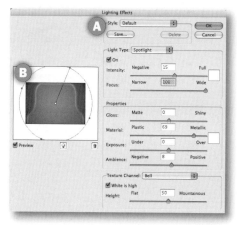

14. Add Lighting Effects to the Bell

Apply the Lighting Effects filter to the bell to enhance its dimensionality. With the Bell layer selected in the Layers palette, choose Filter>Render>Lighting Effects. In the Lighting Effects dialog box **A**:

- Choose Style: Default and Light Type: Spotlight, and check On.

- Set Intensity to around 15 and Focus to around 100, although you can play with these two settings to get an effect you like.

- Choose Bell in the Texture Channel (not to be confused with Bell Transparency) and check White is High. This uses the Bell alpha channel you made earlier in this project to set the contours of the lighting effect.

- Click and drag the center and side anchor points on the preview on the left side of the dialog box to get an effect you like. The configuration of anchor points in the illustration **B** is a good starting point.

Unfortunately, there is a limited preview of the Lighting Effects filter. Click OK to apply the filter, and if you don't like the result **C**, choose Command/Ctrl-Z to undo and try again.

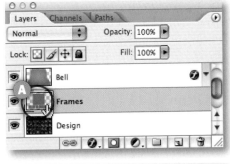

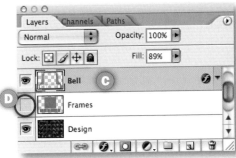

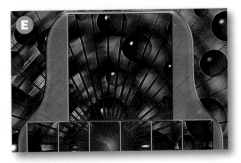

15. Cut Frames in the Bell

Now you'll use the placeholders to cut frames into the bell interface. Command/Ctrl-click directly on the thumbnail on the Frames layer in the Layers palette **A** to load a selection around the large placeholder and each of the thumbnail placeholders **B**. It's important that you now select the Bell layer in the Layers palette **C**. Press Delete/Backspace to cut out the selected areas in the bell interface. Press Command/Ctrl-D to deselect.

Click the Eye icon next to the Frames layer **D** to turn the Frames layer off so you can see the cut-outs in the bell interface **E**. Then click that Eye icon again to turn the Frames layer back on.

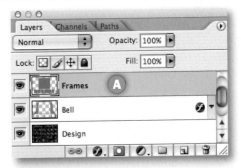

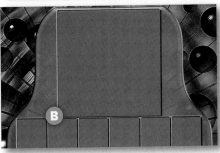

16. Move the Frames Layer

Drag the Frames layer to the top of the Layer stack in the Layers palette **A** to position the image placeholders above the interface in the document **B**.

You've finished building this unique interface for portfolio images. Next you'll try out some images in this interface. These are the Web-ready thumbnails and one of the larger gallery images that were automatically generated by the Web Photo Gallery in the last project.

Colin Smith

17. Add Some Images

Find the folder of HTML pages and images that you saved from the previous project, *Gallery Site with Viewer Feedback*. If you can't find them, use the copies of those files in Chapter 4-Sites That Wow>Ch4-3>C04-03-gallery-end.

Open each of the six JPEG files you'll find in the thumbnails folder that was generated by Photoshop's Web Photo Gallery. Select the Move tool, click in one of those open images, and drag it into the interface image, where it will be located on a separate layer automatically.

Position the thumbnail image on top of one of the placeholders in the interface. Repeat with each of the other thumbnail images that were generated by the Web Photo Gallery. Then open the images folder and do the same with one of the larger images you'll find there—butterfly.jpg, camera.jpg, gameboy.jpg, guitar.jpg, tentacles.jpg, or watch.jpg.

18. Slice the Interface

With the Slice tool, create a slice around each of the thumbnail placeholders and around the large placeholder. You can optimize each slice with the artwork as you'll do here. Or you could turn off the visibility of the content layers, optimize just the bare interface, and swap out the placeholders for content files in a site-building program.

19. Optimize the Slices

Choose File>Save for Web. In the Save for Web window, click on the Optimize, 2-Up, or 4-Up tab to preview each slice with the optimization settings you choose. Select the slices one by one and choose settings that make each slice as small as possible, while retaining its appearance. (Hint: All these slices optimize best as JPEGs.)

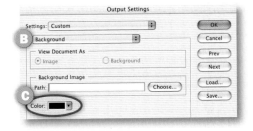

20. Set the Page Background Color

In this step you'll set the color of the HTML page background that will appear around this page when it's viewed in a browser window that's bigger than the green illustration. Click the small arrow at the far right of the Save for Web window **A**, and choose Edit Output Settings. In the Output Settings dialog box that opens, choose Background from the second pop-up menu **B**. Click in the Color field **C**, and choose black from the Color Picker that opens. Click OK to close the Color Picker. Click OK again to close the Output Settings dialog box. Back in the Save for Web dialog box, click Save to open the Save Optimized As dialog box.

T I P

Adding Links. Of course there's lots more you could do with this page. Each of the thumbnails could be made into a remote rollover that causes a different large image to appear in the frame at the top of the interface. Or you could give each thumbnail a link to another page you include in the site. Or perhaps you could put an image slide show in the large frame. These techniques are covered in Chapter 1, *Navigation*, and Chapter 2, *Animation.*

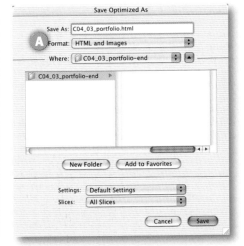

21. Save the Optimized Interface

In the Save Optimized As dialog box, set Format/Save As Type to HTML and Images. Choose a destination folder and click Save. The program will save each slice of the interface as an optimized Web-ready image, along with an HTML file containing a table to hold all the separate image files in place. The thumbnails and large image that were generated by the Web Photo Gallery will not be re-optimized because you turned off those layers before saving.

T I P

Use Your Own Images. Run some of your personal images through the Web Photo Gallery, using the Centered Frame 2- Feedback template and the settings we used in the previous project. Pay particular attention to the size of the thumbnails (100 pixels) and of the large images (360 pixels). You'll end up with automatically resized and optimized images, ready for adding to this portfolio interface.

Jan Kabili

Jan Kabili

Flash Web Photo Gallery Site

Photoshop CS2 has some new Web Photo Gallery templates made with Flash. Try out these galleries complete with interactive slide shows and music.

T I P

Begin in Photoshop or Bridge. If you've already collected your source images in a single folder and intend to use them all, you can run the Web Photo Gallery directly from Photoshop, without selecting images in Adobe Bridge as you did in the Gallery Site with View feedback project.

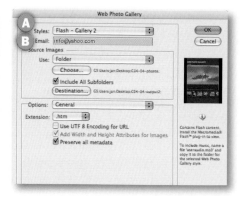

1. Open the Web Gallery Dialog Box

Review the Gallery Site with Viewer Feedback project to remind yourself of the fundamentals of the Web Photo Gallery. Then try out these Flash-based gallery templates, which automatically produce interactive slide shows of your images with music. In Photoshop, choose File>Automate>Web Photo Gallery to open the Web Photo Gallery dialog box. This is the same dialog box you worked with in the Gallery Site with Viewer Feedback project.

2. Choose a Flash Gallery Template

Choose Flash - Gallery 2 from the Styles menu at the top of the Web Photo Gallery dialog box **A**. All of the options you'll choose from this point on are specific to this Web gallery template. Type your email address in the Email field to create a live mail link that opens the viewer's mail program to send a message to you **B**.

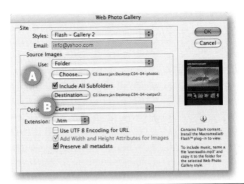

3. Choose a Source and Destination

Set the source of the images to include in the Web Photo Gallery. Choose Folder from the Use menu **A**, and navigate to Chapter 4-Sites That Wow>Ch4-4>C04-04-photos. Click the Destination button **B** and navigate to a folder on your hard drive that will contain all the files generated by the Web Photo Gallery.

CAUTION

Music bloats file size. If you add music to a Web Photo Gallery you may experience a significant jump in file size. Consider whether that trade-off is worth it before you add music.

To include music, name a file 'useraudio.mp3' and copy it to the folder for the selected Web Photo Gallery style.

4. Consider Adding Music

The instructions in the dialog box tell you how to add music to your Web Photo Gallery, an option that is not available for most templates. If you decide to add music, despite the anticipated increase in file size, search your computer for or import a sound file, rename it ***userau-dio.mp3***, and drag it to your Photoshop CS2 application folder>Presets>Web Photo Gallery>Flash - Gallery 2 folder.

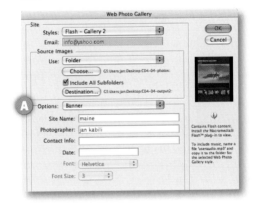

5. Set Banner Options

Choose Banner **A** from the Options menu in the Web Photo Gallery dialog box. These settings determine the appearance of the vertical banner in this design. Enter ***maine*** in the Site Name field and ***jan kabili*** in the Photographer field. This text will appear at the top of the banner. Leave the Contact Info field blank, because your email address has already been included. Leave the date field blank to leave some white space in your design. Don't click OK yet.

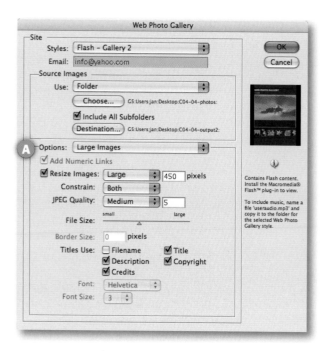

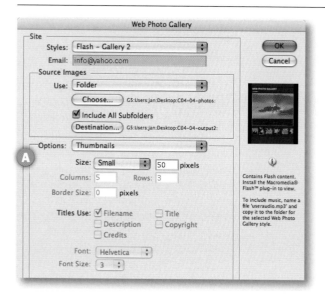

6. Choose Large Image Settings

Choose Large Images from the Options menu **A** to open more settings. These settings govern the display of the large images at the top of the vertical bar in this design. Set these fields as follows:

- Resize Images: With this field checked, choose Large. This sets the largest dimension of each image to 450 pixels.

- Constrain: Leave this set to Both to maintain the proportions of the images.

- JPEG Quality: Medium (5) to try to strike a balance between file size and appearance.

- Titles Use: Check all except for Filename. Values for each of the checked items will appear in each image if available. The information is taken from the File Info dialog box.

7. Set Thumbnail Options

Choose Thumbnails from the Options menu **A**. These settings determine how the thumbnail versions of each image will appear in the banner. Choose Size: Small. This sizes each thumbnail to fit proportionally within a 50–pixel square area. The other thumbnail settings are fixed in this template, so you have no other choices to make here. Don't click OK yet.

INSIGHT

Kinds of Links. Link is the normal state of a link between Web pages. Active Link is the state of a link while it is being clicked. Visited Link is the state of a link that already has been clicked. You can give each of these states a different color in this Web Photo Gallery template.

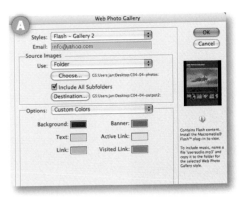

8. Choose Custom Colors

Choose Custom Colors from the Options menu **A**. Click in the Background field to open the Color Picker, and choose a dark color so the light-colored icons on the page will be visible. (Try dark gray (R: 51, G: 51, B: 51.) Click in the Banner field and choose olive green in the Color Picker (R: 126, G: 129, B: 75). Click in the Text field and choose light green (R: 227, 227, 160). Click in each of the three link fields and choose a light green, and click OK.

9. Turn Off Security Options

You won't be setting any security options in this project. See the project Gallery with Viewer Feedback project to learn how to use these options to add watermarks to your images. Select Security from the Options menu, and choose None.

10. Complete the Site

Click OK in the Web Photo Gallery dialog box. Your work is done. Now sit back and let Photoshop do the rest for you: resizing and compressing thumbnail and large images, and automatically creating a SWF file and an HTML page to display those images. When Photoshop is done, your default Web browser opens to display the first page of the Web Photo Gallery site **A**.

If you included a music file in your Web Photo Gallery>Presets folder, it will start playing when the site opens in your Web browser. To turn off the music, click the small sound icon in the controller at the bottom right of the document window **B**.

11. Navigate the Site as a User

Check out your Web Photo Gallery site from the user's viewpoint. In the Web browser, click on a thumbnail at the bottom of the vertical banner **A** to see a large version of the corresponding image in the banner **B**. Use the horizontal scrollbar to access each thumbnail **C**.

We showed you how to prepare your own images with similar information in the earlier topic *Adding File Information to Images.*

12. View Image Information

In the Web browser, move your mouse over a thumbnail **A** to view the title of the image. This is information that we attached to the images in Photoshop's and Adobe Bridge's File Info dialog box. Earlier in this chapter, you learned how to add this kind of metadata to your own images in *Adding File Information to Images.*

To see more image information, click the **?** icon in the controller on the bottom right of the browser window **B**. Title, Description, and Copyright—the fields you enabled in the Large Image settings of the Web Photo Gallery dialog—appear beneath the large image **C**.

Now click the thumbnails icon **D** to hide the thumbnails. This is a nice, clean way to view a single image.

13. Play a Slide Show

Still in the Web browser, click the arrow icon on the controller bar **A**, and wait a few seconds. A slide show of your images begins to play slowly. This is an impressive way to show off your images, particularly if the music is still playing. The viewing area expands to fit wider images **B** and contracts to fit narrow ones. To stop the slide show, click the Stop button to the right of the Play button on the controller.

As you can see, this is an easy way to add interactivity and animation to your Web site.

14. Email Feedback

Viewers can email you, the site owner or manager, directly from the Web Photo Gallery site in a browser. Clicking the email address at the top of the banner **A** opens the viewer's mail program to help him or her create an email addressed to you.

You've finished creating a Flash-based Web Photo Gallery site. Of course, the Web Photo Gallery needs to be uploaded to a Web host server in order to be viewed publicly online. If you have time, try out the other installed Flash Web Gallery site template. You can currently download a third Flash template from the downloads page at www.adobe.com. 📖

Wow Information Site

This home page for an information site has lots of text elements. You'll use tables and CSS to organize and output text graphics and coded text for display on the Web. This project takes place in ImageReady.

1. Decide on Graphics or HTML Text

When you're laying out a page in Photoshop or ImageReady that has lots of text, one of your first decisions is when to use text saved as a graphic and when to use HTML text. The advantage of HTML text is that it is much smaller in file size than text graphics, and is easier to change when you're updating a page. However, you can't guarantee what font or font size the viewer will see. If you save text as graphics, you can be assured of how the text will appear to your audience. However, the total size of the page will be noticeably larger. In general, graphics are the way to go for headlines, logos, and text in fancy fonts **A**, and HTML text makes sense for blocks of small text **B**. In this project, you'll learn how to prepare both kinds of text when you're laying out a page in ImageReady.

Open C04-05-infosite.psd from Chapter 4-Sites that Wow>Ch4-5.

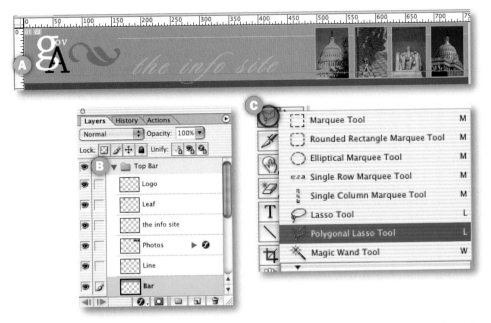

2. Shape the Interface

The layout of this page is simple but elegant. There are no loud graphics to compete with its main product—information. We prepared most of the background elements by creating rectangular color blocks that organize and call attention to the text. In this step you'll set off the secondary navigation (1800s, 1900s, 2000s) by creating a tabbed navigation bar. Choose View>Rulers to turn on ImageReady's rulers. Click in the horizontal ruler and drag out a horizontal guide, positioning it at the baseline of the info site text **A**. Use the Move tool if you need to tweak the guide.

In the Layers palette, click the arrow on the Top Bar layer set **B** to reveal the contents of that layer set, and select the Bar layer. Select the Polygonal Lasso tool from behind the Rectangular Marquee tool in ImageReady's toolbox **C**. Hold down the Shift key (which constrains the tool to making straight lines and 45° angles). Click at the following points: the left edge of the guide, just under the *e* in the word *site*, on the top of the green bar, and at the right edge of the document. Then click around the outside of the document window to come back to the beginning of your selection **D**. Choose Select>Inverse, and press the Delete/Backspace key to cut out a tab shape **E**. Press Command/Ctrl-D to deselect.

3. Add Text Links

Select the Type tool in the toolbox. Choose white and a Sans Serif font in the Options bar. Type a line of text links: *1800s 1900s 2000s* **A**. Click the checkmark on the Options bar to commit the type. Then choose a script font and create another Type layer by typing *link1 link2 link3 link4 link5* **B**. Use the Move tool to position these two type layers as in the illustration.

4. Create Main Links

In this step you'll add text and bullet links to the left side of the page. Click the arrow next to the TextLeft layer set to expand that layer set **A**. Control/right-click the ***link here*** type layer and choose Duplicate Layer from the contextual menu. Repeat this until you have a total of six link here layers **B**.

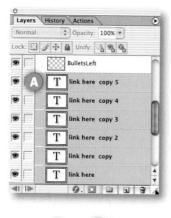

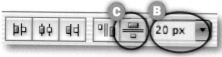

5. Select and Distribute the Links

Now you'll select and automatically distribute the six link layers. With the ***link here*** layer selected, hold the Shift key and click on the ***link here copy 5*** layer at the top of the layer stack **A**. Select the Move tool in the toolbox to display alignment and distribution buttons in the Options bar. Type **20 px** in the box at the far right of the Options bar **B**, and click the Distribute Layer Vertical Space button **C**. This evenly distributes the selected layers vertically, with 20 pixels between each **D**. The ability to select multiple layers and to specify distribution spacing are features found only in ImageReady, not Photoshop.

Now do the same thing with the ***BulletsLeft*** layer. Make five copies and Shift-click to select the six BulletsLeft layers. This time enter **12 px** in the distribute box in the Options bar **E** and click the Distribute Layer Vertical Space button **F**. The bullets are now distributed evenly alongside the text **G**.

Complete the job by repeating Steps 4 and 5 on the text and bullet links on the right side of the pages, which you'll find in the TextRight layer set.

6. Slice the Banner

In this step you'll create slices in the banner at the top of the page. First draw a separate slice around each of the photographs **A**. They merit slicing because they will optimize best in JPEG format, while the text and graphic elements in the banner will optimize best in GIF format.

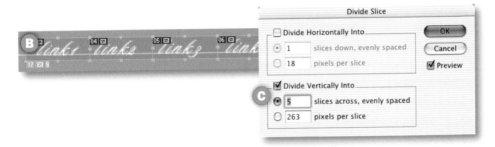

Next you'll slice the text links in the banner, so that each can be assigned a separate URL link when this page is incorporated into a site in Dreamweaver or GoLive. Draw one slice around the five script links that you added to the banner **B**. Then choose Slices>Divide Slices in the main menu bar. In the Divide Slice dialog box, choose Divide Vertically Into and type **5** in the field labeled *slices across, evenly spaced* **C**. ImageReady automatically divides your one slice into five. You can adjust these slices by clicking on their borders with the Slice Select tool and dragging.

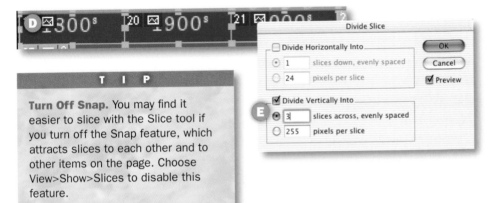

Finally, draw a separate slice around each word in the secondary navigation bar—1800s, 1900s, and 2000s **D**. Choose Slices>Divide Slices, and automatically divide it into three slices across, evenly spaced **E**.

T I P

Turn Off Snap. You may find it easier to slice with the Slice tool if you turn off the Snap feature, which attracts slices to each other and to other items on the page. Choose View>Show>Slices to disable this feature.

7. Group Banner Slices into a Table

In this step you'll group all of the banner slices into a table. When you save this page with HTML, this table will act as a container for all of the GIFs and JPEGs produced by your banner slices.

Select the Slice Select tool in the toolbox and click on each of the slices you created in the banner (known as user slices) **A**. Then choose Slices>Group Slices into Table. A slice border appears around the table, along with a special table slice symbol **B**. Drag the borders of the table to make sure they encompass the entire banner.

I N S I G H T

Why Make Nested Tables? Nested tables are useful for holding sections of your page layout together and in place on the page. They're also a means of creating portable modules. For example, you can take this nested table into a site-building program like Dreamweaver or GoLive and save it as a reusable component that can be easily included in other pages in a site.

I N S I G H T

Yellow Warning Icon. The yellow warning icon next to Table 02 in the Web Content palette means that this slice layout contains some spacer cells that could cause gaps in the table. It can be fixed by adjusting the slice borders with the Slice Select tool. But you can ignore it for now.

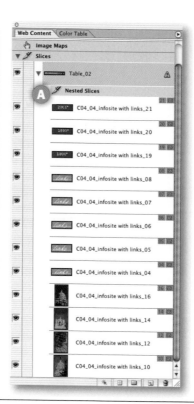

8. View the Table Slices

Open the Web Content palette (Window>Web Content) to view a list of all of your user slices. Notice that although you've only made one table yourself, your slices are listed under Table 02 **A**. That's because when you save a page from ImageReady with standard HTML, the program saves the entire document as one large table—Table 01—with each slice corresponding to a table cell. Any additional tables you create are nested inside of that larger table. That's why these slices are labeled Nested Slices in the Web Content palette.

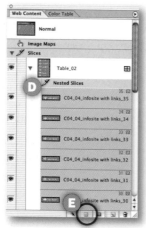

9. Slice and Make a Table of Links

Draw a slice around the top *link here* text link and bullet on the left side of the page **A**. Choose Slices>Duplicate Slice. In the Duplicate Slice dialog box, choose Below Original from the Position menu and click OK **B**. ImageReady makes a new slice that fits nicely around the next link and bullet **C**. This works because each item is the same size and they are evenly spaced. Repeat four more times to create slices around all the links on the left side of the page.

Select all six slices by clicking on one of them in the Web Content palette, holding the Shift key, and clicking on the slice at top of the stack **D**. Click the Group Slices into Table button at the bottom of the Web Content palette **E** to join the slices into another nested table **F**. Repeat with the *link here* items on the right side of the page.

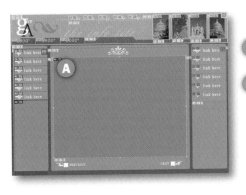

10. Create HTML Text

In this step you'll designate a slice as one that will contain nongraphic HTML text. With the Slice tool, draw a slice around the large empty area in the middle of the page **A**. With that slice selected, open the Slice palette (Window>Slice). In the Slice palette, choose No Image from the Type menu **B**. The palette changes to display a Text box. Type or paste some text into the Text box **C**, and check Text Is HTML **D**. You won't see the text in the document window, because ImageReady doesn't preview HTML text. However, you will see it shortly in a browser preview.

TIP

Expand the Slice Palette. To see all of the options in the Slice palette, click the double-pointed arrow on the Slice tab.

11. Color the Cell Background

The slice you created for the HTML text is a table cell, just like slices that contain graphics. In this step you'll change the background color of that table cell.

Choose the Eyedropper tool in the toolbox **A** and click on a light color in the image. That color appears in the Foreground Color box **B**. Click the arrow next to the Background section of the Slice palette to expand that section. Click in the Color field **C** and choose Foreground color from the pop-up menu. This sets the color of the table cell that will display your HTML text.

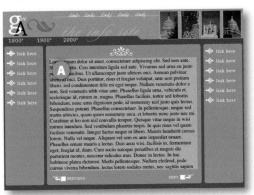

12. Preview the HTML Text

Click the Preview in Browser icon in the toolbox to view the page in your default browser. You'll see the HTML text that you entered into ImageReady's Slice palette against the colored cell background **A**. You can format and change the color of this HTML text when you bring this page into a site-building program.

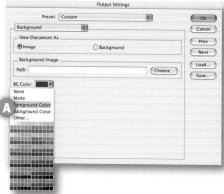

13. Set the Page Background Color

Now you'll choose the color that will appear in a browser window behind your page. Select the Eyedropper tool in the toolbox and click on the dark green border of the page to set the Foreground Color. Choose File>Output Settings>Background. In the Output Settings dialog box, click the arrow on the BG Color box and choose Foreground Color **A**. This sets the Web page background to dark green.

Click the Preview in Browser button to view your page against this HTML background **B**.

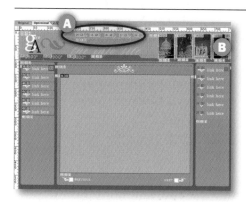

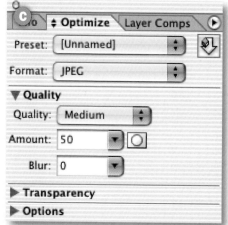

> **TIP**
>
> **More on Optimizing Slices.** To learn more about optimizing slices, take another look at *JPEG Optimization, GIF Optimization,* and *Slicing and Optimizing a Navigation Bar* all in Chapter 1.

14. Optimize the Slices

Click on the Optimized, 2-Up, or 4-Up tab **A** of the document window to preview your page with the slice optimization settings you choose. Select the Slice Select tool in the toolbox. Hold the Shift key and click on each of the photographs in the banner **B**. In the Optimize palette (Window>Optimize) **C**, choose JPEG as the format, and set the compression quality to Medium, striving for the lowest file size that retains the image quality you want.

Select each of the other slices in the image and optimize them as GIFs. Similar slices can be linked so that you only have to choose optimization settings one time for all of them. For example, select all of the link slices. Then choose Slices>Link for Optimization from the main menu bar.

Don't forget that you'll need to optimize the auto slices (the ones with the gray numbers that were created automatically) as well as the user slices (the ones you created).

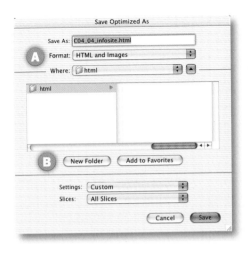

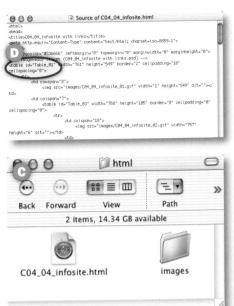

15. Save as HTML

We'll show you how to save this page two ways—first with standard HTML and then with CSS (Cascading Style Sheets). ImageReady produces HTML with tables by default (unless you choose CSS instead). Choose File>Save Optimized As. In the Save Optimized As dialog box, set Format/Save as Type to HTML and Images **A**. Make sure the Slices menu is set to All Slices **B**, choose a destination, and click Save.

ImageReady generates an HTML page with nested tables to hold all your images in place, along with a folder of images that contains GIFs and JPEGs generated by each slice in the source file **C**. Open the HTML page in a Web browser and view the source code there. You'll see tables designated in the HTML code **D**.

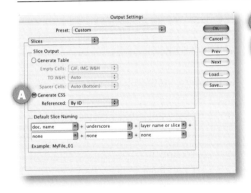

> **T I P**
>
> **ImageReady CSS.** The CSS generated by ImageReady is used to position the output from your slices, as an alternative to HTML tables.

16. Save as CSS

Go back to your PSD file, which is still open in ImageReady. Choose File>Output Settings>Slices. Notice that Generate Table is selected by default. Choose Generate CSS instead **A**. The Referenced setting offers different ways of referencing the styles that position your slices. Leave it at its default, and click OK. Now choose File>Save Optimized As, using all the same settings covered in the preceding step.

This time ImageReady produces images and an HTML file that employs CSS styles, rather than an HTML table to hold your images in place. Open this HTML page in a Web browser and view its source code there to see the CSS code. You'll see slices listed with pixel positions **B**. You can take either kind of output into a site-building program or a text editor and tweak it there. Or use the output as-is in a site. 🔳

Wow Flash Splash Page

We'll finish up with a big splash. You'll make a splash page for a Web site that includes a Flash animation that tests whether a viewer has the Flash player installed on her computer.

T I P

Flash Capability in ImageReady. In case you started reading from the back of the book (we've been known to do it ourselves), we want to be sure you know that you can export movies in Flash format straight from ImageReady. You can also export ImageReady layers as individual Flash files for import into Flash, and you can create Flash movies with variables and dynamic data in Image-Ready. Take a look at our Flash projects: Chapter 2, **Vector-Based Flash Movie**, and Chapter 3, **Creating Dynamic Flash Web Banners**.

1. Start with a Splash

Many sites use a splash page as the gateway to the site. This splash page is all that an introductory page should be. It uses animation to catch viewers' attention, and a sexy three-dimensional graphic to entice them to delve further into the site. Most importantly, it serves a real purpose. This splash page offers viewers a test of whether they have the Flash Player—which is necessary to enjoy a Flash-based Web site. And if they don't, there's a quick link to download the player.

We used Photoshop to make the dimensional graphic for this page. You'll work in ImageReady to animate the graphic and export it as a Flash movie.

In ImageReady, open C04-06-splash.psd from Chapter 4-Sites That Wow>Ch4-6.

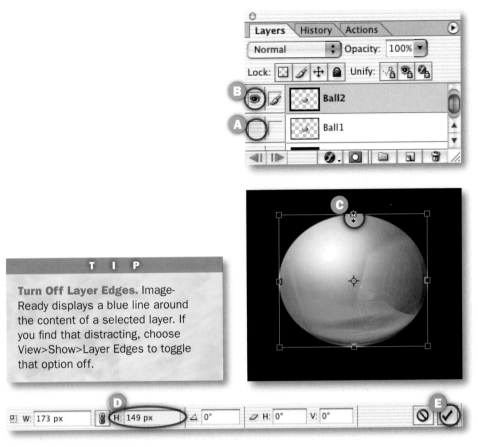

2. Transform the Ball

You'll be amazed at how easy it is to make layered artwork for an animation of a sphere pulsing. In the Layers palette, double-click the layer name on the Ball layer and rename that layer **Ball1** to correspond to the animation frame on which it will be first visible. Then Control/right-click the Ball1 layer, choose Duplicate Layer from the pop-up menu, and name the duplicate layer **Ball2.** Click in the Visibility field of the Ball1 layer to turn its Eye icon off **A**, and click in the Visibility field of the Ball2 layer to turn its Eye icon on **B**. With the Ball2 layer selected, choose Edit>Transform>Scale. Hold the Alt/ Option key as you click on the center anchor point at the top of the bounding box **C** and drag down to compress the height of the ball from the top and bottom. If you want to be precise, keep your eye on the Height field in the Options bar, dragging down until the original number there (173 px) is reduced to 149 px. **D**. Click the big checkmark on the Options bar **E** to exit transform mode.

> **TIP**
>
> **Turn Off Layer Edges.** Image-Ready displays a blue line around the content of a selected layer. If you find that distracting, choose View>Show>Layer Edges to toggle that option off.

3. Transform Another Ball

Repeat the preceding step, duplicating the Ball1 layer and naming the duplicate layer **Ball3**. Turn off the visibility of the Ball1 and Ball2 layers and turn on the visibility of the Ball3 layer. Compress Ball3 more than Ball2 by Option/Alt-dragging the center anchor point at the top of its transform bounding box down until the Height field in the Options bar reads 107 px.

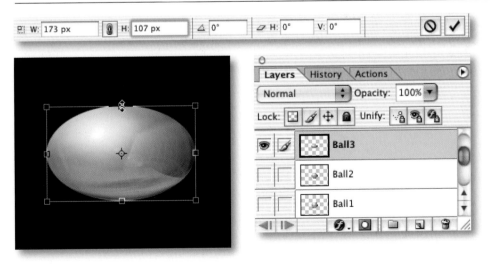

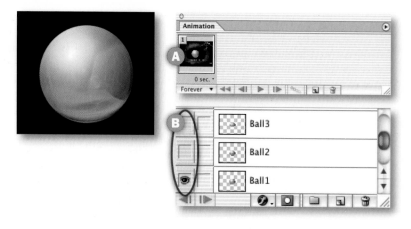

4. Make Frame 1 of the Animation

Now that you've made the layered artwork, you're ready to create the animation in ImageReady. This simple animation is made by clicking in the Visibility field of each ball layer to turn its Eye icon on or off on each frame.

Open the Animation palette, which automatically displays Frame 1 **A**. In the Layers palette, set the layer visibility as follows **B**:

Ball1 layer on
Ball2 layer off
Ball3 layer off

5. Make Frame 2 of the Animation

Click the Duplicate Animation Frame icon **A** at the bottom of the Animation palette to create Frame 2. With Frame 2 selected, set layer visibility as follows:
Ball2 layer on
Ball1 layer off
Ball3 layer off

6. Make Frame 3 of the Animation

Click the Duplicate Animation Frame icon at the bottom of the Animation palette to create Frame 3. With Frame 3 selected, set layer visibility as follows **A**:
Ball3 layer on
Ball1 layer off
Ball2 layer off

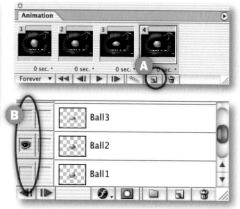

7. Make Frame 4 of the Animation

Click the Duplicate Animation Frame icon **A** at the bottom of the Animation palette to create Frame 4. With Frame 4 selected, set layer visibility as follows **B**:
Ball2 layer on
Ball1 layer off
Ball3 layer off

8. Set the Animation Time Delay

In this step you'll set the time delay between frames. With Frame 4 high-lighted in the Animation palette, hold the Shift key and click on Frame 1 to select all the frames. Click the Time Delay label under any frame **A** and choose 0.2 sec.

Click the Play arrow **B** at the bottom of the Animation palette to preview the animation in ImageReady. Click the same button to stop the preview. Sweet!

9. Add Text

Select the Type tool in the toolbox, and choose white and a Sans Serif font in the Options bar. Type: ***To enjoy this site you will need to have Flash® Player installed***. Use the Move tool to move the text into place under the ball **A**. (Select-ing the Move tool also commits the type and exits text edit mode, so you're ready to add another type layer.)

Type: ***If you see a ball moving in the center of the page click HERE*** Press Return/Enter, and type: ***Other-wise, get Flash® Player HERE***

Highlight the last two lines of text, and click the Align Text Right icon in the Options bar. Use the Move tool to move this text into place at the bottom-right corner of the image **B**.

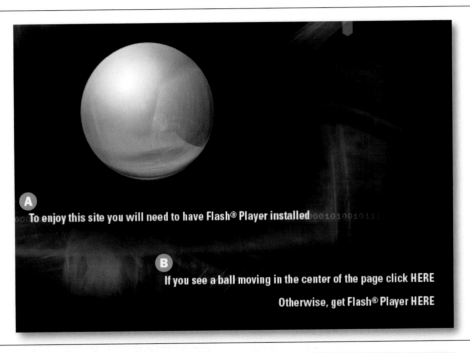

TIP

Registered Trademark Symbol. To insert a registered trademark symbol, press Command-R/Alt-0174. Highlight the symbol and click the Character palette icon in the Options bar. In the Character palette, click the Super-script button.

10. Make Image Map Hot Spots

Select the Image Map Rectangle tool in the toolbox **A**. Drag rectangular hot spots around each of the two words HERE. Select a hot spot with the Image Map Select tool **B**. In the URL field of the Image Map palette **C** (Window>Image Map) add a relative link (like contact.htm) to a page you plan to add to the site. For the second hot spot add a full link (including http://) to an exter-nal site where a viewer can download the Flash® Player.

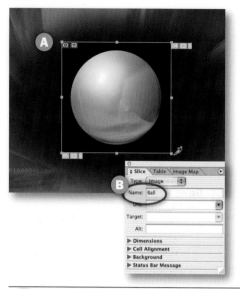

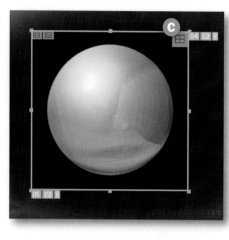

11. Prepare a Slice Around the Ball

If the fully round ball is not visible, turn on the Eye icon on the Ball1 layer in the Layers palette. Select the Slice tool in the toolbox and draw a slice around the ball no bigger than its black glow **A**. In the Slice palette (Window>Slice), name the slice **Ball B**. Choose Slices>Group Slices into Table from the main menu bar. A table symbol now appears in the Ball slice **C**. Putting this slice alone in a nested table as you just did, rather than leaving it as a cell in a larger table, which is the default behavior, will help keep the area from collapsing in the HTML file when you remove the ball image later in this project.

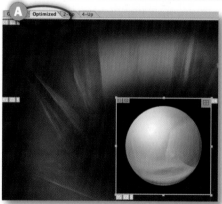

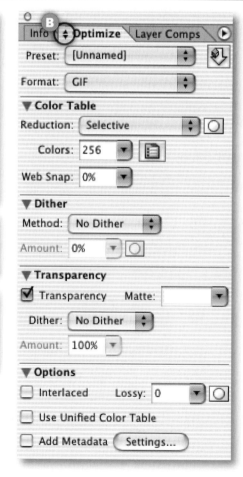

12. Optimize the Slices

The file now contains one user slice around the ball and several auto slices that ImageReady made to fill in the surrounding area. You'll optimize these slices in this step.

Click on the Optimized tab in the document window **A** so you can see a preview of the image with the optimization settings you choose. Open the Optimize palette (Window>Optimize), and click the double-pointed arrow on its tab **B** to see all its settings. Select the Slice Select tool in the toolbox **C**, and click on the Ball slice in the image. In the Optimize palette, choose the following settings:

- Format: GIF (This has to be a GIF because it's an animation. JPEG does not support animation.)

- Reduction: Selective

- Colors: 256

- Dither Method: None

- Transparency: Checked

- Add Metadata: Unchecked

Repeat this on one of the auto slices.

T I P

Optimizing an Animation. To learn more about optimizing an animation, see Chapter 2, **Animation**.

13. Set the Page Background Color

Choose File>Output Settings>
Background. In the Output Settings
dialog box, click in the BG Color field **A**
and choose black (#000000) in the Color
Picker that opens. Click OK in both
dialog boxes. This sets the background
color of the Web page that will show
in a browser window that is stretched
larger than this image.

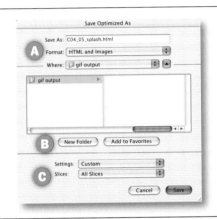

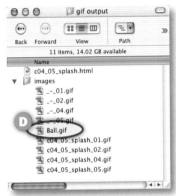

14. Save with a GIF Animation

Choose File>Save Optimized As. Set
Format/Save As Type to HTML and
Images **A**. Click New Folder **B** and make
a new folder in which you'll save these
files. Set Slices to All Slices **C**. Click
Save. ImageReady generates a folder of
images that contains the Ball.gif animation **D** generated from your Ball slice.
It also produces an HTML file, with a
nested table to hold the animation
in place.

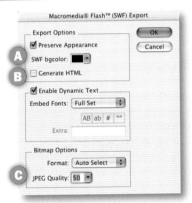

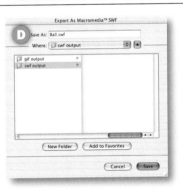

15. Export ball.gif as a SWF

In ImageReady, choose File>Open and
navigate to Ball.gif in the folder of images you generated in the last step. With
Ball.gif open in ImageReady, choose
File>Export>Macromedia® Flash™ SWF.
In the SWF Export dialog box, click in
the SWF bgcolor field **A** and choose black
from the Color Picker. Uncheck Generate HTML **B** to save the SWF without an
HTML file. Set JPEG Quality to about 50
C. (This setting will apply to the graphics
in this animation.) Click OK. In the next
Export dialog box, click Save to save the
animation as Ball.swf **D**.

INSIGHT

Technique Summary. To review—you saved an HTML file that incorporates a GIF
animation, and then re-exported that GIF animation as a SWF Flash movie. You can
substitute the GIF animation for the SWF animation by opening the HTML file in a
site-building program like Dreamweaver.

16. Replace the GIF with the SWF

In Dreamweaver or another site-building
program, open the HTML file you saved
in Step 14. Delete Ball.gif and substitute
the Ball.swf file that you exported in the
last step. The Flash animation is now
incorporated in your splash page! ▨

Index

A

absolute links, 40
action droplets, 116
action sets, 103, 107–108, 119
actions, 108–109. See also automation
    assigning function keys to, 108
    Button Mode, 109
    conditional, 118–123
    creating, 103
    customizing, 109
    described, 102
    loading, 108
    nested, 104
    pausing, 109
    playback of, 108
    pre-made sets, 103
    presets, 3
    recording, 103–105
    running, 111
    sharing, 108
    testing, 103, 122
    troubleshooting, 103, 122
    uses for, 102
Actions palette, 103, 108
Add Metadata option, 13
adjustment layers, 103
Adobe Bridge. See Bridge
Adobe Photoshop One-Click Wow !, 2
alignment
    buttons, 10
    text, 11, 52
alignment guides, 10
alpha channels, 176
Alt Tag, 21
Angle layer style setting, 87–88
animation frames. See frames
Animation palette, 47, 52–54, 58, 74
animations, 42–99
    duration, 75
    fade-in, 138
    file size, 49, 99
    Flash, 196–201
    fly-in, 137
    frames. See frames
    GIF, 43, 49, 55–63, 69, 201
    ImageReady and, 43
    interactive, 70–79

JPEG format and, 56, 69
Las Vegas resort, 80–85
layer masks, 80–85
layer styles, 86–89
looping, 68
manual, 47
modifying, 55
optimizing, 49, 54–55, 62, 69, 85, 90
pausing, 53, 61
photos, 56–63
playing, 53–54, 61, 71, 83, 97, 199
previewing. See previews, animation
radar screen, 44–49
reducing speed, 68
remote, 70–79
reopening, 55
rollover-triggered, 70–79
saving, 49, 62, 85
slices, 57–58, 72
slide shows, 64–69
smoothness of, 83, 89
stopping, 53, 61
text, 95
time, 75
time delay, 58, 85
traffic light, 56–63
tweened, 47, 137
vector-based Flash movies, 92–99
unifying layer properties, 91
viewing, 15
warped text, 50–55
.atn extension, 108
audio, 183
Auto Select Group option, 10
auto slices, 16, 19, 57, 79
automation, 100–149. See also actions
    batch processing, 102–107, 109–111
    benefits of, 101–102
    droplets, 116–117
    dynamic Flash Web banners, 137–143
    linked HTML pages, 130, 136
    linked Web pages, 131–136
    multiple pages in single file, 124–129
    multiple Web graphics, 112–115
    multiple Web pages, 131–136
    outputting Web pages, 131–136

B

Background Contents field, 7
background images, 171

background layers, 7, 26, 86, 112
backgrounds
    color, 9, 27, 50, 166, 181, 185, 194
    patterned, 29, 156, 160–161
    slice, 21
    Web-safe, 27
banners
    dynamic, 183–184
    slicing, 191
    Web, 137–143, 165, 183–184
Batch dialog box, 107, 111
batch processing, 102–107, 109–111
bevel style, 178
Bicubic Sharper method, 119
bit depth, 7
bitmapped images, 92, 99
blending modes, 177
Blur option, 12
blurring
    alpha channels, 176
    images, 12
borders, 9, 165
Bounding Box option, 54
boxes, 161
Bridge
    batch processing from, 107
    described, 8
    opening, 8, 106
    opening images from, 106
    selecting images from, 107, 164
Bridge labels, 163
browsers
    color and, 7
    image dimensions, 6
    image resolution, 6
    previewing in, 33, 49, 55, 62, 68, 85, 98
Brush tool, 46
Button Mode, 109
button states, See Rollover States
buttons
    aligning, 10
    angle, 77
    borders, 9
    color, 31
    creating, 9, 22
    distributing, 23
    duplicating, 10
    Glow effect, 72–73, 78
    halos, 28–29
    hot spots, 38–41
    links, 38–41
    on navigation bar, 8–15

Watch over Jan's shoulder...

...as she leads you through one-on-one Photoshop CS2 for the Web training from the comfort of your own desktop!

With the purchase of this book you get access to a sampling of high-quality streaming video instruction from Software Cinema and Peachpit Press with Jan Kabili!

BONUS TRAINING MOVIES

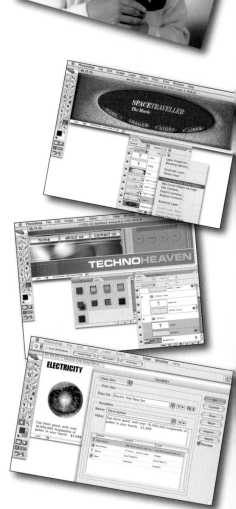

Learning Photoshop for the Web is now as easy as getting online. SOFTWARE CINEMA and PEACHPIT PRESS are pleased to introduce you to the newest and easiest way to master Photoshop CS2 for the Web. Using new advances in streaming media, we are able to bring you online video instruction in vivid, full-resolution detail. You will learn quickly and naturally as Jan walks you through each technique as if she were right there with you. As part of purchasing this *How to Wow* book, you can experience a sampling of these dynamic, interactive Photoshop movies at no cost! Simply go to www.software-cinema.com/htw for log-in instructions.

Jan Kabili has a knack for teaching the hidden secrets of Photoshop for the Web—always with a practical emphasis on quality, flexibility, and speed. In her *How to Wow* video series for SOFTWARE CINEMA, Jan holds nothing back. It's all here, every trick and technique for making creative Web graphics in Photoshop CS2 and ImageReady CS2, demonstrated in real time, with original images by award-winning illustrator Colin Smith. From navigation, to animation, to automation, to home pages that wow, these are techniques you will use every day. After learning these easy and useful methods, you'll wonder how you ever handled Photoshop and ImageReady without them.

How to Wow: Photoshop CS2 for the Web training, with many hours of one-on-one instruction by ***Jan Kabili***, is also available on DVD. Go to www.software-cinema.com/htw to purchase Jan's DVDs at a special discount for readers of this book. If you ever wished you could take a full semester class to learn Photoshop for the Web with Jan, here's your chance!

Note: Specific tutorial movies may differ from the examples shown here

software**CINEMA**®
A Dean Collins Production